The Middle Kingdom of Ancient Egypt

DUCKWORTH EGYPTOLOGY

The Middle Kingdom of Ancient Egypt

History, Archaeology and Society

Wolfram Grajetzki

Duckworth

First published in 2006 by
Gerald Duckworth & Co. Ltd.
90-93 Cowcross Street, London EC1M 6BF
Tel: 020 7490 7300
Fax: 020 7490 0080
inquiries@duckworth-publishers.co.uk
www.ducknet.co.uk

A catalogue record for this book is available
from the British Library

ISBN 0 7156 3435 6

Typeset by Ray Davies
Printed and bound in Great Britain by
CPI Bath

Contents

Preface   vii
List of Illustrations   ix
Introduction   1

1. History   7
  1.1. The end of the Old Kingdom   7
  1.2. The Heracleopolitan kings (*c.* 2161/2131-1990/1970 BC)   8
  1.3. The early Eleventh Dynasty at Thebes (pre-2065-2008 BC)   10
  1.4. The second part of the Eleventh Dynasty (*c.* 2008-1938 BC)   17
  1.5. The early Twelfth Dynasty (*c.* 1938-1837 BC)   28
  1.6. The late Twelfth Dynasty (*c.* 1837-1759 BC)   51
  1.7. The Thirteenth Dynasty (*c.* 1759-1685 BC)   63

2. Archaeology and Geography   77
  2.1. Upper Egypt   78
  2.2. Lower Egypt   121
  2.3. The neighbouring lands   133

3. Society   139
  3.1. Outside the ruling classes   143
  3.2. The ruling classes: people with administrative titles   151
  3.3. The king and his family   161

Chronology   167
Appendix   169
  A. Kings of the Middle Kingdom   169
  B. Viziers of the Middle Kingdom   172
  C. Treasurers of the Middle Kingdom   173
Notes   175
Further Reading   191
Bibliography   193
Illustration Sources   197
Index   199

Preface

This volume provides an introduction to the history of the Middle Kingdom. At the outset, it should be emphasised that for any period of Egyptian
history before the Late Period it is not possible to write a political history,
in the sense of a sequence of major political events such as ministerial
appointments or military successes or setbacks. Our knowledge of such
historical events is extremely limited, so this book offers instead a guide
to the sources, listing data for each reign and providing a general outline.
Following this chronological sketch, the most important archaeological
sites are described from south to north, as the Egyptians ordered their
geography. This section on archaeology includes also the history of many
regional centres, such as Beni Hasan, Elephantine and Asyut, just to
mention the most important. In a book of this size, individual sites and
monuments cannot be covered from every angle, but for more details the
reader can consult the bibliography in the endnotes. The third, final part
turns to discussion of Middle Kingdom society.

The focus throughout is on the full range of material evidence from this
period. For example, beside the biggest tombs and houses, the smaller
ones are also mentioned. The Western tradition of almost exclusive attention to aesthetic aspects of culture is very selective. Sculpture, painting,
architecture and literature tend to be classified as art, and these aspects
of the culture are treated as superior to others. As a result, for art, religion
or literature in the Middle Kingdom, important studies already exist, and
their findings need not be repeated. Here instead I aim to give a different
picture of the Middle Kingdom, intended to be closer to the far wider scope
of the surviving sources. Works of literature and high-standard art works
can have played only a minor part in the life of most of the people. The lives
of the Middle Kingdom have yet to be recovered from archaeology, and only
then can the artistic achievements be set in any adequate context.

I would like to thank Nick Reeves, Deborah Blake and Ray Davies from
Duckworth for all their support and Stephen Quirke for reading my
English. For pictures I am grateful to Hugh Kilmister, Tracey Golding and
Sally MacDonald (Petrie Museum University College London), and Prof.
Dr M. Egg (Römisch-Germanisches Zentralmuseum Mainz).

Illustrations

For illustration sources see pp. 197-8.

Plates

(between pp. 116 and 117)

I. Head of a statue of Senusret I, found in his funerary temple at his pyramid at Lisht.

II. Double statue of Amenemhat III in a naos, found in the 'Labyrinth' at Hawara.

III. Head of a sphinx of Amenemhat III, found at Tanis.

IV. Bead with the name of Sekhemre-khutawy.

V. Statue of a vizier, father of the vizier Ankhu, Thirteenth Dynasty.

VI. Two block statues and standing figure of a woman found at Kom el-Khatein (Delta).

VII. Bronze statuette of a woman.

VIII. Life-size statue of the high steward Nakht, found at Lisht.

IX. Decoration of the interior of a coffin from the cemetery of the lower officials at Beni Hasan.

X. Ini and his wife receiving offerings; paintings on Ini's coffin found at Gebelein.

XI. The two long sides of the coffin of the lady 'Ankhet begotten of Iti' found at Rifeh.

XII & XIII. Coffin fragments found at Rifeh, decorated with palace façades typical of coffins of the late Twelfth Dynasty.

XIV. Mummy mask found at Harageh, late Middle Kingdom.

XV. Pyramid of Senusret II at Lahun.

XVI. Mastabas found next to the pyramid of Senusret II at Lahun.

XVII. Two canopic jars of the 'lady of the house', Senebtysy, found at Harageh.

XVIII. Stela of Djari, el-Tarif, Thebes.

XIX. Stela of the treasurer Khenty-khety-em-sauef Seneb, Harageh tomb 136.

XX. Relief fragment found at Abydos, showing the 'treasurer' Ameny-seneb hunting in the marshes.

XXI. Stela of Mentu Sahathor and his family found in a small niche in his mastaba at Abydos.

XXII. Objects found in Abydos tomb 793.

Illustrations

XXIII. Pectoral found in the tomb of the 'king's daughter', Sathathoriunet, at Lahun.

Figures

1. Map of Egypt. xii
2. Rock inscription naming King Qakare. 2
3. Satet temple on Elephantine. 37
4. Reliefs of Senusret I found at Koptos. 39
5. Pyramid complex of Senusret II at Lahun. 49
6. The first to fourth Upper Egyptian nomes. 79
7. The First Cataract region around Elephantine. 81
8. House H 70 at Elephantine. 82
9. Qubbet el-Hawa near Elephantine: tomb of Sarenput I. 85
10. Qubbet el-Hawa: painting in the tomb of Sarenput II 86
11. A burial chamber found at Edfu, very close to the town. 88
12. Deir el-Bahri, the funerary complex of Nebhepetre Mentuhotep II. 90
13. Reconstruction of the Amun temple of Senusret I at Thebes. 91
14. The fifth to eighth Upper Egyptian nomes. 93
15. Valley temple of Senusret III at Abydos (South). 96
16. The house of the governor of Wahsut. 96
17. The eighth to twelfth Upper Egyptian nomes. 98
18. Two tombs of governors at Qaw el-Kebir. 100
19. Scarabs found in different Middle Kingdom tombs at Qaw. 101
20. The tomb of Nakht-ankhu at Rifeh. 103
21. The thirteenth to nineteenth Upper Egyptian nomes. 104
22. Depiction in the tomb of Hapidjefa (I). 106
23. Family of governors at Meir. 108
24. A governor's family of the Twelfth Dynasty at Beni Hasan. 113
25. The twentieth to twenty-second Upper Egyptian nomes, the Fayum and the first Lower Egyptian nome. 117
26. The temple at Medinet Maadi. 120
27. Burial found at Qasr as-Saga, late Middle Kingdom. 120
28. The mastaba of the high priest of Ptah Senusret-ankh at Lisht. 122
29. The burial of Ankhet at Lisht. 123
30. Part of a settlement found next to the pyramid of Amenemhat I. 124
31. Saqqara South and Dahshur in the Middle Kingdom. 126
32. Mastaba no. 1 at Dahshur. 126
33. The Delta and its nomes. 129
34. The Middle Kingdom temple at Ezbet Rushdi. 132
35. Egypt and the Near East during the Middle Kingdom. 134

Illustrations

36. Plan of the excavated Middle Kingdom town at Lahun. 140
37. A typical house found at Tell el-Dab'a; early Twelfth Dynasty. 145
38. Expression and status of servants of an official. 147
39. The families of Sobekhotep and Zahi. 155
40. Building B, Wahsut (Abydos). 157
41. Drawing of Plate XI. 166

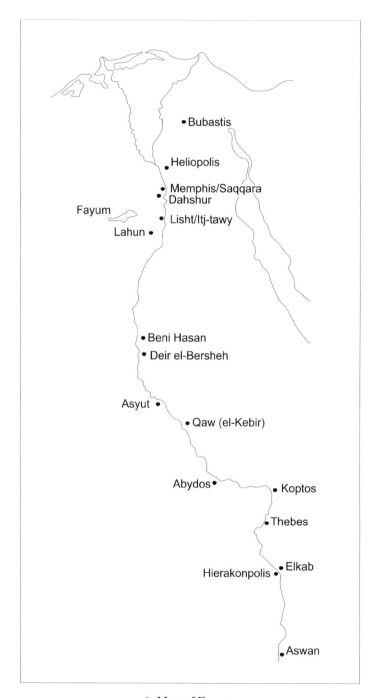

• Bubastis

• Heliopolis

• Memphis/Saqqara
• Dahshur

Fayum

• Lisht/Itj-tawy

Lahun •

• Beni Hasan

• Deir el-Bersheh

Asyut •

• Qaw (el-Kebir)

Abydos •

• Koptos

• Thebes

• Elkab

Hierakonpolis •

• Aswan

1. Map of Egypt.

Introduction

For the ancient Egyptians of later times, the Middle Kingdom was the classical period of their arts, history and literature. Insofar as a political history can be retrieved from our sources, the Twelfth Dynasty in particular emerges as one of the strongest to rule the land. Eight monarchs ruled the country for almost two hundred years, and brought to all parts of Egypt an unprecedented stability and wealth. However, it is not only this political stability that was considered exemplary in later times; the arts and literature of the Middle Kingdom also often served as prototypes in the New Kingdom and the Late Period. The language of the period remained the classical language for royal and religious writing till the end of the use of the hieroglyphic script, and even in the Ptolemaic Period temple inscriptions referred to Middle Kingdom kings as the temple founders.[1]

Not much has survived from this glory on the level of the monumental architecture. The temples and tombs of the Middle Kingdom were mainly built in the finest limestone, and this was later quarried away for other building projects or simply burnt for lime. Therefore great parts of the architecture of the period are lost. Along with that architecture many depictions in reliefs were destroyed, and the information of their contents with them. The sculpture of the period is better known, but it is certain that a high proportion of statuary too has vanished. As a consequence of this destruction many sites of the Middle Kingdom do not attract the Egyptologist or the tourist very much. The mastabas of the Old Kingdom and the Theban rock-cut tombs are much better preserved than the destroyed mastabas of the Middle Kingdom; the latter are therefore less often targets of archaeological research. This just increases the lack of knowledge about the Middle Kingdom. The Old and New Kingdom are in many respects well-known periods, whereas most Egyptologists know the Middle Kingdom only from its literature and eclectically selected works of art, such as the royal sculpture of the late Twelfth Dynasty.

The Middle Kingdom is the period of Egyptian history between the Old Kingdom, when the great pyramids were built, and the New Kingdom, when Egypt controlled parts of the Near East as well as Nubia. The Old Kingdom ended in a period of political disunity for Egypt – the first such between ages of unity, which is therefore known in Egyptology as the 'First Intermediate Period'. The kings and the ruling class seem not to have had access any longer to the same resources as in the Old Kingdom, while many provincial cemeteries flourished to an extent not known before or afterwards.[2] Modern historians often call the First Intermediate Period a time of decline, but there are innovations in art, language and religion, demonstrating great vitality at many sites. However, the ruling class of the Middle Kingdom saw this time as a period of disorder and impoverishment, a topos perhaps most directly expressed in the literary composition 'Prophecy of Neferty', which may echo events of this age:

> The land is shrunk – its rulers are many,
> it is bare – its taxes are great;
> the grain is low – the measure is large,
> it is measured to overflowing.[3]

This period of political instability for the ruling class can be seen as the background to the Middle Kingdom. However, it is hard to judge what real impact the First Intermediate Period had on the Middle Kingdom. Is there a change in the concept of kingship or the Egyptian view of the past? In former times the rise of pessimistic literature was always seen as one example of direct influence. However, new research has shown that almost all of these works of pessimistic literature belong to the late Middle Kingdom, some two centuries after reunification. Therefore it is hard to believe that this literature reflects so directly the events of the First Intermediate Period. It is equally difficult to judge the effect on the ideology of kingship. Were the rulers of the Middle Kingdom considered less divine than Old Kingdom kings, as often proposed?[4] The sources do not give tangible evidence for that view. For the present it seems safer to say instead that the wealth of the various provinces in the Middle Kingdom is the one direct result of First Intermediate Period developments.

Sources for a history of the Middle Kingdom

Before reading an outline of a history of the Middle Kingdom, it is important to be aware of the main sources for the chronology of ancient Egypt in general. First is the king list of Manetho, an Egyptian priest who lived in the third century BC, and compiled in Greek a history of Egypt in three volumes for the Ptolemies – the Greek-speaking rulers of the country at that time. The works of Manetho are preserved only in later copies, notably by Christian writers who used a shortened version, perhaps compiled after the death of Manetho. The more accurate copies by the third-century Christian writer Africanus are known, in turn, only from excerpts quoted by later authors, whereas a modified version by Eusebius (about AD 260-340) is preserved in Armenian and Latin translations of the fifth century. Excerpts of both Africanus and Eusebius in the original Greek are preserved in the works of George Syncellus, compiled around AD 800. Despite this complicated transmission history, the Manetho king list is still useful for historians because it presents an outline for the whole of Egyptian history, including the Middle Kingdom. Manetho divided Egyptian history into thirty dynasties: the second half of the Eleventh, the Twelfth and the first half of the Thirteenth comprise the Middle Kingdom of Egyptological histories, if the Middle Kingdom is defined as a period of unity. That is to say, the country was at least for most of that time united under one king. The periods of political disunity before and after this Middle Kingdom are now known as the First and Second Intermediate Periods – times when the country was divided into several kingdoms. Manetho himself did not make this distinction into Intermediate Periods (times of disunity) and Kingdoms (times of unity). However, it is clear even from the Manetho list of kings that significant change occurred, for, whereas he listed all rulers of the Twelfth Dynasty by name, he did not report the names of the kings of the First and Second Intermediate Periods (or at least they are not preserved in the later copies).

The list of Manetho is problematic in several respects. As recorded in his Greek version, the names of the kings are sometimes difficult to identify with the Egyptian originals. Manetho or his copyists seem to have made several mistakes. Names seem to have been confused and also the lengths of reigns which appear after the names of kings are often in disagreement with the evidence of sources contemporary with the kings. The later copies often give different versions of names or time spans.

As an example the Middle Kingdom in Manetho (from Africanus via Syncellus) is given here:

Dynasty XI
The Eleventh Dynasty consisted of sixteen kings of Diospolis (or Thebes) who reigned for 43 years. In succession to these Ammenemes ruled for 16 years.

Dynasty XII
The Twelfth Dynasty consisted of seven kings of Diospolis
1. Sesonchosis, son of Ammanemes, for 46 years
2. Ammanemes, for 38 years: he was murdered by his own eunuchs
3. Sesostris, for 48 years: in nine years he subdued the whole of Asia, and Europe as far as Thrace, everywhere erecting memorials of his conquest of the tribes. Upon stelae he engraved for a valiant race the secrets parts of a man, for an ignoble race those of a woman. Accordingly he was esteemed by the Egyptians as the next in rank to Osiris.
4. Lachares, for 8 years: he built the Labyrinth in the Arsinoite province as his own tomb.
5. Ameres, for 8 years
6. Ammenemes, for 8 years
7. Scemiophris, his sister, for 4 years

Dynasty XIII
The Thirteenth Dynasty consisted of sixty kings of Diospolis, who reigned for 453 years.[5]

3

Another important source for the sequence of kings is the hieratic manuscript list known in Egyptology as the Turin Canon, an ancient Egyptian king list written in the Ramesside period (about 1250 BC), and now in the Egyptian Museum of Turin. The papyrus is not well preserved, but originally presented a list of all Egyptian kings down to the beginning of the New Kingdom with the full length of their reign and their years, months and days. For the Eleventh Dynasty only the last kings and some lengths of reigns are preserved. For the Twelfth Dynasty most of the names are missing, but there are still some year lengths of reigns preserved. The kings of the Thirteenth Dynasty are for its first part quite complete, though the lengths of reigns are generally now missing. The second part of the period is very damaged. However, the Turin Canon is the most important source for the order of kings of the Thirteenth Dynasty, and appears consistent with the evidence from that time. So far as it can be confirmed from sources contemporary with those kings, the lengths of reigns and the order of kings seem to be reliable.[6]

Finally there are hieroglyphic king lists of the Ramesside period, preserved in royal temples and in one case in a private tomb. These lists give quite a large number of kings, but not always in their chronological order. Kings of the First and Second Intermediate Period (including the Thirteenth Dynasty) are often omitted. Among these sources, the Karnak list is of especial importance for the Thirteenth Dynasty and Second Intermediate Period. It comprises the depiction, in registers around the walls of a small chamber in the Karnak temple, of kings, or more probably statues of kings there that had to be moved because of building work under Thutmose III in the Eighteenth Dynasty. The list does not follow any clear overall chronological order, but it is a useful document because it names otherwise unknown or not very well-known kings. In general these lists are not so much helpful for reconstructing the history of the Middle Kingdom, as useful for revealing which kings were later regarded as important or not, in particular contexts.[7]

Archaeology of course provides the bulk of the evidence for the Middle Kingdom. It has yielded, and continues to yield, rich sources for material culture, arts, crafts and religion. Many tombs and some stelae are decorated with autobiographical inscriptions. Several monuments are inscribed with kings' names and dates. However, two important points should be made. 1. For the Middle Kingdom the tombs of many high officials have not yet been found, whereas such monuments are a major source for the history of the Old and New Kingdom. Most residential cemeteries of the Middle Kingdom are badly damaged or have been only sporadically excavated. 2. Inscriptions and works of literature provide much important historical information, but they always provide one point of view, in almost all cases that of the ruling class. It will therefore never be possible to write a social history from written sources. For the Egyptian 'historians', religious events, offerings and the correct action of a king

4

according to the gods are more important than the search for the causes and effects of specific events and activities.

One important remark on year datings should be made. The ancient Egyptians dated by years of a king's reign. With a new king a new dating was started. In the Turin Canon, the main source for the length of reigns of the Eleventh and Twelfth Dynasty and the main source for the order of the kings of the Thirteenth Dynasty, the full length of each reign was given; this includes months and days. The Turin Canon is sadly not very well preserved and therefore there are still many questions about the chronology of the Middle Kingdom. Many kings left dated monuments, which give a clue to length of a king's reign. On a dated monument or document the year dating started with the first year of a king's reign. A king reigning just for one day would have a dating 'year 1, first month, day 1'. An important point is that the following year was calculated as starting from the next New Year's Day. A king whose reign started one month before the New Year's day counted the days after New Year as within his second year. Therefore, when on a monument a year 46 appears for a certain king and in the Turin Canon it is stated that this king reigned forty-five years, the two sources of information do not contradict one another; the king reigned into his forty-sixth year, but did not complete it, and entered the king list with a reign of forty-five years plus x months/days.

Another problem for calculating an absolute chronology is the practice of coregencies. In the Middle Kingdom a king might, on reaching an advanced age, choose his successor and rule together with him for the remainder of his reign. The successor counted the years from the start of the coregency as part of his own reign, creating an overlap. Unfortunately, the surviving sources do not always specify when each coregency started. In the later king lists these overlaps caused by coregencies are not marked, complicating the task of adding up the number of years for the whole period.

1

History

1.1. The end of the Old Kingdom

The Old Kingdom (about 2700-2150 BC) is the first classical period of Egyptian history. The first kings of the Fourth Dynasty built the largest stone pyramids, and were able to concentrate the capacity of the whole country for these building projects in their residence in the region of Memphis. However, over time national resources were no longer concentrated in the residence region. The kings of the Fifth Dynasty still built pyramids, but these buildings are smaller. They also erected temples which functioned for the worship of the sun god Re and for the cult of the ruler himself. At the end of the Fifth Dynasty the custom of building these temples came to an end, but the kings of the Sixth Dynasty had other temples made for the king's cult in multiple provincial centres. This seems a significant mark of the growing status of the provinces. At the end of the Old Kingdom the provinces became more and more powerful. There were now many relatively rich cemeteries all over the country with well-furnished tombs of local governors, demonstrating that a high proportion of the country's resources remained outside the residence region.

At the end of the Old Kingdom, the country seems to have fallen apart into several political units ruled by more or less independent rulers, following the long reign of Pepy II, lasting, according to the king lists, sixty-four or even ninety-four years. Egyptologists call the resulting period of disunity the First Intermediate Period. In Memphis there is a high number of little-known kings in the aftermath of the Old Kingdom. They left just a few monuments; only one pyramid of these kings is known, for a ruler named Ibi. It is a small monument, demonstrating the decline in royal resources. On a formal level the kings in Memphis seem to have been accepted as the rulers of the whole country, still issuing decrees to the provinces. However, in practice many local governors acted, or claimed to act, independently. The most famous example is Ankhtyfy, who had a decorated tomb-chapel at Moalla in Upper Egypt and who reports in its inscriptions how he conquered the neighbouring provinces. Despite this rise in local self-promotion, there is so far only one example of a ruler who took over at least parts of the royal titulary: Khui.[1] His name is written in a cartouche, the oval frame denoting kingship, but he is only known from one relief fragment found in Middle Egypt near Dara. Indeed it is hard to give a precise date for this local king. A big, almost king-size tomb was excavated at Dara, and is often connected with him. However, his name was not found at the monument itself, and so the link between King Khui and this tomb remains unclear.

At a certain point a new line of kings appeared in the North. They are called in later sources 'Heracleopolitan', presumably because they came from Heracleopolis or even had their residence there. They seem to have ruled in the tradition of the Old Kingdom and were still buried in pyramids. However, these northern kings are little known; many of them appear on only a few objects, while others are known only from later king lists. Some of them have the name Khety, and there are some inscriptions found in Upper Egypt referring to the 'house of Khety'. It seems plausible, though it is not certain, that 'house of Khety' was an expression referring to this line of kings.

At about the same time that the kings of Heracleopolis ruled the North, or a little later, in the South Theban rulers seem to have declared independence. The Thebans adopted parts of the royal titulary, notably the Horus name, among the most important expressions of kingship. Over a period of about a hundred years these Theban rulers conquered parts of their neighbouring provinces and finally under King Mentuhotep II the whole country. Thus the second part of the First Intermediate Period seems to have been a constant struggle between the Heracleopolitan and the Theban rulers for control of Egypt. The events in detail are still much disputed. There are not many extant sources relating to these events, and the period may have had a less military character than we might think. Most of the written sources come from the Theban kings and their subjects, while there are only a few tombs in Middle Egypt (at Asyut) with biographical inscriptions which give us an idea of the events from the Heracleopolitan point of view. However, from the few inscriptions we gain the impression that the kingdom in Thebes was a small but dynamic kingdom. There are several references to struggles and the officials serving the Theban kings seem to have been loyal to their kings. These officials often refer to their kings in their inscriptions. Many of them mention the extension of the growing empire, and it is possible, on the basis of these monuments, to reconstruct its rise.

1.2. The Heracleopolitan kings (*c.* 2161/2131-1990/1970 BC)[2]

The names of these kings are preserved mainly in the Turin Canon, but the part of the papyrus listing the rulers of this period is particularly heavily damaged. Otherwise the kings of the period are known only from a handful of smaller objects, providing little information. The known kings of the period include the personal name Khety and the throne names Wahibre, Nebkaure and Merykare. The pyramids of the period remain unexcavated, or at least unidentified. The pyramid-complex cult of a certain Merykare is mentioned in several titles of officials buried at Saqqara, and so it is presumed that the burial place of at least that king was somewhere in the same area, rather than at Heracleopolis. It is not known how long the cult of each king lasted after his death. Royal cults might survive for many generations, and therefore these officials are not necessarily contemporary with Merykare, and may even belong to the Middle Kingdom. At Asyut there are several tombs of local governors belonging under the Heracleopolitan kings. Their autobiographical inscriptions provide the only substantial body of written information on the northern kingdom, but it is quite a complicated matter to fit them into the wider historical picture. Finally there are two literary compositions set under these kings: 'The Eloquent Peasant' and 'The Teaching of Merykare'. Both texts were composed in the Middle Kingdom, and provide at least indirect information about the period. However, it must remain an open question how much they can be used as direct historical sources. In terms of archaeology there are many cemeteries dating to the First Intermediate Period, providing a uniquely detailed view on the material culture of the time. In general they give the impression that the provinces were quite rich in the First Intermediate Period. Large royal monuments are missing but private monuments are abundant.

As already mentioned, only the contemporary inscriptions found at Asyut seem to refer to episodes in the military struggles between the Thebans and the Heracleopolitan kings. Asyut was part of the Heracleopolitan kingdom, and so the surviving texts there represent a northern perspective on the events. Three tombs contain biographical inscriptions. The earliest tomb, belonging to Khety (I), does not mention any fight with the Thebans, but the tombs of Iti-ib and Khety (II) report struggles. Iti-ib boasted that he brought security to his province. The description of combat is sadly extensively damaged, but it seems likely that Iti-ib was the winner; otherwise this kind of inscription would not appear in his tomb. The inscriptions of Khety (II) are dated to the time of the Heracleopolitan king Merykare, who is not datable for sure but is mentioned twice in the tomb. His chronological relation to the Theban kings is not known. In the (again poorly preserved) inscriptions of Khety (II) a war is mentioned again: '... all people are in confusion, the towns ... fear is in their limbs.' In the 'Teaching of Merykare' the 'Southland' is mentioned several times, and there is reference to an attack on the town Thinis and the destruction of tombs. There are also Asiatics mentioned as having invaded the eastern Delta. The problem for the historian is again that these events are not linked to names of the kings known from Thebes; an uprising in Thinis is mentioned on a Theban stela dated to the time of Horus Seankhibtawy Mentuhotep II and it might be argued that both sources refer to the same event, but this is uncertain. In these sources the Heracleopolitan realm seems to have been very much on the defensive.

1.3. The early Eleventh Dynasty at Thebes (pre-2065-2008 BC)

Sources

The political unification of Egypt after the First Intermediate Period came from the South. In the First Intermediate Period Thebes was the centre of a small kingdom which managed after a rule of about a hundred years to unify the country under one king. The position of Thebes in the Old Kingdom is uncertain, as few monuments known from this period survive at the site. However, this does not mean that the city was unimportant in earlier times. The town and its cemetery were later greatly expanded and overbuilt, with extensive reuse of rock-cut tombs in particular, making it possible that a high number of Old Kingdom monuments disappeared without any traces.

The general order of the kings of the early Eleventh Dynasty is known from later Eleventh Dynasty inscriptions. The New Kingdom king lists tend not to mention the rulers of the early Eleventh Dynasty, presumably because they did not rule over the whole of Egypt. For example, the Abydos list of Sety I starts the Eleventh Dynasty with Nebheptere (Mentuhotep II); he may have been the first Eleventh Dynasty king to secure undisputed control over the Abydos region. Political events are normally not mentioned on these king lists. They have to be reconstructed from contemporary sources. Only the second and the third king (Wahankh Intef II and Nakhtnebtepnefer Intef III) are known for sure from contemporary documents, while the first king appears only in later sources. There are not many inscriptions of these kings set up by themselves. From Wahankh Intef II is preserved a broken stela found at his tomb with some kind of biographical inscription, providing important information. There are only a few other monuments set up by these kings, such as decorations of temple buildings. Inscriptions on them do not provide much information. There are several stelae of officials serving under the two kings. They sometimes also record biographical inscriptions and therefore give further information about these reigns. However, the residence cemetery of the early Eleventh Dynasty is very damaged and an unusually high number of documents is surely lost.

The beginning of the Eleventh Dynasty

The Karnak king list is a depiction of kings' statues on a wall in the Karnak temple; compiled under Thutmose III (Eighteenth Dynasty), it names the 'member of the elite' and 'foremost of action', Intef, without giving royal titles. However, this Intef can be considered as the founder figure of the Eleventh Dynasty for two reasons: a person without royal titles makes no sense in this list, and the name Intef would support a date in the early Eleventh Dynasty. This Intef without royal titulary may also be known from contemporary sources. A stela in Cairo, found at Thebes, belongs to the 'member of the elite, foremost of action, great overlord of the Theban province, and great pillar, who keeps alive the two lands'.[3] He was clearly the governor at Thebes in the First Intermediate Period. Inscriptions found in Denderah also mention an Intef, who bears the title 'great overlord of Upper Egypt'. If the two are identical, as seems possible, Intef would have been at first a local ruler just ruling Thebes. In this respect he would initially have been no different from other contemporary governors, but presumably he managed later to extend the area of his rule over Denderah, as demonstrated by the find spot of inscriptions and the title 'great overlord of Upper Egypt'. However the identity of the persons named on the fragments is not certain, for the name Intef is too common for us to be able to reach any firm conclusions.

Another ruler in the Karnak list who must belong to the early Eleventh Dynasty is Mentuhotep-aa (the name is partly destroyed) who bears the Horus name 'the ancestor'. This unlikely Horus name seems to be a later artificial creation. A Mentuhotep-aa had a statue in the Heqaib sanctuary at Elephantine and appears there as 'father of the gods', a plural form of a title 'father of the god' attested for private persons. In this title, when it relates to the royal family, 'god' normally refers to the king, and the plural might indicate that Mentuhotep-aa was the father of two or more kings. This is only one possible interpretation: 'gods' might equally refer to a generation of kings, a new dynasty.[4] Mentuhotep-aa's name and title are enclosed by a cartouche. However, the title 'father of the gods' makes it likely that he never was king. The Elephantine statue belongs stylistically to the early Twelfth Dynasty, and so was set up posthumously.[5] It indicates that Mentuhotep-aa was treated – perhaps together with Intef – as father of the Eleventh Dynasty; at least it shows that later generations still honoured him.

Intef I (Horus Seherutawy) (pre-2065 BC)

The first king of the Eleventh Dynasty likely to have claimed a royal titulary is Horus Seherutawy ('he, who contents the two countries') Intef I. He is securely known only from later sources: no contemporary inscription with the name Seherutawy Intef I can be attributed with certainty to him.[6] A relief found at Tod, belonging to a temple building of Mentuhotep II, provides vital evidence for revealing the position of Seherutawy Intef I. The relief shows three kings with the name Intef and with their Horus names. The first king mentioned is Seherutawy Intef I, the second is Horus Wahankh Intef II and for the last the Horus name is destroyed but must be King Horus Nakhtnebtepnefer Intef III.[7] Since the Old Kingdom the royal titulary or 'great names (of the king)' had comprised five titled names, with the birth, throne and Horus name as the most important elements. For Seherutawy Intef I and the following two kings with the name Intef, only the birth and the Horus names are attested. It seems likely that the other parts of a royal titulary were never worn by these kings, rather than that these names did not survive in our records. It seems therefore that Seherutawy Intef I did not appear as full king or was hesitant to take over the full range of royal attributes, as can be seen from the incomplete royal titulary and the non-royal style of his burial place (see below). It is possible that some of the fragments mentioned above naming a certain local governor Intef belonged to Seherutawy Intef I before he became king. However, this uncertainty of assigning monuments to single people again demonstrates how little we know about the time and the persons involved. The exact length of his reign is not known but must have been less than sixteen years. For the following kings the lengths of reigns are preserved in the Turin Canon, while the length of the reign for Seherutawy Intef I is destroyed. However, the summary for the length of the dynasty is preserved as 143 years for the whole dynasty from Men-tuhotep-aa I to Mentuhotep III, including six years at the end. From this it can be calculated that his reign did not exceed seventeen years, and was most probably shorter, since Mentuhotep-aa may also have been included in the list and some of those years would then belong to him.

The tomb of Seherutawy Intef I is of a type known in Egyptology by the Arabic word *saff*, 'row' or 'line'. It has been attributed to him because it is one of altogether three such tombs of royal dimensions found at Thebes; one of the others can be linked by inscriptions to the following ruler (Wahankh Intef II). The remaining two belong therefore most probably to Seherutawy Intef I and Nakhtnebtepnefer Intef III. The one with the earliest pottery has accordingly been attributed to Seherutawy Intef I. This tomb is a huge open space sloping down towards the rear, about 300 m long and 54 m wide, cut into the ground with a colonnade fronting the burial chamber at the back. Today the place is called Saff el-Dawaba.[8] The *saff* tomb is the regular elite tomb type in the early Eleventh Dynasty at Thebes and other sites in southern Upper Egypt (Dendera, Gebelein). It seems remarkable that the king did not choose a pyramid complex, the typical form of royal funerary monument for the Old Kingdom.

Intef II (Horus Wahankh) (c. 2065-2016 BC)

The successor of Seherutawy Intef I is generally thought to be Horus Wahankh Intef II, often called Intef-aa 'Intef, the great' in contemporary inscriptions. If the title 'father of the gods' indicates that Mentuhotep-aa was the direct father of more than one king, then Wahankh Intef II would be the brother of Seherutawy Intef I. However, the interpretation of the title 'father of the gods' remains open, and it seems unwise to draw any conclusions from it. The full filiation of Wahankh Intef II remains there-fore unknown. His mother is mentioned as a certain Neferu.[9] Her name appears only after the name of the king who calls himself often 'Intef-aa, born of Neferu'; nothing else is known about her.

According to the Turin Canon Wahankh Intef II reigned forty-nine years; on a stela of the king his fiftieth year is mentioned – both dates refer to the same year.[10] There are several inscriptions of private individuals preserved datable to his reign, providing us with a rough outline of events and the step-by-step growth of his kingdom. While there is nothing known about the politics of Seherutawy Intef I it becomes clear from the few sources on Wahankh Intef II that one aim of his reign was to extend the borders of his small Upper Egyptian realm. The extent of his kingdom at the beginning of his reign is not known for sure. It is not certain whether he ruled several Upper Egyptian provinces, or just the Theban province. However, several inscriptions of officials and also of the king himself confirm that at the end of his reign larger parts of Upper Egypt were under his control. Some texts seem to refer to fights with the Heracleopolitan kings, because a 'house of Khety' is mentioned.

From a stela of a certain Hetepi, not datable within the reign of the king, it becomes clear that the area ruled by the Theban king at one point extended from the south at Elephantine to around Abydos in the north. The full text of the stela is given here in translation as an example of an early Eleventh Dynasty biographical inscription. Hetepi reports:

Horus Wahankh, King of Upper and Lower Egypt, Son of Re, Intef, born of Neferu, beloved of Nekhbet. A king's offering to Anubis, who is before the divine booth at all his places ... Hetepi says: I am the beloved one of his lord and the praised one of the lord of this country. His majesty made glad his humble servant in truth. His majesty indeed said there was none there who ... character, (my) good command except Hetepi. This humble servant made it very well. His majesty praised the humble servant for it. Now his officials said: 'may this face praise you!' The humble servant spoke with his mouth in the middle of the seven provinces of Khen-Nekhen and in Abydos in the Ta-wer nome (eighth Upper Egyptian province), when there was nobody who spoke with his mouth in Nekhen, Wetjes-Hor and Ta-seti (the first three Upper Egyptian provinces) except this humble servant. His majesty praised this humble servant among the troops for having descended to Thinis in un-awareness of Ta-wer in the west. Now famine lasted in this province for many years, but this humble servant was never lenient then. The threshing floor was scorched through its (whole stock of) 220 sheaves and it (i.e. the province) never received a harvest yield from anyone (during) the years of famine while corn ran short, whereas it existed in my entire province. I did everything that was good in the temple of the lady of the universe. I spent all my years as an inspector of those who descended to the temple. I acted so that the priests praised it. I did not allow a man to fight with his brothers ....[11]

The 'sole friend' and 'overseer of the foreign-speaking troops', Djari, reports fights with the 'house of Khety' (Pl. XVIII):[12]

I came forth and the Horus Wahankh, the king, son of Re Intef, born of Neferu, has sent me after I fought with the house of Khety ....

Another important stela belongs to the 'treasurer' Tjetji and was set up under Nakhtnebtepnefer Intef III the successor of Wahankh Intef II. Tjetji reports events under the latter. It is an important document for the administration of the palace, not only for the Eleventh Dynasty but for the whole Middle Kingdom:

> I spent a long period of years under the majesty of my lord Horus Wahankh, King of Upper and Lower Egypt, Son of Re Intef, while this land was under his command from Abu (Elephantine) to Thinis in the Thinite province, I being his personal servant, his chamberlain in very truth.
>
> He made me great, he advanced my rank; he put me in the place of his trust, in his private palace. The treasure was in my hand under my seal, being the best of every good thing brought to the majesty of my lord from Upper Egypt, from Lower Egypt of everything that gladdens the heart, as tribute from this entire land, owing to the fear of him throughout this land.[13]

Another stela, set up for the king himself at his tomb at Thebes, is dated to his fiftieth year and reports the same extension of the small kingdom. The text is partly damaged but seems to mention that the tenth Upper Egyptian province was also conquered:[14]

> Up to the tenth Upper Egyptian province (I placed) its northern (bor)der. In Inet-Hezi I made the (mourning pots); I conquered the whole province of Tjeni (Thinis), after I opened its fortresses ....

King Wahankh Intef II started to renovate and build at several temples in his small kingdom. In the Old Kingdom there is remarkably little evidence for royal building work at provincial temples. Away from major centres of royal cult such as Hieraconpolis, temples seem to have been developed mainly by the local communities. Old traditions, perhaps often going back to prehistoric times, were still strong at many places. The royal building programme in the Old Kingdom seems to have been very much concentrated on the pyramid complex, in the Fifth Dynasty in conjunction with the royal sun temples. Both building types (pyramid complex and sun temple) are involved with the cult of the living and dead king. In the Sixth Dynasty royal *ka*-houses were built across the whole country; these are also temples reserved for the king's cult. By contrast, there are few surviving examples of royal building works at temples not connected with the king's cult. The most notable is perhaps a monolithic granite shrine for the Satet temple at Elephantine erected by Merenre in the Sixth Dynasty. Other examples are harder to interpret. There are clear signs of royal building work on a monumental scale at the temples of Heliopolis, Hieraconpolis and Abydos. However, the gods of these places have exceptionally strong links to kingship, as the cult centres of, respectively, the sun-god

14

Re, Horus the god of kingship, and his father Osiris-Khenty-amentiu the 'dead king'. Therefore these temples too may have a connection to the king's cult. Old Kingdom relief fragments found at Tod and Koptos are not easy to explain; they were found without context and may belong to *ka*-houses. With Wahankh Intef II something new seems to have started. Several temples were renovated or small chapels were added. Local temples became the subject of royal interest, on a scale not known or at least not attested before.[15] The best-documented example is the Satet temple at Elephantine, where the king added one chapel and renovated the main sanctuary, cladding the walls with stone. Several doorjambs and other fragments from it are preserved.[16] At Karnak was found a column with the name of the king and the name Amun; it is so far the earliest known architectural remnant of the Amun temple.[17]

Like Seherutawy Intef I, King Wahankh Intef II was buried in a *saff* tomb at Thebes. The place is today called Saff el-Kisasija.[18] The existence of this tomb was already known to Egyptology long before its excavation, because it is mentioned in the Ramesside tomb-robbery papyri. A mission in year 16 of Ramses IX (20th Dynasty) responsible for checking disturbed tombs passed this royal monument and described it as a destroyed pyramid with a stela in front of it on which a named dog is visible. The tomb chamber itself was found intact. A stela with named dogs was indeed excavated in the nineteenth century but was partly broken; this is the monument that reports important events of the king's reign in his struggle against the North. Like his predecessor, King Wahankh Intef II did not have a full royal titulary, and seems therefore not to have regarded himself as full king.

Intef III (Horus Nakhtnebtepnefer) (c. 2016-2008 BC)

Horus Nakhtnebtepnefer Intef III is the last of the three Eleventh Dynasty kings with the name Intef. Several monuments mention his name, but there are not many concrete events recorded, not surprisingly given his short reign. Nakhtnebtepnefer Intef III was the son of his predecessor Wahankh Intef II and of the king's wife Neferu (also known as Neferukau or Neferukayt). According to the Turin Canon he reigned just eight years. The change of reign from Wahankh Intef II to Nakhtnebtepnefer Intef III is described on the stela of the 'treasurer' Tjetji cited above:

> I am wealthy, I am great, I furnished myself from my own property, given to me by the majesty of my lord, because of his great love for me – Horus Wahankh, King of Upper and Lower Egypt, Son of Re, Intef, who lives like Re forever – until he went in peace to his horizon.
> Now when his son had taken his place Horus Nakhtnebtepnefer, King of Upper and Lower Egypt, Son of Re Intef born of Neferu, who lives like Re for ever – I followed him to all his good places of heart's content ... I passed all my time on earth as personal chamberlain of the king. I was wealthy; I was

great under his majesty. I am a man of character, praised by his lord every day.[19]

The mother of Nakhtnebtepnefer Intef III is well known from a stela found at Denderah set up by the 'royal sealer', 'sole friend' and 'steward', Redi-ui-Khnum, who was the administrator of the estates of the 'queen's mother', Neferukayt. Each queen had her own estate administered by a staff of stewards and other managers. Neferukayt bears the titles 'king's mother', 'king's daughter' and 'beloved king's wife'. She was therefore probably the daughter of Seherutawy Intef I and the wife of Intef II. The queen bears the title 'mistress of Upper Egypt'. On the stela it is described how Redi-ui-Khnum organised the provinces from the first province in the South (Elephantine) to the tenth Upper Egyptian nome (province) in the North, presumably the parts of Egypt ruled by the Thebans at this time. The stela is not dated by a king's name but seems to belong to the first years of Nakhtnebtepnefer Intef III.[20] The most important parts of the stela are translated here:

> I (Redi-ui-Khnum) have spent a long period of years under my mistress, the royal ornament Neferukayt ... being a king's daughter and a king's beloved wife. She had inherited it all from her mother. She has resettled Upper Egypt, the van of men from Elephantine to the Wadjit nome [the tenth Upper Egyptian province] with women together with estate managers and officials from the whole country.
>
> I grew up under the feet of her majesty since my earliest youth .... Then she placed me at Denderah in the great cattle farm of her mother, rich in record, a foremost enterprise, the greatest estate of Upper Egypt ....
>
> I managed the estate successfully. I enlarged all its departments ....[21]

The queen is also attested in the filiation of the king, in which he is often called 'born of Neferu'. Neferu is in this case therefore most likely the abbreviation of Neferukayt. On a fragment found in the king's tomb appears a woman called Neferukau, referring doubtless to the same woman.[22]

Little building activity is known. King Nakhtnebtepnefer Intef III added to the Satet temple at Elephantine.[23] An inscription with the name of the king in the sanctuary of Heqaib at Elephantine reports that there was some monument in ruins, most likely the sanctuary of Heqaib, and that he rebuilt it.[24] Like his predecessors the king was buried at el-Tarif in a huge *saff* tomb, known today as Saff el-Baqar. It is today badly damaged,[25] but fragments of reliefs and of sarcophagi demonstrate that it was once richly adorned.[26]

In terms of material culture the early Eleventh Dynasty clearly still belongs to the First Intermediate Period. In this period each region in Egypt had developed its own style. This is especially clearly visible in funerary material, better known than any other aspect of culture in this

period. Coffins, wooden models placed in tombs, pottery and tomb architecture differ from place to place. The quality of reliefs, paintings and the
style of sculpture which adorned the tomb chapels of richer individuals has
often been described as in decline. It is true that these objects often seem
to display a certain lack of craftsmanship and perfection (Pl. XVIII), in
comparison to the classical Old Kingdom. However, it should be remembered that at many sites where monuments of the First Intermediate
Period have been found, little or nothing of formal art had been produced
in the Old Kingdom. Therefore art production at these sites often represents
not a decline but a new beginning. The high-quality monuments of the Old
Kingdom in the provinces may have been produced by craftsmen of the
residence region, men who came for only a short period to these places before
returning to the residence or going to another place. In the First Intermediate
Period this did not happen on the same scale, as these places may have lost
direct contact with the workshops of the royal residence.

Art production in the Memphite region kept up a certain high standard
throughout the First Intermediate Period, to such an extent that it is often
hard to tell whether a particular object belongs to the Old Kingdom or the
following period. The workshops seem to have continued production here
without interruption, although major royal monuments are missing, or at
least have been not yet found.

Already under the early Eleventh Dynasty Thebes seems to have been
a substantial urban centre. At el-Tarif there is a huge cemetery of the
officials of the period, around the tombs of their kings. The normal tomb
type at this site as already mentioned is the *saff* tomb, with an open court
cut into the ground, a row of pilasters at one side and burial shaft and cult
rooms behind it. Far the largest *saff* tombs belong to the kings, but many
of their officials were buried in similar, smaller structures. These tombs
were mainly decorated with stelae. The cemetery at el-Tarif has been
extensively looted over the last centuries and therefore not much of the
decoration is left. Many stelae in different museums all over the world
dating to the Eleventh Dynasty must come from el-Tarif, but almost none
of them were found at their original site. Many more must have been taken
away already in antiquity, and reused or burnt for lime. We have therefore
only a limited picture of the officials serving the kings of the early
Eleventh Dynasty.

1.4. The second part of the Eleventh Dynasty (*c.* 2008-1938 BC)

Sources

There is a wide range of sources for the second part of the Eleventh
Dynasty. King Mentuhotep II and King Mentuhotep III are well known
from many temples in Upper Egypt, though these buildings are much
damaged. Most of the preserved scenes show the kings together with

various gods. They are an important source for religious beliefs and expression of kingship, but do not often provide information on political history. Of the funerary temples, only that of Mentuhotep II is known and excavated. The building must have once been fully decorated with reliefs, but they are again only preserved in fragments and so far have not been fully collected and published. The courtiers of the kings are better known, although their tombs are also badly damaged; there are some stelae decorated with biographies. There are finally several rock inscriptions naming the king, some events and officials. Other rock inscriptions (for example at the alabaster quarries of Hatnub) are hard to date; they provide important information, but it is still difficult to fit them in our general picture of the events. Altogether, therefore, the information on the period remains patchy. A new discovery, such as a new biographical inscription, could instantly change our view of the second part of the Eleventh Dynasty. It is particularly remarkable that it is still not known how and when the unification within the reign of Mentuhotep II happened. There are surprisingly few sources which relate to that key event.

Nebhepetre Mentuhotep II (c. 2008 to 1957 BC)

Nebhepetre Mentuhotep II[27] was the son of Nakhtnebtepnefer Intef III and a woman called Iah. His main wife, and the mother of his successor, was the 'king's wife' and 'king's mother', Tem. Another wife was Neferu, the sister of the king; finally there were five women buried in the royal funerary complex with the titles 'king's wife', 'sole royal ornament' and 'priestess of Hathor'. Their status is disputed.[28] Several other women known from burials around the king's temple may have been some kind of concubines.[29] The only son known for sure is the successor Mentuhotep III, perhaps the man shown as 'king's son' in the funerary temple of the king.[30] Mentuhotep II reigned fifty-one years; during this time Egypt was finally reunited. Mentuhotep II appears in later sources (most often as Nebhepetre) together with Menes (founder of the Old Kingdom) and Ahmose (founder of the New Kingdom) as one of the great kings of Egypt.[31] In the view of later periods he was therefore the founder of one of the classical eras of Egypt. This view is confirmed by the fact that he is the first king to appear in several king lists after a gap covering almost all kings of the First Intermediate Period.

In the course of his long and momentous reign, Mentuhotep II changed his names twice. This modification of name has generally been seen as a reflection of important political events. Already in the Old Kingdom, the royal titulary had consisted of five main titles each with a name, and in a fixed sequence: the Horus name, the *nebty* ('two ladies' – the goddesses Nekhbet and Uto representing Upper and Lower Egypt), the gold Horus name, the throne and finally the so-called birth name. Mentuhotep II bore at first a simple titulary: Horus Seankhibtawy ('who causes the heart of the two lands to live'), son of Re Mentuhotep. This titulary follows the model of the Intef kings who also only had a Horus and a birth name. The only dated monument with this titulary is a private stela from year 14.[32] The second change of names must have happened before year 39, when the last name is already attested. No datable monument is connected with this second Horus name, Netjeri-hedjet, and a nebty name, also Netjeri-hedjet. With this Horus name there is connected for the first time in the Eleventh Dynasty a throne name: Nebhepetre. The king therefore not only modified his Horus name but also added further elements of a full royal titulary. Royal names are always also part of royal propaganda. It seems therefore likely that the change of name was connected with a change in politics or even with major conquests in the north, but nothing for sure can be said about this. By year 39 he is finally called Horus Sematawy – 'who united the two countries'. The name refers clearly to Egypt's reunification. It is not known when the king took this name. At about the same time he seems to have changed the writing of his throne name (a different *hepet* sign was chosen) and he took over the full royal titulary including the gold Horus name, not previously attested in this dynasty.

The most important event of the reign is the unification of the country. His Horus name, Sematawy, in the last phase of his reign clearly refers to this event. Some reliefs found in several parts of Upper Egypt and once belonging to chapels seem to be the only direct evidence from the king himself relating to the unification. On a fragment found at Gebelein Mentuhotep II (here named Netjeri-hedjet) is shown smiting enemies, which is a rather conventional scene in Egyptian art. However, the person subdued by the king is an Egyptian and not a foreigner, as normally appears in these scenes. The inscription to the image says: 'overthrowing the heads of the two countries, founding of Upper and Lower Egypt, the foreign lands, the two riverbanks, and the nine bows ....' At the back of a chapel found at Denderah Mentuhotep II is depicted striding forwards in the stance of a king smiting his enemies, but instead of an enemy he is holding two plants: the lotus and the papyrus, representing Upper and Lower Egypt. It is tempting to see in this depiction a reference to the unification of Egypt (see p. 94). On a stela of the steward Henenu, who served Mentuhotep II, appears the phrase 'he suppressed the south, north, east and west'.[33] Finally in the autobiographical inscription of an official named Intef, who served under Wahankh Intef II, Nakhtnebtepnefer Intef III and Horus Seankhibtawy Mentuhotep II, there is mentioned a 'year of a rebellion in Thinis', which seems to relate to some battles, although nothing more is known.[34]

There is also some evidence that the king undertook a military campaign to Asia, most likely to south Palestine. In the tomb of the 'overseer of the troops', Intef, the siege of an Asiatic fortress is shown.[35] It is not known whether this relates to a real event. Asiatic people are also shown in the reliefs of the funerary temple of the king at Deir el-Bahri. It remains unknown whether this refers to historic events or whether it is a symbolic representation.[36] In a rock inscription of a certain Tjehemu found at Abisko (Lower Nubia) campaigns against Asiatics are mentioned. However, it may not necessarily refer to an expedition to Asia, for people called Asiatics (Aamu) also lived in the eastern desert:[37]

> Inscription made by Tjehemu in the year of overthrowing the hill countries. I started to fight in the army in the time of Nebhepetre, when he travelled south to Ben (= Buhen?). [...] He (the king) crossed the whole land to kill the Aamu (Asiatics) of Djaty, when it would approach (in opposition), and Thebes was in fight. It was the Nubian who fought; then (he) overthrew Djaty with the result that he raised sail in sailing southwind.[38]

The campaigns of the king against Nubia are a little better known. Nubia is the neighbour of Egypt to its south. In its northern parts the country is not very fertile and therefore not densely populated. However, it has enticing raw materials (gold, copper) and, for this reason if not as a security threat, it was already in the Old Kingdom often the target of military campaigns. In the First Intermediate Period many Nubian soldiers seem to have served under Egyptians. Mentuhotep II started to attack the country again. A fragment of an inscription from Deir el-Ballas reports a victory over Wawat (Lower Nubia). A block from Gebelein shows the king smiting Nubians (Setiu), Asiatics (Setjetiu) and Libyans (Tjehenu).[39] An inscription carved in the rock near Aswan, and dated to year 41 of the king, reports: 'coming of the royal sealer and sole friend, overseer of sealers Khety, born of Satre from Wawat [Lower Nubia]'.[40] Finally reliefs on a chapel in Denderah indicate that various Nubian tribes had to pay tribute.[41] For all these depictions and texts originally from temple decoration, it might be doubted that they refer to real events. However, the inscription found at Abisko demonstrates that troops under the leadership of the king were there. It is not known whether Lower Nubia was already conquered by the king, or whether these campaigns just refer to short forays to force the Nubians to pay tribute.

Mentuhotep II started a large-scale royal building programme. The king built at several sites in Upper Egypt. In Denderah he erected a small chapel which was at the beginning of the twentieth century still fully preserved. Other sites with evidence of his building programme are Abydos,[42] Deir el-Ballas (the blocks found there may originally have come from Nubt),[43] Armant,[44] Gebelein,[45] Elkab[46] and Elephantine.[47] Substantial parts are also preserved from the Mont-temple of the king in Tod, where it is even possible to reconstruct part of the plan.[48] The reliefs found here and in the other temples are of the highest quality. However, most often only single blocks are preserved. The temple of Mentuhotep II at Abydos seems to have been an important building, whereas at least some of the other remains may come from a small chapel such as the one found at Denderah. There is so far no building with the name of the king anywhere north of Abydos. In the North the king may not have undertaken bigger construction projects. All the sites with remains mentioning Mentuhotep II are located inside an area which was already ruled by Wahankh Intef II. It may reflect the core region of his reign. The main monument of the king's reign was clearly his mortuary temple in Deir el-Bahri (Thebes), built in several phases (p. 89).[49] The king left the old royal necropolis of the early Eleventh Dynasty el-Tarif to build his mortuary temple in a valley surrounded by the high cliffs of the western desert.

Mentuhotep II seems to have reorganised the administration of the royal court, and indeed of the whole country. The royal court of the early Eleventh Dynasty was essentially arranged like the court of a provincial governor. There was a treasurer ('overseer of sealed goods'), responsible for the goods coming to the palace and there was the steward ('overseer of an estate'), responsible for the lands supplying the palace and the king with agricultural products. Both offices are already known in the Old Kingdom administration of private estates, but did not belong to the organisation of the royal court. When the small Theban province became a kingdom, these offices suddenly became state offices. Mentuhotep II also seems to have introduced into his state many offices coming from the royal court of the Old Kingdom, but not attested in the early Eleventh Dynasty at Thebes. At the head of the administration there was placed the vizier, who had this important position in almost all periods of ancient Egyptian history. The treasurer was second only to the vizier, presumably because he administered the luxury goods coming to the palace. The steward (in the Twelfth Dynasty called 'high steward') managed the estates of the state and the king. The 'scribe of the royal document' filled an office taken from the administration of the Old Kingdom. He seems to have been the personal scribe of the king. The importance of these people is clearly seen in their monuments. They have the biggest tombs and the highest quality sculpture. It is not easy to say whether the king also reorganised the provincial administration. The Middle Kingdom rock-cut tombs of Beni Hasan started in the Eleventh Dynasty. They show that the new regime placed loyal people in this region most likely to gain better control over the area. It is unclear under which king this happened. Mentuhotep II also reorganised the use of certain titles. Ranking titles (p. 158) announce the position of an official in relation to the king and to other officials. For example, the title 'member of the elite' (*iry-pat*) was in the Old Kingdom a sign of the highest position at the royal court. Only people with a special status were allowed to bear the title. At the end of the Old Kingdom and in the First Intermediate Period the title lost its exclusive character. Almost everybody boasted of being a 'member of the elite'. Under Mentuhotep II there were again only a few people with the title. The ranking titles were now obviously again restricted to a small number of important officials. They were only given to the highest court officials and appear in the provinces for the governors and perhaps a small number of other people who had a special status. The ranking titles were never found in connection with officials of a lower status.

Some officials seem to have come from the North to work for the new regime. A certain Khety reports that he served 'in the domain of the North'.[50] The name of the treasurer Khety, a different official, may also indicate that this high official came from the North. Khety is a common king's name under the Heracleopolitan Dynasties. Finally there is good evidence that artists from the Memphis region now worked in Thebes.[51]

The high courtiers of the last years of his reign are especially well known compared to other reigns of the Middle Kingdom. There are many rock inscriptions naming officials. These officials are also mentioned in the funerary complex of the king in Deir el-Bahri, and the tombs of many of them are preserved. Two viziers are attested under Mentuhotep II. There is Bebi,[52] known only from a fragment found in the funerary temple of the king, and Dagi, who started his career as 'overseer of the gateway' and was appointed vizier under Mentuhotep II.[53] He is attested with both functions in the funerary temple of the king and is also known from his important tomb in Deir el-Bahri. Khety was the treasurer in office in the second part of the king's reign. He appears together with the king, the 'king's mother' and the 'god's father', Intef, in a relief at Shat er-Rigal. He was leading figure in the *sed* festival[54] of the king.[55] The *sed* festival was perhaps the most important celebration of kingship in ancient Egypt, attested since the First Dynasty; on the basis of New Kingdom examples (Amenhotep III, Ramses II), it would have been celebrated in about the thirtieth year of a king's reign, and thereafter every three years. A prominent role in the *sed* must have amounted to a display of exceptional royal favour of an official. Khety had an important tomb in Thebes. Its decoration in sunken relief is today badly damaged but originally included depictions of the king on stelae.[56] This is new; no mastaba or tomb of the Old Kingdom has in its decoration the depiction of a king. Another treasurer attested under Mentuhotep II and most likely the successor of Khety is Meketre, who also appears several times in the decoration of the king's funerary temple. He is mainly known from the wooden models found in his tomb, which dates to the end of the Eleventh or early Twelfth Dynasty. The third important court official was the 'steward' or 'steward in the entire country' as the title was sometimes given in the Eleventh and early Twelfth Dynasty. There are two people with the office attested; one is Buau Mentuhotep, known only from his coffin, found in a small shaft tomb. He may have stayed in office only a short while, having no time to prepare a big tomb. Henenu is known from the smashed stelae found in his tomb. He is still attested under Mentuhotep III. Of the other officials the 'overseer of the troops', Intef, has been mentioned in connection with the depiction of the siege of an Asiatic town.

With unification, art production received a new impetus. The king commissioned important building projects and the tombs of officials were built on a scale not known from the First Intermediate Period. However, in terms of material culture there is still a variety of styles and local developments throughout the country under Mentuhotep II. It is generally impossible to date an object without an inscription to the time before or after the unification and even for inscribed objects this is often not easy. Reliefs of the royal mortuary complex at Deir el-Bahri and in the different temples built by the king in Upper Egypt generally display a high quality. The raised relief is often bold in comparison with reliefs of the Old Kingdom (which are sometimes rather flat), giving the figures a robust appearance. Other reliefs, especially in the mortuary temple, are stylistically more similar to Old Kingdom prototypes. This supports the idea that artists in the Memphite region, where into the early Middle Kingdom they followed Old Kingdom traditions, worked in Thebes after the unification.[57] There is also a wide range of relief styles found in the much damaged tombs of the highest court officials. The reliefs in the tomb of the treasurer Khety are sunken, and, in comparison to the solid figures in many royal reliefs, perhaps appear quite slim and attenuated. The workmanship is of a high level but obviously made by artists working in a different tradition. However, there are many other tombs of court officials, and even some of queens, which display a rather crude provincial style. These indicate a lack of trained artists and craftsmen. Evidently, after the unification, with the prosperity of the country, suddenly there was a strong demand for well-trained artists. In the provinces at places such as Sedment, Qaw or Badari the change from the time of the early to the late Eleventh Dynasty is not visible in terms of material culture. Coffins and wooden models, typical grave goods for ruling-class burials, are often hard to date. These object types developed slowly and their development seems not to have been interrupted by political events. Especially at Memphis, although much written material has been found there, it is almost impossible to date objects precisely. The inscriptions of officials buried there refer to cults of kings, but not explicitly to the reigning king. In the (inscribed) archaeological material the Eleventh Dynasty does not appear in Memphis and in the North.

Mentuhotep II was in later times worshipped as a god. He appears as such on private monuments,[58] but there are also many later royal donations to his temple.

Mentuhotep III (c. 1957-1945 BC)

The mother of Sankhkare Mentuhotep III was the 'king's wife' and 'king's mother', Tem,[59] wife of Mentuhotep II. The latter was therefore most probably the father of Mentuhotep III. According to the Turin Canon, Mentuhotep III reigned twelve years. Little is known about his reign, but he seems to have followed the line of his father Mentuhotep II. There is clear evidence for building work at several temples in Upper Egypt. An inscription in the Wadi Hammamat mentions an expedition to Punt. The tomb of the king has not yet been securely identified. A huge unfinished tomb in Thebes near the temple of Mentuhotep II used to be identified as his burial place. Recent research has shown how uncertain this is, proposing instead that the complex may have been planned for Amenemhat I early in his reign.[60]

The most important historical monument of Mentuhotep's III reign is a long rock inscription in the Wadi Hammamat dated to year 8 of the king. It reports an expedition of the steward Henenu, who describes how he went to Punt and on the way home brought statues for the king:

> My lord has send me to go with great ships to Punt to bring for him fresh myrrh from the highest rulers of the desert ... then I went forth from Koptos on the way his majesty had ordered upon the road, which his majesty commanded me. A troop from the South was with me ... I went forth with a troop of 3000 men .... Now I made twelve wells in the bush and two wells in Idehat, 20 cubits in one and 30 cubits in the other .... Then I reached the Sea; then I made this ship, and I dispatched it with all things, when I had made for it a great oblation of cattle, bulls and ibexes. After my return from the Sea, I made what his majesty commanded and brought for him all the gifts, which I had found at the shores of God's land. I returned through the Wadi Hammamat, I brought for him fantastic blocks for statues for the temple ....[61]

Monuments of this king are found predominantly at places where Mentuhotep II had already built. Some remains seem to come from larger buildings, as at the Osiris-Khenty-amentiu temple at Abydos,[62] to which a *ka*-chapel of the king also belonged,[63] and Elephantine,[64] while the remains at other places may just come from redecoration of existing temple structures, as at Armant.[65] Substantial parts are preserved from the temple of Mont at Tod. The king seems to have rebuilt there the temple of his father Mentuhotep II and adorned it with reliefs of the highest quality.[66] At Thebes, Mentuhotep III erected a small sanctuary in the high desert mountains.[67] A statue with the name of the king in the offering formula was acquired at Qantir,[68] and suggests that in later times the king was deified. However, many objects found at Qantir were brought here later; therefore the origin of the small statue remains unknown.

The court of the king is not well documented; some of the officials already known from the reign of Mentuhotep II may still have been in office, such as the vizier Dagi, the treasurer Meketre and the steward Henenu of the Punt expedition. Another official who is datable to the end of the Eleventh Dynasty is the 'overseer of the quarry', Khety, known only from his tomb where three stelae with autobiographical inscriptions were found. On one of the stelae Khety reports (only translated in part):[69]

1. History

I am a god's sealer in overthrowing the foreign lands. I was in Sinai (?) and saw it; I travelled in the countries of Temhet. I was in the domain of the North; I sealed its treasury at the mountain of the domain 'Horus of the turquoise street'... I travelled on the order of this my lord (the king) and did what he loved ... I have defended the Asiatics in their own countries ... I returned in peace to the palace and brought to him (the king) the best of the foreign countries.

The events described may have happened under Mentuhotep II, Mentuhotep III or even under Mentuhotep IV. Only for Mentuhotep IV is it known for sure that he sent an expedition to Sinai. For Mentuhotep II it seems plausible that he fought in Asia and therefore it is difficult to assign the events mentioned in this inscription to a particular king. Khety is not known from other sources apart from his tomb.

Nebtawyre Mentuhotep IV (c. 1945-1938 BC)

The last king of the dynasty does not appear in the later king lists and, on that evidence alone, it has been argued that he was a usurper. The Turin Canon does not mention the king but records seven years without naming a king at the end of the Eleventh Dynasty. It remains unclear whether these seven years were filled with the reign of Nebtawyre Mentuhotep IV, or whether there followed other kings. However, this part of the Turin Canon is not well preserved and it is not clear whether these seven years refer to a period without a king or whether the scribe of the manuscript could not read a king's name appearing in the manuscript he was copying. The monuments of the reign of Mentuhotep IV are not abundant, and consist mainly of expedition inscriptions. They show no signs that the king may have been in trouble, or that he was a usurper, although this is the kind of information official Egyptian inscriptions do not provide anyway. There is a fragment of a bowl found at Lisht with the name of the king on one side and with the name of Amenemhat I on the other.[70] The name of Mentuhotep IV is not erased, indicating that the later king respected his reign. However, already under Senusret I his name and person seem to have been ignored. In an inscription on a statue found on Sinai at Serabit el-Khadim there are listed four kings: Kheperkare (Senusret I), Sehetep-ibre (Amenemhat I), Nebhepetre (Mentuhotep II) and Sankhkare (Mentuhotep III). Mentuhotep IV is missing. The last king mentioned is Senusret I, under whom the inscription was probably cut. However, nothing is known about the intention of the inscription and it seems therefore unwise to draw any further conclusions.[71]

Mentuhotep IV is otherwise known only from a number of rock inscriptions, where he appears as the son of the 'king's mother', Imi. The most important of his inscriptions were found at the Wadi Hammamat, five others at the Wadi el-Hudi (south-east of Aswan) and one in the North at Ayn Soukhna, which is on the route from Memphis to Sinai. The inscriptions at the Wadi Hammamat are of special interest because they report the search for and selection of a sarcophagus and material for statues for the king. The expedition leader was the vizier Amenemhat. The inscriptions at the Wadi Hammamat are dated to the second year of the king. In one of the inscriptions is mentioned the first *sed* festival of the king in his second year. The *sed* festival was normally celebrated after thirty years, and there is no evidence, though much speculation, for why the king performed the festival so early in his reign. The main texts of one of the Wadi Hammamat inscriptions reports:

> This wonder happened to his majesty: that the small cattle of the deserts came down to him; there came a pregnant gazelle, going with her face toward the people before her. Her eyes looked backward, but she did not turn back, until she arrived at this noble mountain at this block, it being still in its place for this lid of this sarcophagus. She gave birth upon it while this army of the king was looking. Then they cut her neck before the block and brought fire. It descended in safety.[72]

Another inscription reports:

> My majesty sent forth the 'member of the elite', overseer of the city and vizier, overseer of royal works, favourite of the king Amenemhat with an army of 10,000 men from the southern provinces of Upper Egypt beginning from the Theban province to bring for me a noble block of pure stone which is in this mountain.[73]

Four Wadi Hammamat inscriptions mention the vizier Amenemhat as leader of the expedition. It has been assumed that he was the future King Amenemhat I and that he was the real power in Egypt at this time. The latter assumption is not proven, though the hypothesis that the vizier and the later king are identical is at least possible.

The five inscriptions of the reign at the Wadi el-Hudi mention the bringing of amethyst, which is the main material collected in the area.[74] The inscription at Ayn Soukhna, only recently discovered, reports a troop of 3000 men bringing turquoise.[75] Turquoise is always mentioned in the inscriptions on Sinai, for which Ayn Soukhna must have been some kind of port or landing-stage on the Egyptian side.

Nothing is known about the end of the reign of Mentuhotep IV and of the end of the Eleventh Dynasty. The biography of a courtier found at Lisht names Amenemhat I and three kings before him (their names are not preserved) demonstrating that the administration of the country went on without much of a break from the end of the Eleventh to the Twelfth Dynasty.[76]

The court of Mentuhotep IV is not well known; his vizier was the Amenemhat in the Wadi Hammamat inscriptions. The treasurer and high steward was perhaps still Meketre, if he died under the next king.

2. Rock inscription naming King Qakare.

Nubian kings? (c. 1945-1938 BC)

In Lower Nubia in the area from Bab el-Kalabsha to Abu Simbel were found a number of rock inscriptions naming three kings: 1. Horus Ankhkhnumre, Wadjkare Zegerzenti; 2. Horus Geregtawy Iy-ib-khenti-re Intef; and 3. Horus Senefertawyf Qakare In (or perhaps Intef) (Fig. 2). Their position is uncertain but it seems plausible that they belong to or shortly after the Eleventh Dynasty. The name Intef and the construction of the Horus name with *-tawy* ('the double land') are typical for this period. The kings have a fuller royal titulary than the kings of the early Eleventh Dynasty, indicating a later date. This seems to point to a date under or after Mentuhotep II, who was the first king of the period with the same longer titulary. The 'Nubian kings' are only known from these rock inscriptions, no other objects or buildings with their names being so far known. The end of the Eleventh Dynasty is somewhat mysterious and therefore it had been assumed that these kings belong into this period. However, there is no proof for that view. Only for Wadjkare Zegerzenti is a longer text known, referring to military actions against enemies of one of these kings:

> Order made to the son of the ruler, that he might overthrow the enemies of his father, the Horus Ankhkhnumre the King Wadjkare, son of Re Zegerzenti in the north of Per-senbebet, looking at Zekha and Wag.[77]

Two possibilities may be put forward concerning the position of these kings:
1. They may have been the last kings of the Eleventh Dynasty, only reigning for a short time. Against this idea might count that these kings are only attested in Lower Nubia. However, Mentuhotep IV is also almost exclusively attested outside of the Nile valley and there seems no doubt that he ruled over Egypt.
2. A second possibility is that these kings formed an independent Nubian kingdom at the end of the Eleventh and the early Twelfth Dynasty. In an inscription of the vizier Intefiqer under Amenemhat I, found in Lower

Nubia, appears the phrase 'as one has to act against him who rebelled against the king'. The 'rebel against the king' may be a reference to one of these Nubian kings.[78]

1.5. The early Twelfth Dynasty (*c.* 1938-1837 BC)

Sources

There is again a wide range of sources for the first half of the Twelfth Dynasty. For all kings the pyramids are known and excavated. However, the state of preservation varies, as does the standard of excavations and their publications. Thus, a king such as Senusret I, with a better preserved pyramid and tombs of officials around, is more accessible to us than a king such as Amenemhat II whose pyramid and contemporary cemeteries are more ruined and less explored. The names of Twelfth Dynasty kings are found all around the country; in particular, rock inscriptions left by mining or trading expeditions often provide valuable information. In the first half of the Twelfth Dynasty many provincial cemeteries in Middle Egypt flourished. The tombs of the local governors are often fully decorated, sometimes even with biographical inscriptions providing further valuable data on life in the provinces at this period. The tombs of the local bureaucrats working for these governors are also known. Though usually not decorated, they contained painted coffins often inscribed with long religious texts, an essential source for religious beliefs of the period. However, some other cemeteries used in the First Intermediate Period stopped being used as burial grounds under Senusret I (notably Sedment and those in the Badari/Qaw region). For the First Intermediate Period those sites were an important source for the lower levels of society. Presumably these people were being buried somewhere else in the Twelfth Dynasty, and their tombs have yet to be found. Perhaps this relocation of burial grounds points to some reorganisation of society, but this remains an open question.

Sehetepibre Amenemhat I (c. 1939/1938-1909 BC)

The first king of the Twelfth Dynasty is Sehetepibre Amenemhat I, who was probably the vizier mentioned in the Wadi Hammamat inscriptions of Mentuhotep IV, although final proof of this identification is lacking. Three major literary compositions ('Prophecy of Neferty', 'Instruction of King Amenemhat I for his Son Senusret I', 'The Tale of Sinuhe') relate most likely to events under Amenemhat I. None of them needs to have been written under the king, but the three works supply us with at least indirect information on his reign. However, there are still many open questions about this time. Monuments of the king in the country are not abundant, although he reigned thirty years. The number of court officials datable to his reign is also not very high. Most of their tombs are still missing.

The mother of Amenemhat I was a woman called 'king's mother', Nefret, who appears on an offering table found at the pyramid complex of the king at Lisht. In the 'Prophecy of Neferty' the mother of a king named Ameny (most likely Amenemhat I) is mentioned as a woman from Ta-seti – the 'land of bows' (first Upper Egyptian nome).[79] The father of the king appears in later sources as 'god's father', Senusret. Both parents are obviously of non-royal origin. The title 'god's father' refers in this case to the position as a father of a king and is not a position in administration or in a temple. Therefore the social background of this man remains unknown. The relation of Amenemhat I to the last Eleventh Dynasty king Mentuhotep IV is not known for sure, but a bowl with the name of both kings was found at Lisht, as mentioned above. Amenemhat I seems to have respected his predecessor of the Eleventh Dynasty.[80]

The events of the first years of the reign of Amenemhat I are rather unclear. In the beginning the king seems to have had the titulary Horus Sehetepibtawy, *nebty* Sehetepibtawy, gold Horus Sema; this was changed at some point early in his rule.[81] There is an inscription at Ayn Soukhna, most probably datable to year 7, which perhaps gives a new Horus name, Horus Wehem-mesut, indicating that the change of name occurred early in his reign. The new titulary is significant, for Wehem-mesut means 'Renewal of births' or 'Renaissance'. It seems clear that the king saw himself as the founder of a new era. However, the inscription at Ayn Soukhna is heavily damaged, and the reading of the name is far from certain.[82] The idea of King Amenemhat I as the founder of a new era is also clearly expressed in the literary composition called today 'Prophecy of Neferty'. The story is set under King Snofru of the Fourth Dynasty. The king hears the saying of the 'lector-priest of Bastet' named Neferty. Neferty describes how the country will fall into disorder, but declares that at the end of this bad period there will come from the South a king named Ameny bringing order to Egypt. Ameny is a short form of Amenemhat and Amenemhat I is usually identified as the king whose coming is celebrated in this composition.[83]

The main event of Amenemhat's I reign seems to have been the founding of a new capital in the North, near the modern village Lisht, where the king also built his pyramid. The new Residence was called Itj-tawy-Amenemhat, 'Amenemhat is the one who grasps the Two Lands'. The precise timing of this move is not known and it is possible that the king stayed for a longer period at Thebes; therefore it has been proposed that the king started a substantial funerary monument there, which was never finished.[84] The tomb complex is located in a valley in West Thebes south-west of the funerary complex of Mentuhotep II; no archaeological evidence has been found there with any royal name, and it may therefore belong either to Mentuhotep III or to Mentuhotep IV, although at least Mentuhotep III reigned more than ten years and one might expect a more finished funerary complex for him.[85]

While it is not known for sure when the king moved his capital to the area of the modern village Lisht, at the new site Itj-tawy-(Amenemhat), there is some evidence that it was quite late in his reign. Possibly the king first tried to establish a capital in Memphis,[86] because at Saqqara, the necropolis of Memphis, many burials have been found of high-ranking persons, probably datable to this time.[87] It is not clear why the king did not stay in Memphis, but instead established a capital elsewhere. The move further to the south to Lisht may reflect a decision to be closer to the Fayum. The Fayum is a great lake, now salt, but connected to the Nile in the desert south-south-west of Memphis. Especially from the Middle Kingdom there are many attestations of increased interest in this region, which was very fertile and may have brought much more new ground into agricultural use. This new interest in the province seems to have already started with Amenemhat I, with the foundation of the new capital, although the first building work there so far known is from his son Senusret I. Another reason for the new site of the capital may be a more symbolic one. Itj-tawy is located directly on the border of Upper and Lower Egypt. Its name Itj-tawy, 'seizer of the Two Lands', thus appears in a new light. The capital was built exactly at the place where the Egyptians themselves sited the middle of their country.

Not much is known about the capital. In hieroglyphic writing the name of the town is often surrounded by a wall, indicating that it may have originally been more fortified palace than densely populated town. However, around the pyramid of Amenemhat I were found settlement remains of the Thirteenth Dynasty. They may be the remains of the suburbs of the town. Unlike many Egyptian towns there is no god which can be connected with Itj-tawy.

The pyramid of Amenemhat I at Lisht was finished in great haste. The name of the successor Senusret I appears more than once in the remains of the funerary temple, indicating that at least this temple was built at a time when Amenemhat I and Senusret I ruled together, or even that it was finished after the death of Amenemhat I. Furthermore some blocks mentioning both kings were used in the foundation of the funerary temple. The temple was therefore built when the two kings reigned together.[88] There is also a dated inscription at the pyramid, giving the 'year 1' without naming a king. One may argue that the inscription dates to Amenemhat I and is a proof of the beginning of the pyramid-building in his first year. However, considering the evidence from the blocks just mentioned, it seems more likely that 'year 1' refers to Senusret I, which is the first year of the coregency and year 20 of Amenemhat I. The pyramid-building seems therefore to have started only in the third decade of the reign. This may also be the time when the new capital was founded.[89] The name of the capital Itj-tawy appears for the first time on a private stela dated to year 30 of Amenemhat I and year 10 of Senusret I.[90]

Like many Egyptian rulers Amenemhat I was involved in several military campaigns against the lands adjacent to Egypt. There are references to campaigns and wars against all three main neighbours of Egypt: Nubia, Asia and Libya. Amenemhat I is well attested in several rock inscriptions in Lower Nubia at Abu Handal (about 150 km south of Aswan, near Korosko), where campaigns against Lower Nubia (Wawat) are mentioned. One inscription dates to year 29 of Amenemhat I and records: 'In year 29 of Sehetepibre (Amenemhat I) we came to vanquish Wawat'.[91] One undated inscription was set up by a certain Intefiqer and speaks a clearer language: 'Then the Nubians of the entire remaining part of Wawat were slaughtered. Thereupon I sailed victoriously upstream, slaughtering the Nubians on the riverbanks and then I sailed downstream plucking corn and cutting down their remaining trees. I set fire to their houses, as one has to act against him who has rebelled against the king.'[92] The inscription mentions the famous vizier Intefiqer, who also appears in another inscription in Lower Nubia and who seems to have been involved in these campaigns. Finally a reference to the Nubian wars is to be found in the 'Instruction of King Amenemhat I for his Son Senusret I', preserved on several manuscripts and ostraca of the New Kingdom: 'I repressed those of Wawat (name of Lower Nubia), I captured the Medjay (name of Nubian tribes in the eastern desert)'. There are also indications of war or campaigns against Asia in the same work of literature: 'I made the Asiatics do the dog walk'.[93] In the 'Prophecy of Neferty' Asiatics are mentioned: 'Asiatics will fall to his sword' [...] One will build the 'Walls-of-the-Ruler', to bar Asiatics from entering Egypt; They shall beg water as supplicants'.[94] On the stela of the 'overseer of troops', Nesmont, and in the biographical inscription of Khnumhotep at Beni Hasan[95] are references to military actions on the eastern border of Egypt. The defence system Walls-of-the-Ruler is also mentioned in the 'Tale of Sinuhe'. Sinuhe, the hero of the story, is leaving Egypt and recounts: 'I reached the Walls-of-the-Ruler which were made to repel the Asiatics and to crush the sand-farers'. The Walls-of-the-Ruler are mentioned only in these two literary compositions. Their exact location is not known. The Wadi Tumailat, the area of Tell ar-Rataba, has been proposed.[96] Finally there are references to campaigns against the Libyans. In the 'Prophecy of Neferty' it is simply mentioned that 'the Libyans fall to his flame'. The 'Tale of Sinuhe' is rather more substantial. At the time of the death of Amenemhat I his son was involved in a campaign against them: 'His majesty, however, had despatched an army to the land of the Tjemeh [Libyans], with his eldest son as its commander, the good god Senusret. He had been sent to smite the foreign lands and to punish those of Tjehenu [another Libyan tribe]'. All these military campaigns remain mysterious. For Lower Nubia it has been assumed that the country had been conquered up to the Second Cataract, although this is not certain. The campaigns against the Libyans and the Asiatics may just have had the aim of looting their lands, and protecting Egypt against attack. There are no indications that these campaigns were combined with the annexation of territory.

At several places in Egypt Amenemhat I seems to have installed governors, who were loyal to him and to the new ruling family. The first tomb of a governor at Meir dates most probably to the beginning of the Twelfth Dynasty. The new governors here were therefore most likely put in place by Amenemhat I. Senebi (I) was the first in office.[97] Khnumhotep (I) from Beni Hasan left in his tomb a biographical inscription where he said that he was installed in office by his majesty, most likely Amenemhat I, who is mentioned in the same inscription. At this place there was already a family of governors in office. The appointment of a new official may represent an attempt to install a new loyal line of people here.

There are indications that the rule of the king was not accepted everywhere in the country and that there was some kind of civil war. The stela of the 'overseer of troops', Nesmont, is one of our main sources for this:

I trained the troops in ambush and at daybreak the landing stage surrendered. When I grasped the tip of the bow, I led the battle for the two lands. I was victorious, my arms taking (so much spoil) that I had to leave (some) on the ground. I destroyed the foes, I overthrew the enemies of my lord, and there being none other who will say the like.[98]

Most important seems the phrase 'I overthrew the enemies of my lord', referring clearly to struggles inside Egypt. From the further text we learn that the base of the struggles was Thebes.

Like the kings of the Eleventh Dynasty, Amenemhat I rebuilt or renovated several temples in the country. In the Eleventh Dynasty royal building activity is so far only attested in Upper Egypt. For Amenemhat I there is also evidence that he built or renovated temples in Lower Egypt. A block found at Koptos showing the king and his *ka* in front of Min demonstrates that he built at the main temple of this town.[99] A block and a statue fragment were also found at Tod.[100] At Abydos was found an offering table with the name of the king.[101] Further building work in Upper Egypt is attested at Armant.[102] In the Delta near Khatana (near Tell el Dab'a) there was found a completely preserved gateway inscribed with the name of the king. An inscription added under Senusret III states that it belonged to a Djadjau (some kind of administrative building). Nothing was found from the building itself and it is not even certain that the blocks were found in their original location.[103] At Bubastis a block with his Horus name was found with a dedication to Bastet and is therefore most likely from this site.[104]

The king is known from an inscribed statue fragment found on Sinai, where he is the first attested Middle Kingdom king with his own monument.[105] The preserved fragment with his name is small and there may be some doubt that it was made under the king. Some later inscriptions on Sinai mention earlier Middle Kingdom kings, including Amenemhat I. However, there is also the inscription at Ayn Soukhna mentioned above. That region was a coastal station for expeditions heading to Sinai, and the inscription of the king there confirms the impression from the Sinai fragment that the king sent an expedition to the Sinai copper and turquoise mines, evidently in his seventh year.

An important innovation of Amenemhat I is the introduction of the coregency. The old king chose his successor, who then ruled beside him as full king. With this institution the succession of kings seems to have been ensured. The 'Instruction of King Amenemhat I for his Son Senusret I' is an important literary composition relating to Amenemhat I and the new institution of coregency, and seems to justify it. The king tells his son how to relate to his subjects:

> Beware of subjects who are nobodies, of whose plotting one is not aware. Trust not a brother, know not a friend. Make no intimates, it is worthless. When you lie down, guard your heart yourself, for no man has adherents on the day of woe.[106]

Then the instruction gives an unparalleled description of an attack on the king:

> It was after the meal, night had come. I was taking an hour of rest, I lay on my bed, for I was weary. My heart began to follow sleep. Suddenly weapons for my protection were turned against me, while I was like a snake of the desert. I awoke at the fighting, alert, and found it was a combat of the guard. Had I quickly seized weapons in my hand, I would have made cowards retreat in haste. But no one is strong at night; no one can fight alone; no success is achieved without a helper.
> Thus bloodshed occurred while I was without you; before the courtiers had heard I would hand over to you; before I had sat with you as so to advise you. For I had not prepared for it, had not expected it, had not foreseen the failing of servants.[107]

If the king survived an attack on his life, the episode would have been ample cause for a coregency between Amenemhat I and his son. However, there has been debate among Egyptologists over whether Senusret I really had a coregency with his father Amenemhat I or not.[108] Stela Cairo CG 20516 shows in the roundel a date of year 30 of Amenemhat I and year 10 of Senusret I, implying that these years are identical and that the coregency started in the twentieth year of Amenemhat I. Other sources seem to confirm this impression. In the roundel of stela Louvre C1 both kings are mentioned. In the text the two kings are referred to as 'they'. In Nubia at Abu Handal were found rock inscriptions which all seem to belong together and are attestations for military campaigns to Lower Nubia.

Some of them mention a year '9',[109] others a year '29'.[110] Only one dating is connected with a king's name: year 29 of Amenemhat. The only other king appearing in these inscriptions is Senusret I. It seems plausible that the inscriptions of year 9 and 29 refer to the same campaign. The evidence from the building work at Lisht has already been mentioned, indicating that both kings built together at the pyramid of Amenemhat I. In year 30 of his reign the king seems to have prepared, and perhaps celebrated, his *sed* festival, which is mentioned on blocks found at Lisht and on a statue which comes – according to the inscription – from Mendes.[111]

The high officials of the king are not well known. The vizier at the beginning of his reign may have been Ipi. His tomb was found at Thebes.[112] The vizier Intefiqer is attested in the last years of the king; he was a leading figure in the military campaigns; it is likely that other viziers were in office before him, but they are not yet known.[113] Treasurer and high steward was Meketre,[114] followed by Intef[115] and another man named Ipi,[116] who was in office around year 7. No other treasurer is known for sure for the following years.

In terms of material culture the reign of Amenemhat I still belongs in many ways to the First Intermediate Period. Many provincial towns had their own styles in pottery, arts and crafts. They are not very different from those of the Eleventh Dynasty. Provincial cemeteries flourished at the beginning of the Twelfth Dynasty. There are the decorated tombs of the local governors and next to them the smaller shaft tombs of the officials working for the governors. This situation is perfectly visible at Meir, Asyut, Deir el-Bersheh and Beni Hasan. Other people, the 'common population' of these local centres, seem to have been buried elsewhere; their tombs have yet to be discovered. The burials of the more 'common' people are different. They are not often buried with objects especially made for the tomb. Undecorated coffins are very common; pottery vessels for the eternal food supply are also essential. In burials of women, jewellery, most likely previously worn in daily life, is typical. Sometimes this seems to be quite expensive and provides evidence that even 'common' people had access to some small wealth. These tombs never contain objects relating to the profession of these people. Without inscriptions – known only from the burials of the ruling class – it is not known where and how these people worked. These tombs display only the social status – rich or poor – and the sex of the dead.

The tomb furnishings of the local ruling classes seem to be quite uniform, but contain a high proportion of objects especially produced for the tomb. There are decorated coffins, wooden models of craftsmen working in workshops and people preparing food. The dead, often wrapped in linen, but not often mummified, are sometimes adorned with jewellery, including scarabs, which become common at the beginning of the Middle Kingdom. In detail there are differences from local centre to local centre. Coffins found at Asyut are often adorned with double lines of inscriptions.

Coffins found at Upper Egypt (Gebelein, Edfu) are often decorated on the outside with scenes of daily life. Each centre still kept its own style, which tends to go back to the First Intermediate Period. The best-documented cemetery so far is Beni Hasan, where the tombs of the governors datable to the time of Amenemhat I are still painted in a style which seems to come directly from the First Intermediate Period. The tombs of the governors at Meir, starting under Amenemhat I, display a more elaborate 'residential' style, and it seems likely that artists and craftsmen from the residence decorated these tombs. Tombs at the residential cemeteries display a totally different, elaborate style. The reliefs in the tomb of the treasurer and high steward Meketre are of the highest quality. The relief is very fine with high-quality painting on it. The wooden models found in the tomb belong in quality to the best ever made in Egypt. Models of similar quality have been found at Saqqara and it seems most likely that the models from the tomb of Meketre were produced by artists from Memphis. In Memphis the traditions of the Old Kingdom were still strong, to such an extent that it is often hard to decide whether a tomb belongs to the First Intermediate Period, to the Eleventh or to the early Twelfth Dynasty.

In Lisht and Memphis court officials were buried in mastabas. They are often damaged and it is therefore hard to gain a clear picture of their original appearance. The inside rooms were decorated with reliefs, but with a reduced decoration programme compared with Old Kingdom mastabas or even compared with the rock-cut tombs of the early Middle Kingdom at Thebes. The local governors of several provinces were buried in rock-cut tombs, decorated with reliefs or paintings. Some of them, such as those at Beni Hasan, are quite well preserved. At other provinces such rock-cut tombs are not known and one wonders whether they are all destroyed, not yet found or whether governors at other sites were buried in undecorated rock-cut tombs or in mastabas.

Sculpture at the beginning of the Twelfth Dynasty displays strong connections to the Old Kingdom (Pls. I and VIII). Officials are often shown sitting with a short wig, a naked chest and a short skirt. This is similar to many statues of the Old Kingdom, although in detail there is never a doubt whether a work of art belongs to the Old or the Middle Kingdom. An innovation of the early Twelfth Dynasty is the block statue. A person is shown sitting on the ground and the whole body is treated like a block. Little more than outlines of the legs are shown, while only the head is fully sculpted (Pl. VI).

The few royal monuments display a style which seems to be very much influenced by Memphite artists. The reliefs of Amenemhat I found at Koptos or at his mortuary temple at Lisht are of the finest quality but they did not show any of the robust figures and the high plastic relief so common in the Eleventh Dynasty.[117]

Kheperkare Senusret I (c. 1919-1875/1874 BC)

The reign of Kheperkare Senusret I is among the best documented in Egyptology. The pyramid complex of the king is the best preserved of the whole Middle Kingdom. There are many rock inscriptions at several sites providing detailed information, and officials of the king left several dated inscriptions at Lisht, Abydos and elsewhere.

The family relations of the new king are not known for sure. Amenemhat I is clearly the father of Senusret I, but the name of his mother is not certain. A Neferitatenen appears on a statue as 'king's mother'; she seems to be the most likely candidate. The inscription of a statue of this woman was copied in the nineteenth century, but the statue is now lost. The inscription mentions 'King Senusret born to King Amenemhat and born of the king's mother Neferitatenen'. The name of the mother – otherwise not known from the Middle Kingdom – raised questions about the accuracy of the copy of the inscription.[118] The wife of Senusret I was a certain Neferu. She bears the title 'king's daughter' and was therefore most probably a daughter of Amenemhat I and sister of Senusret I. She was also the mother of Amenemhat II.[119] Two daughters of Senusret I are known, Itakayt and Sebat.[120] Two possible 'king's sons' are also known. Ameny, who appears in an inscription dated to the time of Senusret I in a tomb at Beni Hasan was most likely the future King Amenemhat II. Amenemhatankh, who occupied some religious functions at Memphis, is known from various monuments. He was buried at Dahshur.[121] His relation to Senusret I is not certain.

While the number of monuments in Egypt belonging to Amenemhat I seems to be rather limited, under Senusret I there was great activity all around the country. Senusret I started a large-scale building programme. The king seems to have renovated many or even all important temples of the country. At some places such as Koptos, Abydos, Karnak, Medamud and Heliopolis he seems to have built new large-scale temple complexes. At the temple at Heliopolis the obelisk of the king is still standing. It is the oldest in situ royal obelisk in Egypt. The Amun temple of Senusret I in Karnak is the core of the great temple of later periods and was still standing in the New Kingdom. The intention of the massive building project is not known, but it may have similar purposes to that of the Intef kings, who started to decorate local temples on a larger scale. The position of Senusret I in Egypt was perhaps not very stable. The building programme may have given him the chance to be present in the whole country. It seems to have occupied the whole length of his reign. The building work at Heliopolis clearly belongs to the early decade, because the building inscription on the 'Berlin leather roll' (see p. 40) dates to year 3. The involvement of the treasurer Mentuhotep, who was in office after year 22, in building the Karnak temple seems to indicate that at least some temples were built or rebuilt only in the second part of the king's reign.

1. History

The temples renovated or rebuilt are:

Satet temple at Elephantine (Fig. 3)

The whole temple of the goddess Satet, which had already received much attention from the kings of the early and later Eleventh Dynasty, was rebuilt in limestone. The temple of the Eleventh Dynasty was a mud-brick building with only some important parts such as the doorways made in stone. The temple of Senusret I seems to have been richly furnished with

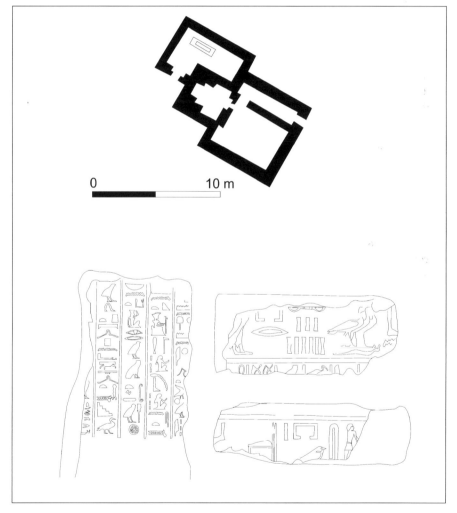

3. Satet temple on Elephantine (reconstructed plan)
and some relief fragments found there.

37

offering tables, statues and stelae.[122] There was also a long inscription, sadly now badly damaged.[123] The excavators were able to reconstruct the plan of the building.

Amun temple at Thebes

Here the king built the 'white chapel', so called by Egyptologists to distinguish its white Turah limestone blocks from the Hatshepsut 'red chapel' of red quartzite blocks. The 'white chapel' was demolished in the New Kingdom and used as building material. Modern excavators were able to reconstruct the entire monument. It is one of the few well-preserved examples of Middle Kingdom non-funerary architecture. There are two colossal figures of the king from Karnak, demonstrating the large-scale building of the main new temple. The Amun temple of Senusret I was the core of the large temple complex of later periods. Not much survived from this building. It was made of limestone which was later quarried away. The king also ordered the production of several statues of Old Kingdom kings; they may have been placed in the Amun temple. The main person responsible for building work in Karnak seems to be the treasurer Mentuhotep.[124] There are several statues of this important official from Karnak.

Min temple at Koptos

The Min temple at Koptos, which was already heavily damaged when the first excavators arrived, was also most likely totally reshaped by Senusret I. Several relief fragments with depictions of the king were found, none of them in its original context (Fig. 4). Two fragments now in London show the king running at the *sed* festival in front of Min. It also seems clear that the king built a large relief-decorated gateway to which the London fragments may belong.[125] There is also a fragment with the name of Amenemhat I. It has been argued that the block comes from the same building phase (although the style is different). Then the temple would have been built in the first decade of Senusret I when he was still ruling with his father Amenemhat I. There is no proof of this, although it seems possible.[126]

Osiris temple at Abydos

Like so many other temples the Osiris-Khenty-amentiu temple at Abydos seems to have been totally rebuilt, to the extent that in the Thirteenth Dynasty the complex was still called the temple of King Kheperkare (Senusret I). Few remains are preserved, but they include the foundation deposits.[127] Abydos was already an important town in the early dynasties, when the kings of the time were buried here. In the Old Kingdom the place

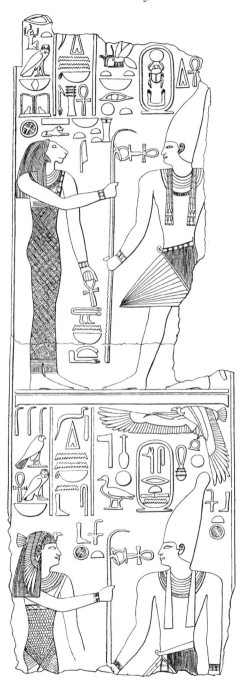

4. Reliefs of Senusret I found at Koptos.

kept its importance, but it gained a special role at the end of the Old Kingdom with the rise of the cult of Osiris, the ruler of the underworld. In the Middle Kingdom it became customary for officials to set up a stela at Abydos or even to erect a small chapel there. The underlying idea for these people was certainly to be close to Osiris. This custom seems to have started under Senusret I: the first stelae from Abydos, dated with a king's name, belong to the first decade of his reign. The quality and workmanship of these stelae vary, but especially under Senusret I and Amenemhat II there are many examples of the highest quality.

A high official much involved in the royal building work at Abydos seems again to have been the treasurer Mentuhotep (see p. 44), who was also responsible for construction work at Thebes. Some phrases in the inscriptions on one of his stelae seem to refer to the work in Abydos and his involvement. Mentuhotep was in office after year 22.[128] This date might give an idea that the building work at the temple was also performed in the second part of the king's reign.

Atum / Re temple at Heliopolis

There is good evidence for building activity in Heliopolis. The obelisk of Senusret I here has been mentioned above. The 'Berlin leather roll' (a copy on a New Kingdom leather roll of a temple inscription) reports building activity of the king at Heliopolis in his third year (and is therefore datable to the time of the coregency of Amenemhat I and Senusret I), and there is a block found at Matariya with the names of Senusret I and Amenemhat I, perhaps connected with the building work mentioned on the 'Berlin leather roll'.[129] Finally, there are blocks in Cairo that most likely come from Heliopolis.[130] The text of the 'Berlin leather roll' may here be translated in part. It is one of the oldest examples of the 'Königsnovelle' (kingship novella), a text genre often found in royal inscriptions of the New Kingdom and following the same outline. The king is sitting in his palace and asks his courtiers what to do.

> Year 3, month 3 of Akhet, day 8, under the majesty of the king of Upper und Lower Egypt Kheperkare, Son of Re Senusret (true of voice), may he live for ever in eternity.
>
> The king appeared with the double-crown; and a sitting took place in the Hall, a consultation with his followers, the Friends of the Palace and the officials of the private chambers, with commands for their hearing, a consultation for their instruction: See my Majesty is planning works, being mindful of a deed of excellence for the future. I will make a monument, and lay down durable decrees for Harakhti, as he bore me to do what should be done for him, to create what he commanded done. He placed me as shepherd of this land; he knew who would gather it together for him ....
>
> And these Friends said, answering to their god: Utterance is in your mouth, and Perception around you! O sovereign (may he live, be prosperous and be healthy) whatever is to happen, that is your plan: the royal appear-

ance as the uniter of the two lands to stretch the cord in your temple. It is noble to look to tomorrow, as something excellent for one's lifetime .... Great are you, as you make monuments in Iunu [Heliopolis], the sanctuary of the gods, before your father, the lord of the Great Mansion, Atum, the bull of the ennead. Create your mansion; provide for the offering stone, that it shall do service for the statue and be well disposed for your image for the fullness of all time .... The rope was let loose, the line put on the ground, made into this temple.[131]

Other building work is attested, often with only small blocks, at the following temples:

A brick with the name of the king and an offering table[132] were found at Hieraconpolis.[133] Blocks with the name of the king were found at the Mont temple at Armant,[134] the Nemty temple at el-Atawla (Egyptian Per-Nemty)[135] and Bubastis.[136] The Eleventh Dynasty temple of Tod seems to have been totally rebuilt. It is one of the few Middle Kingdom temples where we have an idea of the original plan.[137] A long inscription of Senusret I there refers to political unrest in his reign.[138] At Abgig (Fayum) the king erected a tall round-topped obelisk (12.62 m), decorated at the top.[139] At Kom Ombo,[140] Edfu,[141] Esna[142] and Bilifya (Egyptian Nebuau, twentieth Upper Egyptian nome)[143] were found blocks with the name of a King Senusret, possibly also belonging to temple buildings of Senusret I, although another King Senusret cannot be totally excluded.

Lisht, pyramid of the king

The pyramid of the king was built at Lisht.[144] The building project seems to have started only in year 10 – the first year of his sole reign. The course of the building work is relatively well known from the control notes – dated ink inscriptions on the building stones done by workmen or their scribes. Therefore it seems that the main pyramid was constructed after year 10, while the funerary temple and the causeway were started around years 22 and 24.[145] Unlike the Old Kingdom when the whole pyramid complex had one name, in the Middle Kingdom the single parts of the pyramid had different names. The pyramid of Senusret I itself was called Senusret-peteri-tawy, 'Senusret is viewing the two lands'. Two other names are known but it is not certain to which part of the complex they applied (pyramid town or funerary temple): Kha-Senusret, 'Senusret appears', and Khnem-sut-Kheperkare, 'united with the places of Kheperkare'.[146] Around the main pyramid were erected the pyramids of queens and king's daughters. The pyramid seems to have been finished. In many ways, with its valley temple, causeway, funerary temple and a satellite pyramid, it represents a copy of a Sixth Dynasty pyramid complex.

41

Senusret I seems to have reorganised or at least confirmed the frontiers of the Egyptian nomes.[147] On the 'white chapel' in Karnak are listed all the provinces with their measurements, their main towns and their main deities. There are also two boundary stelae attesting that at least the borders of some of the provinces were marked by such stelae. These stelae show the Horus name and the son-of-Ra name of the king at the top. Normally the bird signs of the Horus (a falcon) and of the son (a goose) are orientated in the same direction. On these boundary stelae they are placed back to back looking in different directions, as if each is looking into a different province on either side of the boundary marked by the stela.[148] There is also evidence that the king, as his father Amenemhat I had previously done, installed several loyal governors at different parts of Egypt. Sarenput (I) was installed as governor at Elephantine. He reports in his tomb the favours he received from the king, including provision for workmen for building his tomb. At Qaw el-Kebir appears at about this time a strong ruling family, perhaps also put in place by Senusret I. Other governors seem to have been confirmed in their positions, such as Djefai-Hapi (I) and Djefai-Hapi (II) in Asyut.[149]

In year 25 there was most probably a devastating famine. It is mentioned in two inscriptions and seems to have affected the country for many years. Dated monuments and documents are rare for the following years. The inscription at Tod already mentioned may refer to the looting of the temple after this famine, although this is not certain.[150]

In his foreign policy Senusret I seems to have followed what his father started. Several campaigns against Lower Nubia are attested. A 'year 9' found in a Lower Nubian rock inscription most likely belongs to King Senusret I, which is year 29 of Amenemhat I. In the time of his sole reign he continued with Nubian campaigns. It has been assumed that these campaigns were so successful that Lower Nubia was totally occupied. The main campaign under Senusret I was in year 18 against Kush (Upper Nubia). There is a stela of the 'overseer of the double granary', Mentuhotep, dated to that year, found at el-Girgawi near Korosko. A stela found in Buhen (Florence 2540 A + B) reports the same campaign in year 18 against Kash (Kush). There are two inscriptions in Egypt which probably also refer to this campaign. In the tomb of Sarenput (I) at Qubbet el Hawa (the burial place for the ruling class of Elephantine) it is simply mentioned that the king seems to have stopped at Elephantine on his way to Kush (here again written Kash). Clearer evidence can be found within the inscription in the Beni Hasan tomb of the governor Amenemhat, who followed the king on his campaign. These Nubian campaigns are connected with the foundation of fortresses, such as Buhen, indicating that this conquest went far beyond anything known before. It seems to be the first time that Egypt conquered an area outside its home country and kept it under permanent control. In the Old Kingdom there had probably been only loose supremacy over certain economically important points. At

Buhen in Lower Nubia, for example, in the Old Kingdom there was a small settlement, which seems to have controlled copper mining and production at this place, while the area around was perhaps not under direct Egyptian command. By contrast the Middle Kingdom fortress of Buhen is a huge fortified building, which seems to have had more than a local function.[151]

The king is finally also known from several expedition inscriptions. Those of the Wadi el-Hudi report the bringing of amethyst.[152] There are at least three expeditions to the Wadi Hamammat.[153] One of the expedition inscriptions dates to year 38 of Senusret I and was guided by the 'herald' Ameny. The rock inscription gives a detailed list of all expedition members. 17,000 people were involved, among them 20 'governors', 30 'followers of the lord' and several kinds of soldiers, such as 700 'soldiers of the province' and 300 'soldiers of the ruler's crew at Thebes'. The aim of the expedition was to bring 60 sphinxes and 150 statues.[154]

References by private individuals to building projects are not many and are often unclear. The 'sealer under charge', Mery, reports:

> My Lord [Senusret I] has sent me as messenger because of my loyalty that I may work at the place of eternity, which is greater in name than Rasetau, it is foremost above all places: a magnificent region of goods. Its walls touch the sky, the lake which was dug reached the river, the gates which reached the sky are made from limestone Turah.[155]

The reference to the 'place of eternity' may indicate that the text refers to the pyramid of Senusret I, under whom the stela is dated (year 9). However, it also seems possible that the inscription refers to building work at the Osiris-Khenty-amentiu temple at Abydos, especially because the building work at the pyramid seems to have started only after year 10 of the king.

The king celebrated in year 31 his first *sed* festival, mentioned in an inscription in Hatnub:[156] 'year 31 of the first *sed* festival of Kheperkare, the royal sealer Amenemhat born of Sat-hedj-hetep: the great one came to Hatnub to bring stone for the king of Upper and Lower Egypt, Kheperkare', and on the kiosk at Karnak.[157]

The king was still adored as a god in the New Kingdom, but the attestations for this are not plentiful.[158] According to the Turin Canon, Senusret I reigned forty-five years; the number of months and days of his reign are lost. A year dating found on a bowl at Elephantine may also date to this king, and confirm that he completed the forty-fifth year of his reign.[159] He had a short coregency with his son Amenemhat II.[160]

The men around the king, the highest officials, are relatively well known. The vizier in the early years was Intefiqer, who was perhaps already in office under Amenemhat I. His tenure of the position seems to have been quite long, because the next known vizier is a certain Senusret, attested only at the very end of the king's reign. Intefiqer was deeply involved in several royal expeditions. He was buried in a small mastaba next to the pyramid of Amenemhat I at Lisht. Only two treasurers are known for sure for the king's reign. There is a certain Sobekhotep, known from a dated inscription (year 22) and his successor Mentuhotep, who seems to be the most important official of the reign. He was most likely responsible for the building projects of the king at Abydos and Thebes. At Abydos he had an important chapel with an impressive stela decorated on all sides. His tomb was found at Lisht next to the pyramid of Senusret I and still contained a finely painted sarcophagus. Several high stewards are known: Nakht (Pl. VIII) (involved in building the pyramid), Intef (son of Satamun), Hor (leader of an expedition to the Wadi el Hudi) and a second Intef (son of Satuser).

In terms of material culture, the Middle Kingdom started under Senusret I. Before his reign, pottery and funerary culture, such as coffins, are still much influenced by, or in the tradition of, the First Intermediate Period. Under Senusret I this seems to have changed slowly. The building programme of the king may be one reason for this. Craftsmen of the residence were now working throughout the country. It is attested by inscriptions that royal craftsmen worked for Sarenput I, who was governor at Elephantine. However, especially in the arts there is still a strong Old Kingdom influence. The pyramid complex of the king seems to be almost a copy of a Sixth Dynasty complex.[161] Even the reliefs in it follow Old Kingdom prototypes.[162] The capital Itj-tawy was clearly the centre of the developments in the country. This is visible from the cemeteries at Lisht, which are most likely the burial grounds of the capital. The sarcophagus of the 'treasurer' Mentuhotep is decorated on the outside with a palace façade. Similar decorations on coffins appear only later in the provinces (Pls. XII-XIII). Therefore it seems plausible that this decoration pattern was developed in the capital and later copied elsewhere. A similar development is visible in terms of pottery style. Before Senusret I each region had its own style. The pottery of Upper and Lower Egypt, in particular, developed in the First Intermediate Period in markedly different directions. Under Senusret I pottery became more uniform throughout the country, although there are certainly still small local variations. The new pottery style is indeed first visible at Lisht and seems then to have slowly spread over the whole country.

Another remarkable feature of the reign of Senusret I is the production of literary compositions. There are so far no works of literature preserved from the Old Kingdom (only religious compositions or biographical inscriptions on the walls of the chambers in the pyramid and on the walls of the tomb chapels). Therefore the literature of the Middle Kingdom seems to be something new, although the possibility cannot be excluded that literature in a narrower sense (non-religious and non-autobiographical texts for tombs) were already produced in the Old Kingdom. Only in the late Middle Kingdom were such texts put in tombs, the only place where a text has a

good chance of survival. The first known texts which can be called literature were most likely written under Senusret I or in the time of the
coregency between him and his father Amenemhat I. The 'Instruction of
Amenemhat' and the 'Prophecy of Neferty' have already been mentioned.
The most famous Egyptian story, the 'Tale of Sinuhe', was also most likely
written under Senusret I or shortly after. Sinuhe, one of the highest court
officials, was involved in events around the death of Amenemhat I. Afraid
of being accused of being connected with the death of the king, Sinuhe flees
the country and escapes to Palestine, where he undergoes some adventures. Senusret I called Sinuhe back to Egypt, knowing that he was
innocent. The story is known from several copies and was doubtless
popular already in the Middle Kingdom. Another important work of
literature seems to have been the 'Loyalist Teaching', possibly even written by the 'treasurer' Mentuhotep. This composition focuses on the
importance of being loyal to the king and need to care for workers.

Nubkaure Amenemhat II (c. 1877/1876-1843/1842 BC)

The reign of King Nubkaure Amenemhat II is in many ways an enigma.
Although the king ruled more than thirty years, few monuments are
datable to his time. His family relations are unclear. It can be assumed
that he was the son of Senusret I, but this is not precisely stated anywhere.
A 'king's son', Ameny, appears under Senusret I in a tomb inscription in
Beni Hasan. It seems possible that he is identical with Amenemhat II. The
mother of Amenemhat II was the 'king's mother', Neferu, who was buried
in a small pyramid at the pyramid complex of Senusret I. She was also a
'king's wife' and a 'king's daughter' and was therefore most likely a
daughter of Amenemhat I.[163] The wife of Amenemhat II is not known. A
queen called Kemi-nub buried within his pyramid complex at Dahshur
belongs to the Thirteenth Dynasty. The burials of three women with the
title 'king's daughter' (Ita, Ita-weret, Khenmet) in the same complex may
date to his reign. These women may be daughters of the king, although
this is not certain.[164]

At Memphis there were found several pieces of a huge annal stone
dating to Amenemhat II and preserving events of his reign. The biggest
fragment was found reused as part of a pedestal statue beneath a colossal
figure of Ramses II (Nineteenth Dynasty). The rescued fragments relate
to events at the beginning of Amenemhat II's reign. The complete monument may have recorded most parts of his rule, although this is only a
guess. Single entries are described in a short telegram style, but they are
nevertheless an important source for the tasks of the king and for royalty
in ancient Egypt. Political events, so important for modern chroniclers,
are mentioned but do not receive the same attention as we may like to
give them, whereas donations to several gods and temples are most
important. The number of objects given is often not very high: 'for Mont

in Armant: one *des*-vessel made of Asiatic copper; for Mont in Tod, one *des*-vessel made of Asiatic copper'. Donations of royal statues and many other objects are mentioned for the mortuary temple of Senusret I, but also donations of statues for private people are recorded: 'making of wood, a statue of the overseer of the marshland-dwellers Ameny, for whom offerings (?) were made in the temple Djefa-Amenemhat (the mortuary temple of Amenemhat II)'. At one point an expedition against Asia is mentioned. The text relates the destruction of Iuai and Iasy which may have been the goal of the same expedition. The location of these places is not known. 1554 people were captured and brought to Egypt. Several foreigners are mentioned bringing tribute: the 'children of the rulers' of Asia, the 'children of the ruler of Kush', 'Webatsepet' and finally nomads are recorded. The number of objects they delivered is not high. A cultic function seems to lie behind a report of the catching of birds with a net. The expedition to Asia and destruction of two towns or settlements could be seen as an act of demonstration of power by the new king in connection with the ritual of 'smiting the enemies', which seems to have a key function in Egyptian kingship. The inscription seems to date to the early years of the king although it is impossible to give an exact year date.[165]

Amenemhat II built his pyramid at Dahshur. It is not known why the king chose a different site to Lisht, where his two predecessors were buried. The pyramid has been excavated only superficially and is also badly damaged, so not even the measurements of the building itself are known in detail. An important point seems to be the plan of the complex. Senusret I had copied the complex of a late Old Kingdom pyramid. The pyramid of Amenemhat II is set within a huge rectangular wall, which seems to be similar to the Third Dynasty Djoser enclosure at Saqqara. However, the complex of Amenemhat II was orientated east-west instead of north-south (Djoser enclosure). Next to the entrance of the complex were found two massive pylon-like structures of unknown function. Only further research may reveal a detailed plan and the concept of this building. The entrance to the pyramid itself was found on the north side and leads to the burial apartments under the middle of the pyramid.

The most interesting find in the pyramid complex is the set of three gallery tombs each with two burials of princesses and other high ranking persons; four of them were found undisturbed. These galleries were found behind (west of) the pyramid. The tombs of the 'king's daughters', Khenmet, Ita and Ita-weret and of the women Sathathormeryt still contained beautiful jewellery. The tombs of the treasurer Amenhotep and of the queen Kemi-nub were found disturbed; they both date to the Thirteenth Dynasty.

Several inscriptions of officials seem to relate to the building work at the pyramid. A certain Sahathor reports on his miniature limestone chapel, now in London:[166]

causing to go to the pyramid 'Amenu-sekhem' to supervise the work on his fifteen statues of hard stone of a million (years), which happened indeed in two months to the day (?). Never had the like occurred with any other supervision …

Sahathor further reports:

I visited the Mine-land [Sinai] as a youth and forced the chieftains to wash gold. I brought turqouise [from there]; I reached Nubia of the Nubians, I came there to overthrow it by the fear of the lord of the two lands.

King Amenemhat II is otherwise not well attested in Egypt.[167] There are some expedition inscriptions from Sinai, where at least three expeditions of the king were conducted (in years 2, 11 and 24). There was at least one (undated) expedition to the Wadi el-Hudi, mentioned on a stela found at Dabod (Lower Nubia).[168] At the Wadi Gasus a stela was found reporting the return of an expedition guided by the 'overseer of the gateway', Khenty-khety-wer, in year 28 of the king.[169] There are remains of a limestone gateway excavated at Hermoupolis, which was – according to the text on it – erected in front of a half-destroyed temple 'which his majesty found decayed'.[170] This is one of the few examples of a temple building which seems to have been totally rebuilt by the king. There is some evidence – mainly from inscriptions on statues – of a special interest in Heliopolis, but not much has survived of it; the most important object is a colossal sphinx found at Tanis, but certainly originally coming from this site.[171] In the annal inscription found at Memphis building work at temples in the east Delta and in Heracleopolis is mentioned.[172] At Memphis was found a lintel with the name of Amenemhat II. As with the annal stone, it is not certain whether the block comes originally from a building of the king at Memphis or from another place.[173] In Tod was found a treasure of silver objects in four boxes; two of the boxes had the name of the king written on them. The silver vessels discovered are obviously not made in Egypt and are a demonstration of Egypt's foreign contacts in the Middle Kingdom.[174] The vessels are most likely of Aegean origin. In the undisturbed tomb of the 'king's daughter', Khenmet, already mentioned, jewellery was found which seems to be also of Aegean production, additional evidence for widespread foreign contacts in the Middle Kingdom.

While the number of royal monuments of Amenemhat II seems not very large, there are many stelae of private individuals containing his name.[175] However, this does not mean that we are well informed about the royal court of the king. Courtiers must have been buried next to his pyramid, but these cemeteries are not yet well excavated. Rehuerdjersen seems to have been the treasurer in the first part of his reign. He had a tomb at Lisht and a stela with his name is most likely from Abydos. Merykau is another treasurer. He is known from a stela found in the eastern desert dated by the king's name. Siese was the treasurer in office at the end of the reign. He is known from four finely sculpted limestone slabs found in his tomb next to the king's pyramid at Dahshur. He seems to have reached this position from being 'high steward' and was later also given the honorific title of vizier. His tomb, wrongly identified as a pyramid by the Lepsius expedition in the mid-nineteenth century, was decorated in its underground part with pyramid texts. Another official buried next to the pyramid of the king is the 'overseer of the gateway', Khenty-khety-wer, mentioned above.

Biographical inscriptions on stelae are often quite useful in revealing otherwise unknown aspects of the king's reign. The 'overseer of the chamber', Snofru, reports: 'I came to direct (the building work at) this first temple of Nubkaure [Amenemhat II]'.[176] Another official, the 'overseer of the chamber', Senitef, refers to the same temple: 'I was the one who directed (the work on the) this first temple of the majesty of the king Nubkaure'.[177] The nature of this 'first temple' is not known, but it may be a temple building at Abydos, because both stelae are from this place. A longer biographical inscription is found on another stela and reports the career of a high court official:

> I was born in the time of the majesty of the king Sehetepibre [Amenemhat I] when he departed in peace. I was a child when I knotted the head band in front of his majesty Kheperkare [Senusret I]. His majesty appointed me as the scribe of the prison of hearing. He praised me for it very much. His majesty appointed me as the scribe of the *tema* [unknown word]; his majesty praised me for it very much. His majesty appointed me accountant of grain in Upper and Lower Egypt. He praised me for it very much; His majesty appointed me as the scribe of the great enclosure. He praised me for it. His majesty appointed me as scribe of the royal document and overseer of the works in the whole country ... the scribe of the royal document Samont.[178]

Amenemhat II seems to have had a coregency with his successor Senusret II of about three years.[179] A rock inscription at Aswan mentions the joint reign.[180] Amenemhat II himself reigned, including the coregency, about thirty-five years.

Khakheperre Senusret II (c. 1845/1844-1837 BC)

The family relations of the new king are not entirely clear. His mother is not known; Amenemhat II was most likely his father, although this is nowhere stated specifically. The main wife of the king is a certain Khenmet-nefer-hedjet-weret (I), who clearly outlived her husband and seems to have occupied an important position under her son Senusret III. She does not have the title 'king's daughter' and may therefore be of non-royal origin.[181] Two possible sons of Khakheperre Senusret II are known: Senusret-seneb-wer,[182] who appears in a list of statues together with the 'king's daughters', Itikayt[183] and Neferet,[184] and a certain Kha-kau-Re, who appears in a rock inscription at Hatnub.[185] Neither individual is connected with the name of a king and the identification of these 'king's sons' as sons of Senusret II is open to doubt. Khakaure is the throne name of Senusret III. It is possible that this person is simply a son of another (later) king or an official with the title 'king's son'.

At the beginning of his reign King Senusret II chose a site for his pyramid (Pl. XV) at the entrance of the Fayum. That region seems now to have become the focus of royal interest, after already receiving some attention from kings earlier in the dynasty. The pyramid of the king shows some radical changes from the pyramids of the early Twelfth Dynasty (Fig. 5). The entrance was now no longer in the north but in the south. It was placed next to the shafts of royal women, providing the impression for potential robbers that it was simply another shaft tomb, placed outside the pyramid building. The pyramid was also the first with a core mainly built

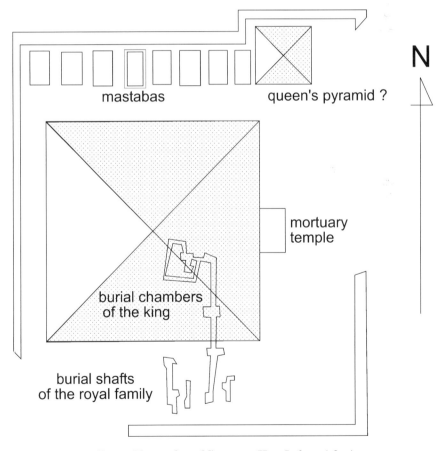

mastabas queen's pyramid ?

N

mortuary temple

burial chambers of the king

burial shafts of the royal family

5. Pyramid complex of Senusret II at Lahun (plan).

in mud brick, and not in loose stones like the pyramids of the first kings of the Dynasty. However, the pyramid was erected on a rock about 12 m high. Only the covering and a framework of internal retaining walls were built in stone, while the space in between was filled with mud brick. North of the pyramid, but still inside the pyramid enclosure, were eight mastabas cut into the rock (Pl. XVI), but without any sign of a shaft. Slightly further north, just outside the pyramid enclosure, was also found an elaborate tomb with several chambers, paved walls and a sarcophagus all made in a style known only from royal tombs. It has been assumed that this was the real tomb of the king, but this is far from certain.[186] In the north, next to the mastabas, there is also a satellite pyramid, which may have functioned as a burial complex of a queen, although no shaft or burial chamber was found. East of the king's pyramid were found the remains of the funerary temple, which was already heavily damaged, but the fragments of fine reliefs demonstrate that it was once richly decorated. The whole pyramid complex seems to have copied the tomb of Osiris. Around the tomb chamber there was a corridor converting the chamber itself into a kind of island, an important symbol of Osiris. The interpretation of the pyramid complex as tomb of Osiris is supported by the fact that around the pyramid were found remains of trees, making the whole complex into a kind of garden.[187] From the same time there is evidence that people were furnished in their burials with objects related to Osiris and kingship. Many royal insignia were found in burials of women belonging to the king's family. The burial chamber of Senusret II was already heavily looted when found, and only a golden uraeus was found. It is not possible to say with certainty how he was equipped, but it seems likely that he was also buried with all the insignia relating to Osiris and kingship. The burial of Senusret II was most likely in furnishings and architecture a copy of the burial of Osiris.[188]

To the south of the pyramid were found several shaft tombs, one of them still containing the treasure of the 'king's daughter', Sathathoriunet (Pl. XXIII), overlooked by tomb robbers. Several boxes contained the finest examples of jewellery.[189] Next to the valley temple, several hundred metres east of the pyramid, a new town was laid out. This was still well preserved when the British archaeologist Flinders Petrie excavated it. The finds are today one of the main sources on life in a Middle Kingdom settlement. The place flourished not only under the king, but seems also to have functioned as a local centre into the Thirteenth Dynasty.

To the first year of Senusret II is dated a stela found at Wadi Gasus which reports the 'establishing of his monuments in the god's land'. For other events of his reign we do not have many records. The stela of a certain Sobekhotep dated to year 6 of Senusret II reports:

> 'His majesty ordered that I go to collect duties at the royal domains of the head of the South and Thebes and that I purify the temples ....'[190]

The court of the king is not well attested. The highest officials were certainly buried around the pyramid complex of the king at Lahun, but all these tombs are very damaged. One of his most important courtiers seems to have been the 'overseer of the gateway', Inpy, who was still in office under Senusret III. His title 'overseer of all royal works in the entire land' may indicate that he was involved in important building works. Senusret II reigned only eight or nine years, while the Turin Canon gives him nineteen years. The highest attested year date is so far on a stela from Toshka, which is hard to read (year 8 or 9).[191] There is no evidence that he had a coregency with his successor Senusret III.

Important changes in the royal titulary occurred in the reign of this king, with the *nebty* title now gaining its own name, different from the other names of the king.[192] In the Old and the early Middle Kingdom the Horus and *nebty* names were always identical (an example from Amenemhat II: Horus Hekenmaat; *nebty* Hekenmaat). Senusret II is the first king whose *nebty* name is different from his Horus name (Horus Seshemtawy; *nebty* Sekhamaat). With this innovation, the fivefold titulary of the king reached its final form, as retained down to the end of the Ptolemaic Period.

1.6. The late Twelfth Dynasty (*c.* 1837-1759 BC)

Sources

There are many sources for the reign of Senusret III. The pyramid of the king at Dahshur is well excavated and partly already published. There are several mastabas of high state officials; there are many stelae datable to the time of this king and the last big provincial tombs were finished under his reign. In stark contrast the sources for the later Twelfth Dynasty are rather difficult. For two of the rulers (Amenemhat IV and Sobeknofru) the burial places are not known. Amenemhat III built two pyramids, but only his pyramid at Dahshur is well excavated and published, while his pyramid and its complex at Hawara are badly damaged. Not many tombs of high officials are datable to the reign of any of these rulers. The cemeteries at Hawara are also much destroyed and were intensively reused for animal burials in the Late Period. There are numerous rock inscriptions of Amenemhat III attesting to the activity of the king in many areas. The inscriptions provide much information on administration and state organisation but few historically important data. The Twelfth Dynasty ends therefore with a lot of question marks.

Khakaure Senusret III (c. 1837-1818 BC)

The new king may have been the son of Senusret II[193] and of his wife Khenmet-nefer-hedjet-weret (I). The latter seems to have lived quite long into the reign of Khakaure Senusret III and had a small pyramid at

Dahshur, next to that of her son Senusret III. However, the pyramid was a cenotaph – the queen seems to have been buried elsewhere.[194] The wife of King Senusret III with an identical name (Khenmet-nefer-hedjet-weret (II)) was buried at Dahshur in the pyramid of the king, which could be entered by a small pyramid next to that of the king.[195] Other wives of Senusret III were Sherit, known from a Lahun papyrus,[196] and Nefert-henut, who had a burial next to the king's pyramid at Dahshur.[197] In the sources of the New Kingdom referring to the king a certain Meresger also appears, but she is so far not attested in contemporary sources. The following daughters are known: Senet-senebtysy,[198] Menet,[199] perhaps Sathathor[200] and Mereret.[201] Amenemhat III seems to be the only known son.

In the chain of remarkable rulers of the Twelfth Dynasty, Senusret III is perhaps the most famous. There are many changes in life, art and culture under this king. It is not known whether these changes were directly influenced by the ruler himself, whatever the specific reasons. Nevertheless his reign marks the beginning of the late Middle Kingdom. Senusret III appears also as an important king and conqueror in the Greek sources, providing evidence that later generations treated him as one of the most important kings of ancient Egypt.

Senusret III is best known for his Nubian policy. Several campaigns against the southern neighbours are attested, and several Nubian forts were built or renewed by the king. This policy was so important for the Egyptians that in Nubia the king was worshipped as a local god. The first of his campaigns seems to have taken place in his eighth year. A rock inscription at Sehel reports on the building of a canal 'beautiful-are-the-ways-of-Khakaure', after 'his majesty went to the south to overthrow the Nubians'. According to the inscription the canal was 250 feet long, 83 feet wide and 25 feet deep. The inscription recording the building of the canal was set up by the treasurer Sen-ankh.[202] It has been suggested that he renewed and cleaned a canal built by King Merenre in the Sixth Dynasty.[203] This canal must have been important for military, but also for trading reasons after the Nubians were conquered. From Elephantine a stela is known which seems to refer to logistical work in connection with this campaign. The inscription mentions 'the great one of the tens of Upper Egypt', Ameny, who built a gate in the fortress of Elephantine and a slaughter house in a working place, while the king 'proceeded to overthrow vile Kush'[204] To the same year is dated a stela found at Semna which reports that the border was created here in that year in order to systematically control the passage of Nubians northwards:

> The southern boundary made in year 8 under the majesty of the king of Upper and Lower Egypt, Khakaure (given life for ever and ever) in order to prevent any Nubian from passing it going north, either on land or in a boat, or any herds of the Nubians, except a Nubian who comes to trade in Iqen [Mirgissa] or on official mission [...].[205]

From this evidence we can conclude that in his eighth year the king conquered Nubia as far as Semna and reopened a canal, most likely for bringing raw materials to Egypt and to have faster access to the new province. A second campaign evidently took place in his tenth year. Two inscriptions found in the far south at Dal and dated to this year of the king include the phrase:

> When one passes it, namely, going northwards in year 10, third month of Akhet, day 9[206]

This inscription implies a campaign deep into the Nubian south, but it seems that it did not have any consequences in terms of conquering these parts of the country. The border was fixed at Semna, north of Dal. In year 16 the king set up two stelae at Semna and Uronarti. The Semna stela is a boundary marker and reports in detail on the royal intentions of the campaign.

> His majesty makes the southern border at Heh, where the fortress 'Repelling-the-Tribesmen' was built. I made my boundary; I went further south than my forefathers. I increased what was bequeathed to me. I am a king who speaks and acts. My heart's intentions are carried out by my arm. I am one who is aggressive in order to seize, impatient to succeed ....

The last campaign was in year 19 and is mentioned on two private stelae and in a rock inscription. The stela of a certain Sasatet reads:

> The overseer of the inner palace Sasatet, he says: I came to Abydos together with the treasurer Iykhernefret to fashion [a figure? of] Osiris-Khentyamentiu, lord of Abydos, when the Khakaure [Senusret III], living eternally, proceeded to crush vile Kash in regnal year 19.[207]

A rock inscription found at Uronarti records:

> Year 19, month 4 Akhet season, day 2 under the majesty of King Khakaure (may he live forever), the lord [i.e. the king] proceeded, living, healthy and well in going downstream from overthrowing Kush ....[208]

In connection with these campaigns the king built, as already mentioned, a chain of fortresses (Semna, Kumma, Uronarti) to establish a defensive system in Nubia. Semna, which had the ancient name Sekhem-Khakaure-maa-kheru ('powerful-is-Khakaure-true-of-voice') was now the most southern point of the Egyptian empire and together with the two other forts formed some kind of borderline.

The precise reasons behind these campaigns are not clear. Already Senusret I seems to have conquered Nubia up to the Second Cataract, although he did not built fortresses there to fix the border. Did the Nubian region secede after Senusret I or were there uprisings against Egyptian rule? Senusret III seems to have entered the regions south of the Second Cataract, but without further conquests.

There is also unequivocal written testimony for campaigns into Palestine under Senusret III. The most important evidence is the stela of the military officer Khusobek, who reports military actions on his monuments. A biographical inscription is found on one of his stelae set up in Abydos, a fine example of a Middle Kingdom biography:

> I was born in year 27 under the majesty of the king of Upper and Lower Egypt Nubkaure (Amenemhat II) (true of voice). As the king of Upper and Lower Egypt Khakaure arose on the throne of the living, his majesty caused that I perform work in fighting behind and beside his majesty with seven men of the residence. And then I was effective beside him. His majesty caused that I be appointed as a follower of the ruler and I was given sixty head (= people).
>
> Journey south by his majesty to overthrow the tribesmen of Nubia. And then I struck the Nubian at Kenkef, beside my town['s troop]. And then I went north, performing service in a ship of the residence. And then he appointed [me] to be the supervisor of the followers. I was given one hundred head as a reward. His majesty proceeded northward to overthrow the Mentiu of Asia. His majesty reached this land called Sekmem .... And then Sekmem fell, together with wretched Retjenu, while I was acting as rearguard of the army. And then the soldiers of the army were engaged in close combat with the Asiatics. And then I struck the Asiatic and his weapons were taken by two soldiers of the army without stopping fighting.[209]

Another important text relating to a campaign or expedition to the Near East under Senusret III was found in the biographical inscription of the 'high steward' and vizier Khnumhotep at his tomb at Dahshur. The inscription is not yet fully published but seems to refer to a journey to Byblos. Further references to Asia under the king are vague. A block found at Medamud states: '... Asia, its products are presented to the palace of the king of Upper and Lower Khakaure'.[210]

Senusret III was in later times one of the most famous kings of Egypt. Herodotus writes of campaigns. However, the events described seem to be a mixture of the enterprises of New Kingdom kings with those of Senusret III.[211]

> Sesostris, the priests said, sailed first with a fleet of warships from the Arabian gulf along the coast of the Indian Ocean, subduing the coastal tribes as he went; then on his return to Egypt (still according to the priests' account) he raised a powerful army and marched across the continent, reducing to subjection every nation in his path .... Thus his victorious progress through Asia continued, until he entered Europe and defeated the Scythians and Thracians ....[212]

The length of the king's reign was for a long time a point of discussion. In the Turin Canon there are mentioned at least thirty years for the king, while Manetho gives him forty-eight years. However, there are hardly any attestations after year 19 for Senusret III. Therefore it has been assumed that the king died in his nineteenth year and was directly succeeded by his son Amenemhat III. However, in the last few years there have been found higher year datings most likely to be connected with Senusret III. They point to a longer reign and most probably to a long coregency with his successor Amenemhat III. The coregency of the kings may have lasted as long as twenty years.[213] A long coregency fits the known data much better. It is known that the king celebrated his *sed* festival, which was normally performed in year 30 of a reign.[214] With a nineteen-year reign it would have to be assumed that he celebrated the festival earlier. This seems possible, but a coregency would make it plausible that he celebrated this festival around his thirtieth year. There are also other indications in support of a long coregency. There is a certain 'overseer of the storerooms', Iu-nefer, known from a stela dated to the time of Senusret III[215] but buried at Hawara, where a pyramid complex was built for King Amenemhat III in the second half of his reign. Burials of important court officials there are unlikely to have taken place earlier in his reign. Without a coregency the burial and the stela were produced about twenty years apart. With a coregency there is now no need to think that the burial took place two decades after the stela was made. The tomb and stela are perhaps more or less contemporary. The case of the 'overseer of the fields', Ankhu, who started his career under Senusret III and seems to have lived into the Thirteenth Dynasty, will be discussed later (pp. 66-7).

The king built his pyramid at Dahshur, but was probably buried at Abydos. In Abydos the king had a funerary complex placed in the desert and oriented to a temple complex, again for the cult of the king. The tomb, which has often been described as a cenotaph, was found looted but still contained remains of burial furnishings. However, it also seems possible that cenotaphs were furnished with burial goods, so that these objects are no proof that the king was buried here. The question of the burial place of the king therefore remains open.[216] At the edge of the cultivation at Abydos a funerary temple was built; in layout and intention it may be identical to the valley temples of the pyramids. The building is not well preserved but was originally richly adorned with high-quality relief and statues.[217] Next to the temple a town was founded, which flourished well into the Thirteenth Dynasty.

There are other clear signs that the king devoted much attention to Abydos. The most direct evidence is the text on the stela of the treasurer Iykhernefret, who reports on his work at Abydos:

King's command to the one who belongs to the elite, foremost of action, royal-sealer, sole friend, overseer of the two gold-houses, overseer of the two silver-houses, treasurer Iykhernefret:

My majesty deigns to have you journey upstream to Thinite Abydos, to create monuments for my father Osiris-Khenty-amentiu, and to adorn his secret image with the fine gold which he has let my majesty bring back from Nubia in exultant victory.

You will surely do this in the best manner of acting for the interest of my father Osiris. For my majesty sends you, confident that you will do everything to the heart's content of my majesty. For you were brought up as a pupil of my majesty. You have indeed grown up as a foster-son of my majesty and sole pupil of my palace. My majesty made you a friend when you were a youth of twenty-six years. My majesty did this because I saw you as one of excellent counsel, keen of tongue, who came from the womb a wise man. Now my majesty sends you to do this because my majesty knows that no one could do it all except you. Go then and return when you have done all that my majesty commanded.

I acted according to all that his majesty had commanded in furnishing all that my lord had commanded for his father Osiris-Khenty-amentiu, lord of Abydos, great power in the province of This. I served as 'his beloved son' for Osiris-Khenty-amentiu, and I furnished [his] great [image] of eternity and everlastingness.

I made for him the palanquin 'Carrier of the beauty of Khenty-amentiu' of gold, silver, lapis lazuli, bronze, sesendjem-wood and *meru*-wood. The gods who attend him were fashioned, their shrines were made anew.

...

I directed the work on the neshmet-bark; I fashioned the cabin. I adorned the breast of the lord of Abydos with lapis lazuli and turquoise, fine gold and all costly stones as ornaments of the god's limbs. I clothed the god in his regalia, in my office of master-of-secrets, my function of robing-priest.

I was pure of hand in adorning the god, a priest whose fingers are clean. I conducted the Procession of Wepwawet when he goes forth to rescue his father. I repulsed the attackers of the neshmet-bark, I felled the foes of Osiris.

I conducted the Great Procession and followed the god in his strides. I made the god's boat sail.[218]

Further building work of Senusret III is attested at Medamud, Armant,[219] Tod,[220] Heracleopolis[221] and Hieraconpolis,[222] and statues of the king have been discovered at Karnak[223] and Deir el-Bahri.[224] Unlike Senusret I there is the impression that the king in most cases only added statues or inscriptions to already existing temple buildings. There are several expedition inscriptions in different parts of the country dated to the time of Senusret III: Wadi el-Hudi,[225] Wadi Hammamat[226] and Sinai.[227]

The court of the king is relatively well known. Viziers were Sobekemhat, Nebit and perhaps Khnumhotep. All are known only from their mastabas excavated next to the pyramid of the king. As treasurers are attested Senankh, who built the canal at Sehel, Sebekemhat, before he was promoted to the office of vizier, and finally Iykhernefret, who was in office in the last years of the king and was responsible for many activities of the king in Abydos mentioned on the stela above. There are not many high stewards datable for sure under Senusret III. The statue of a certain Nesmont was found in one of the small pyramids next to the pyramid of the king. He may date to the time of the king or shortly after. Khnumhotep, the vizier, was before his appointment to this highest office high steward, most likely under Senusret III. He seems to have had an extraordinary career. The son of the governor of Menat-Khufu, he made his career at the royal court and seems to have been sent on a mission to Byblos.

The reign of Senusret III is in many ways a turning point in the Middle Kingdom. New titles appear in the administration; other titles disappear. This seems to indicate a fundamental reorganisation of the country. Egypt seems to have been centralised, focusing on a few centres. Dahshur, Lisht and the Fayum form the focal point of the royal building activities. Other important centres are Thebes and Abydos. The material culture of the country changed, or at least new object types were placed in burials. The wooden models so typical of early Middle Kingdom tombs disappeared, as well as longer religious texts for the interior decoration of coffins.[228] While the tombs of the ruling class in the early Middle Kingdom often look rather stereotyped with their wooden models, decorated coffins and other funerary goods, there is now a wide variety of objects placed in tombs. These are often magical items already used in daily life. Most famous are the magical wands and faience figures of hippopotami and other animals. However, royal courtiers were buried in a different style. The dead person was identified as Osiris and buried like a god. Royal insignia were placed everywhere in the burial, and some mummy masks of private people were even adorned with a uraeus. Royal staves and weapons were placed next to the dead. Common people were buried in a similar way to previously, although there was a trend towards placing more bodies in tomb chambers. Multiple burials became popular on many social levels, while in the early Middle Kingdom they were the exception.

Under Senusret III and also Amenemhat III (Pl. III) the king's portrait was radically innovatory. It no longer showed an idealised young man, but rather the realistic picture of a middle-aged man, unsmiling but with a dynamic expression, which is sometimes described as pessimistic. Many private sculptures followed the royal prototype. Stela production had reached its peak in quality under Senusret I and Amenemhat II. Under Senusret III the mass production of stelae for Abydos chapels begins. Many late Middle Kingdom stelae of private individuals are rather clumsy, only a few still reaching a higher standard (Pl. XXI).

The reigns of these kings also demonstrate a strong revival or influence of the Old Kingdom, especially at the royal court. The royal sarcophagi copied with their palace façade the palace façade of the Djoser complex. It is possible that the funerary complex of Amenemhat III at Hawara was also a copy of the Djoser complex at Saqqara. Pottery vessels found in royal burials have their prototypes in the Old Kingdom.[229] Whether these old models also influenced the administration of the country is an open question.

In the provinces it is evident that under Senusret III the big rock-cut tombs of the governors disappeared. It has been assumed that the king eliminated the power of the local rulers, because they behaved like small kings and were dangerous to central government. One example is the adoption of royal symbols in their tombs or the year datings of them. This view is no longer accepted; the royal symbols in tombs are to be connected with new religious beliefs. They have nothing to do with the usurpation of royal privileges. The disappearance of the big tombs is therefore more likely connected with a general new organisation of the country and new funerary beliefs; indeed at several places local governors are still attested, but they are no longer buried in huge rock-cut tombs.[230]

Nimaatre Amenemhat III (c. 1818/1817-1773/1772 BC)

Not much is known about the family of Nimaatre Amenemhat III. His father was probably Senusret III. His mother is not known. His wives were Aat and Khenmet-nefer-hedjet, who both died early in his reign and were buried in the king's pyramid at Dahshur. For the second part of his reign no new wives are known for sure. As the mother of his successor Amenemhat IV there appeared a certain Hetepti, who was probably also a wife of Amenemhat III. Neferu-Ptah was his daughter. She is the first royal woman in Egyptian history with a cartouche around her name. Therefore it can be assumed that she had a special status, supported by the fact that she had a burial place, which was never used, inside the king's pyramid at Hawara. Her final undisturbed tomb was found about 2 km away from the pyramid of her father at Hawara.[231] It seems strange to have had a burial place in her father's pyramid with her own not far away. It may simply be assumed that her father died earlier than she did. When she died the pyramid could not be opened again and therefore another place was chosen for her.

As already mentioned, Amenemhat III seems to have had a long co-regency of almost twenty years with Senusret III. Remains of an important historical inscription relating to the coronation of Amenemhat III were found at Medinet el-Fayum and may once have decorated the Sobek temple at this site. Only small fragments are preserved, but the same words are found within a longer inscription of the Eighteenth Dynasty in the temple of the ruling queen Hatshepsut at Deir el-Bahri.

Amenemhat III seems to have followed, and in many ways completed, the work of Senusret III. At the beginning of his reign the king started to build a pyramid at Dahshur. Already early on there must have been problems with the construction site. The corridor paving blocks in the pyramid cracked, revealing that the ground was too weak. Therefore the pyramid seems to have lost its status as main pyramid but was used instead as a burial place for the above mentioned queens. Around his fifteenth year the king seems to have started a second pyramid at Hawara (p. 118), not far from Lahun and the pyramid of Senusret II. The position of the new pyramid on the edge of the Fayum is revealing. The king may have finished the cultivation of the river oasis Fayum and concentrated resources in that region. This would explain why there are several temples and two colossal quartzite statues of the king (at Biahmu) in this province, marking the interest of the king in this newly cultivated land.

The complex or the pyramid most likely bore the name Ankh-Amenemhat, 'may Amenemhat live'. The work at the building seems to have been organised from Lahun, where several papyri referring to Ankh-Amenemhat were found.[232] The complex, especially the temple, was described by classical authors as the famous 'Labyrinth'. Inscriptions found at the Wadi Hammamat also refer to building work at Ankh-Amenemhat. The graffito of 'overseer of the gang of stone-masons', Senusret, reports:

> Year 19, first month of spring (peret), 15 (day), the good god, lord of the two lands, lord of the making of things, King Nimaatre (given life, stability and power like Re for ever). Despatching by his majesty to bring for him monuments from the valley of Ra-Henu [Wadi Hammamat] consisting of beautiful bekhen-stone [siltstone] to be established in Ankh-Amenemhat (may he live for ever and ever), in the domain of Sobek of Shedyt: ten statues, in blocks of five cubits [2.5 m]. Quarrying in this year by the beloved of his lord, craftsman of the king ... overseer of the gang of stone-masons, Senusret.[233]

From the surviving monuments, Amenemhat III did not build at many temples in the country. At Serabit el-Khadim (Sinai) the king seems to have erected the shrine for the Hathor temple, which was finished by Amenemhat IV. The activity here does not come as a big surprise because the king sent an exceptionally high number of expeditions to that place.[234] At Elephantine he added his name and the year dating '34' to a lintel which was set up and inscribed by the early Eleventh Dynasty king Nakhtnebtepnefer Intef III.[235] Other building work is not connected with temples but with erecting walls and is possibly of a military character. A fragment of a stela found at Elephantine dated to year 44 seems to be the start of a building inscription.[236] An almost identical stela dated perhaps to the same year (although the full dating is not preserved) was found at Elkab and refers to the building of an addition to a wall of Senusret II.[237] At Bubastis was found a palace building most likely erected by Amenemhat III, as some reliefs with the name of the king are from there, notably a relief showing the king performing the *sed* festival.[238] Blocks with his name have been found at Lisht,[239] Memphis[240] and Heraclcopolis.[241] At Thebes statues of the king were found in the great Ptolemaic Period cachette and also a bark pedestal with the names of Amenemhat III and Amenemhat IV.[242]

The best-preserved temple of the king is still standing today at Medinet Maadi in the Fayum. It was built at the end of the king's reign and its relief decoration was finished by his successor Amenemhat IV.[243] It is a small temple with three chapels at the back.

Amenemhat III is well known from many expedition inscriptions. Some expedition inscriptions found in the Wadi Hammamat are to be connected with the building work of the pyramid complex. Altogether four expeditions (in years 2, 3, 19 and 20) are attested. The expedition dated to year 19 mentions 2000 workmen, a relatively large number. About three expeditions to Wadi el-Hudi are attested.[244] Around twenty-five expeditions are attested for Sinai, where turquoise was the main material. Another inscription dated to year 2 of the king is at Ayn Soukhna[245] (east desert, opposite Sinai, about 40 km south of Suez); this is certainly also connected with expeditions to Sinai – at least some expeditions started their way by sea to Sinai from here.

At the Nubian fortresses of Kumma and Semna the Egyptians started under Amenemhat III to mark high Nile floods. The inscriptions give a sign marking the highest Nile level of a certain year and they include a dating with the king's name. These records provide us with a series of datable inscriptions for the kings at the end of the Twelfth and the early Thirteenth Dynasty, when this custom stopped. Sadly the level seems not have been recorded every year – at least there are gaps; strictly annual datings would have provided a perfect guide to the chronology of the late Middle Kingdom. There is little evidence for military activity by the king in Nubia. An inscription at Kumma made for a certain Samont dates to the ninth year and reports a small campaign in which nobody on the Egyptian side was killed.[246] There is finally a stela found at Kerma (Nubia), south of the Third Cataract, mentioning building work at the 'Wall-of-Amenemhat-true-of-voice'.[247] The stela is dated to year 33 and must have come originally from Egyptian-controlled territory. Kerma, the capital of a Nubian empire in the Second Intermediate Period, was in the Middle Kingdom not part of the Egyptian empire. Other foreign campaigns are not known. There is a pectoral, found at Dahshur, showing the king smiting the Mentiu (Beduins of Asia) and the Setiu (Asiatics).[248] However, the depiction seems generalised and it seems too dangerous to draw any further conclusions from it.

In his year 30 the king celebrated his *sed* festival, which is mentioned on several monuments, the most important being a stela now in the British Museum, London, on which the official Nebpu-Senusret[249] proudly reports that he took part at the festival as bearer of a ceremonial vessel.

There are few sources for the court of King Amenemhat III. Many high officials can be dated to the late Twelfth Dynasty or early Thirteenth Dynasty, but their succession, order and precise dating are far from clear. Khety is the only vizier datable for sure under Amenemhat III. The vizier Ameny can be placed on prosopographical grounds under the king. The treasurer at the beginning of the reign was Iykhernofret. Another treasurer most likely datable to the time of Amenemhat III was a certain Ameny, known from a huge sarcophagus with an inscription invoking Osiris, lord of the Fayum; since the burial place of the king was at Hawara at the Fayum edge, it seems likely that the sarcophagus came from the pyramid cemeteries there, though it was found reused in a Third Intermediate Period context at Tanis.

Maakherure Amenemhat IV (c. 1772-1764/1763 BC)

The mother of the new king was the 'king's mother', Hetepti, who is depicted on a wall decorated under the king in the Renenutet temple at Medinet Maadi (Fayum). She is so far only known from this temple. Her husband was most likely Amenemhat III, although this is nowhere stated. The partly destroyed inscriptions next to her do not call her 'king's wife'.[250] Maakherure Amenemhat IV may nevertheless have been his son. He seems to have had a short coregency with his father before he reigned alone. Some monuments mention both kings together: there are, for example, several stelae of private individuals with the names of both kings in the roundel.[251] Otherwise there is not much evidence for his reign. His burial place is not known. Nevertheless in Sinai he belongs to the better attested kings of the Middle Kingdom; the highest date for him is year 9 in an inscription on Sinai.[252] Altogether there were four expeditions of the king to that place. Another expedition is known by inscriptions to Wadi el-Hudi, dated to year 2.[253] At Semna were found several Nile-level marks dated to the time of Amenemhat IV.[254] Finally there are some private stelae bearing his name as sole king.[255] The custom of placing a king's name on a private stela becomes rare in the Thirteenth Dynasty. Amenemhat IV is the last king for whom the custom is still well attested. This habit seems to be a sign of a strong rulership; it is not attested under weaker kings in the following Thirteenth Dynasty. Other monuments with the name of the king are sphinxes from Abukir (Delta) and Heliopolis, and another in Beirut. In Byblos was found a small and perfectly sculptured obsidian gold chest with his name, attesting contact between Egypt and the town. In a Theban tomb a small box was excavated, decorated with ivory inlays. It shows the official Kemni in front of the king. According to the Turin Canon Amenemhat IV reigned nine years, three months and twenty-seven days. The highest attested year date, year 9, is found in the Sinai inscription cited above. In general the impression is that nothing dramatically changed under the king in comparison to Amenemhat III. Major building projects in his name are lacking, but this may be just a gap in the archaeological record.

Sobekkare Sobeknofru (c. 1763-1759 BC)

Sobekkare Sobeknofru is the last ruler of the Twelfth Dynasty and the first woman who ruled Egypt for whom we have contemporary attestations. For Nitokris, a ruling queen at the end of the Old Kingdom, there are no contemporary monuments. However, little is known about Sobeknofru. Manetho, who called her Skemiophris, states that she was the sister of Amenemhat IV. Assuming that the latter was the son of Amenemhat III, the ruling queen may have been the daughter of Amenemhat III. Following the Turin Canon she reigned only three years, ten months and twenty-four days. Unlike the later and more famous Hatshepsut her memory was not prosecuted and she appears at least in some later king lists, such as in the Saqqara list and the Turin Canon. Inscriptions with her name together with that of Amenemhat III were found at Hawara at the 'Labyrinth'[256] and it is even possible that she finished that complex; at least she seems to have added several inscriptions to it. Another similar inscription without provenance but also naming both rulers possibly comes from the same site.[257] This may also be true for blocks with only her name discovered at Heracleopolis (Ehnasya), no great distance from the Labyrinth. Heracleopolis was still important in Roman times and it is possible that the blocks were transported there from the Labyrinth, especially because we know that the Labyrinth was dismantled by Roman times.[258] The mention of two kings together on a monument is often considered as evidence for a coregency. In the case of Amenemhat III and Sobeknofru, who are separated by the reign of Amenemhat IV, this may indicate that the ruling queen made much reference to the reign of the Amenemhat III, who was most likely her father. The relation must have been important for her, and such monuments could be taken to indicate that her rule was not so stable. This seems to be confirmed by an inscription found at Hawara, which does not give any name but probably refers to her and Amenemhat III: '... her monument for her father ....' However, 'her father' may also refer to a god.[259] Another interesting inscription on a column without provenance (but perhaps also from the Labyrinth) shows the Horus name of Amenemhat III and Sobeknofru facing each other. The Horus falcon of Amenemhat III holds the signs *ankh*, life, and *djed*, stability, to the mouth of the Horus of the ruling queen. The column was certainly inscribed under Sobeknofru and shows her wish to demonstrate her favour for Amenemhat III.[260]

At Tell el-Dab'a were found three statues with her name showing her in a long female dress. The heads of the statues are lost. Therefore it is not possible to say what kind of crown or headdress she wore.[261] Following the dedication inscriptions which mention Sobek Shedety (Sobek, the one from Shedyt), the statues may have come originally from Shedyt (Medinet el-Fayum). Two of the statues show her sitting on a throne, while the third one shows her kneeling on the ground. At the same site was found a sphinx of the queen, which was already much eroded when recorded.[262] In the Louvre there is a statue of her, showing the queen with a female dress and the *nemes* headdress.[263] From Nubia finally there is a Nile-level inscription dated to year 3 of her reign.[264] Unlike Hatshepsut, who is later often shown with the body of a man and who also tends to avoid the female endings in her titulary, Sobeknofru seems to be always shown and depicted as a woman. The titulary always shows the female endings and the statues show a woman with some royal attributes, such as the *nemes* headdress. The *nemes* headdress is known before only from male rulers, simply because all depictions of kings before Sobeknofru belong to men. It is therefore not a sign of taking over particular male attributes. The burial place of the queen is not known, but sites such as Hawara or Dahshur seems to be most likely. On a papyrus found at Harageh a place called Sekhem-Sobeknofru seems to be mentioned.[265] It is possible that this is the name of her pyramid. On a stela dating to the Thirteenth Dynasty is mentioned the 'shena' (production place – the reading is not certain) of the queen, which was most likely located in a building connected with her funerary cult.[266] It seems likely therefore that a funerary cult remained active for a certain time after she had died.

Taken together the sparse evidence suggests that Sobeknofru had a quite 'normal' reign, although the queen seems to have worried about her legality on the throne and therefore refers to Amenemhat III, who was most likely her father. Her building activities seem to be almost exclusively concentrated on the Labyrinth at Hawara. Nothing more is known about the end of the dynasty, but there are no signs that it ended in trouble or violence.

1.7. The Thirteenth Dynasty (*c.* 1759-1685 BC)

Sources

The archaeology and sources for the Thirteenth Dynasty are different from those for the Twelfth Dynasty. The names of the rulers of the period and their order in the early Thirteenth Dynasty are preserved in the Turin Canon. There are still many questions of detail but there is a general agreement on the correctness of the broad outline of the sequence. In perhaps a total of 150 years there are about fifty to sixty rulers attested, giving each of them an average reign of about three years. However, some rulers seems to have had quite long reigns of about ten and even twenty years, making it likely that others ruled only a very short period of time. While the names of the rulers of the first half of the dynasty are quite well preserved in the Turin Canon, the part of the manuscript with the rulers of the second part of the Thirteenth Dynasty is badly damaged. Most of the latter seem to belong within a period when the unity of Egypt was already failing: almost all are known only from monuments found in Upper Egypt, while kings of the first part of the dynasty are known from both parts of the country. Therefore it has been proposed that they constituted their own dynasty: Dynasty Sixteen. (The jump from thirteen to sixteen in the numbering of these dynasties is explained by events in the north: Dynasty Fourteen is the Delta group contemporary with the later Thirteenth Dynasty, while the Fifteenth Dynasty is the subsequent line of foreign rulers, the 'Hyksos'.) However, not all Egyptologists follow this, instead regarding the Sixteenth Dynasty as Delta vassals of the 'Hyksos'. The problem is yet to be resolved.

The Thirteenth Dynasty can be divided into three main periods. The first part is characterised by a high number of short reigns, some less than one year, amounting to perhaps about ten to fifteen years in total. After these kings there is a well-attested group of rulers, some of whom reigned quite a long time. A large number of monuments both private and royal can be dated to this period. Indeed some of the kings of the mid-Thirteenth Dynasty are better known than many of the great rulers of the Old Kingdom. After this phase of perhaps fifty to eighty years there followed a high number of badly attested kings. They are all known only from the south of Egypt, leaving the impression that the unity of the country had come to an end.[267] In the North there appeared at about this time Asiatic people settling in the east of the Delta. Their rulers – the Fourteenth Dynasty – seem to have become at a certain point independent from the kings in Itj-tawy. With this loss of unity Egypt entered the Second Intermediate Period. The exact point of this event is not yet known, but the last Egyptian king attested in the North and in the South is a certain Merneferre Iy. Shortly after or even during his reign the unity of the country seems to have fallen apart. At least his successors are no longer attested in the North.

The residence was most likely still at Itj-tawy. All known royal tombs of the period have been found in the Memphis-Dahshur region. However, there are only a few royal monuments found in situ. The tomb of King Auibre Hor, and the pyramids of Kings Ameny Qemau and Khendjer are the most important examples. There are only a few private monuments connected with royal monuments. There is only a small number of royal rock inscriptions, most of them datable to the time of Khasekhemre Neferhotep I and Khaneferre Sobekhotep IV, and there are only a few private inscriptions referring to a named king. The names of the rulers of the dynasty are therefore relatively well known, but it is still impossible to write a political history. In a similar way it is hard to combine the archaeological records with names of kings. By contrast there are many private monuments, especially stelae and statues, datable to the period. Art production is well documented at least for the early Thirteenth Dynasty. The development of pottery, scarabs, burial furnishings and certain object types is well known for the end of the Middle Kingdom, but it remains hard to correlate these developments with specific reigns and so to place them in a chronological framework which can be related to the political history.

The kings

The Twelfth Dynasty was a period of great political stability. One family ruled the whole country for almost 200 years. The following Thirteenth

Dynasty marks a complete contrast, with many kings ruling only for a short period. Only a few of them seem to have been connected by family ties. There are many theories about the reasons for such a high number of kings, but so far there is no convincing explanation.[268] In general it can be said that the kings of the early Thirteenth Dynasty still ruled the whole country including Nubia as far as the Second Cataract. There is no evidence for local rulers, at least in the early Thirteenth Dynasty; only in its later stages are there indications that people coming from Palestine took over the eastern Delta fringes. The unity of the country must have fallen apart at this point, marking the end of the Middle Kingdom (defined as a period of political unity) and the beginning of the Second Intermediate Period. It has been assumed that many kings of the Thirteenth Dynasty were military usurpers. However, there is little evidence for this. There are also almost no signs that any of the kings of the Thirteenth Dynasty were of foreign origin, as is sometimes assumed; only one king (Khendjer) has a name which sounds foreign, but he is especially well attested in the sources and there he appears as fully Egyptian. His wife has an Egyptian name and he was buried in a pyramid. Nevertheless there are signs that the kingship changed. Some of the better-known kings of the Thirteenth Dynasty provide the names of their non-royal parents on their monuments. In the Twelfth Dynasty daughters of kings were never married to people of non-royal origin. In the Thirteenth Dynasty there is plenty of evidence that a king's daughter might marry an official. Some women in families of officials are called 'king's sister' and there are at least two queens who can be shown to have belonged to important families of officials. It has been assumed that these families were able to place one of their women as 'king's wife'. However, it is also possible to argue that another (male) member of the family had become king. At least some kings of the Thirteenth Dynasty evidently had relations to the administrative elite of the country. This is not attested at all for the Twelfth Dynasty, but a similar situation is found in the Old Kingdom, when it was quite 'normal' that 'king's sons' occupied high positions in the administration of the country and 'king's daughters' were married to officials. The comparison with the Old Kingdom shows that this relationship of the kings to officials cannot be taken as an indication of decline or of weak kingship.

The name of the first king of the new dynasty is still under discussion. In the Turin Canon a ruler with the throne name Khutawyre appears as the first king of the dynasty. There is only one king with this throne name in the Thirteenth Dynasty known from contemporary monuments: Khutawyre Wegaf. Normally there would be no problem in recognising Khutawyre Wegaf as the first king of the Thirteenth Dynasty. However, the early Thirteenth Dynasty date of a king with a similar name, Sekhemre-Khutawy, seems to be indicated by several rock inscriptions in Lower Nubia recording the Nile flood level. These flood inscriptions start under Amenemhat III and seem to end in the early Thirteenth Dynasty. For three kings of this dynasty such inscriptions are known: Sekhemre-Khutawy, Sekhemkare and Nerikare. Only Sekhemkare can be dated securely to the early Thirteenth Dynasty. However, since the last years of the Twelfth Dynasty are well attested in these records it seems unlikely that they stopped at the beginning of the Thirteenth Dynasty only to become common again much later. All three Thirteenth Dynasty rulers therefore seem to belong to the earliest Thirteenth Dynasty. Khutawyre Wegaf does not appear in these inscriptions, whereas three of them are from the reign of Sekhemre-Khutawy, who is known from quite a number of other monuments and appears much later in the Turin Canon. One is dated to year 4;[269] the others to years 2[270] and 3.[271] Is it possible that the writer of the Turin Canon confused Khutawyre with Sekhemre-Khutawy? Here it should be noted that the first part of the Thirteenth Dynasty seems to have been very short. Many kings may have reigned for less than a year. Therefore there may not have been a long gap between the end of the Twelfth Dynasty and King Sekhemre-Khutawy, making it unnecessary to assume confusion in the Turin Canon between Khutawyre Wegaf and Sekhemre-Khutawy. It should also be remembered that the flood inscriptions were not recorded every year; there are gaps of several years among the Twelfth Dynasty examples. King Sekhemkare, who most likely had the birth name Amenemhat, is dated by two Nile rock inscriptions, one dated to year 3[272] and one to year 4.[273] The gaps would also account for the omission of Khutawyre Wegaf, because he reigned only two years.[274]

The first phase of the Thirteenth Dynasty: trouble on the throne (c. 1759-1744 BC)

The name of the first ruler of the Thirteenth Dynasty is, then, still disputed, but it seems likely that it was a certain Khutawyre Wegaf. A person called Wegaf is also known from a seal, where he bears the titles 'royal sealer' and 'great overseer of troops'. The name Wegaf is rare and therefore it seems possible that the 'great overseer of troops' and King Wegaf are identical.[275] Another group of sources perhaps related to the family of the king are monuments of the 'royal sealer' and 'overseer of fields', Ankhu. Ankhu states in a tomb inscription that he served as temple scribe for Khakaure (Senusret III) and that he followed the 'king's son', Amenemhat III, while he was still young. This must have happened during the long coregency of the two kings. The inscription dates Ankhu securely to the end of the Twelfth Dynasty. In the same inscription Ankhu is called 'born of the king's sister Merestekhi'. On other monuments relating to Ankhu the woman does not have this title. She seems to have been appointed at one point in her life to 'king's sister', obviously when her brother, who was one of the first kings of the Thirteenth Dynasty – perhaps Wegaf himself – became king.[276] In the Twelfth Dynasty it is not yet attested that any member of the king's family was married to a person of non-royal origin, and therefore the event must have happened at the beginning of the Thirteenth Dynasty. Whether Ankhu's uncle was Wegaf or another king of the earliest Thirteenth Dynasty is not really certain, but it indicates strongly that at least some kings of this dynasty came from the main administrative families of the country. Wegaf ruled only two years and is known only from a few monuments. In the Turin Canon a king named Sekhemkare appears as his successor. He is perhaps the king Sekhemkare Amenemhat V, who is known from a magnificent statue found at Elephantine. The Nile rock inscriptions show that he reigned at least three years. In the Turin Canon, behind the name and reign of Sekhemkare, there follows in the same line the entry 'lacuna, six years'. This has given rise to much speculation. Was there a gap in the papyrus being copied by the Ramesside scribe of the Turin Canon, or could he not read the names of kings written there? The question remains open. There is the possibility that in this lacuna belong some or at least one of the unplaced kings who are known from monuments datable to the early Thirteenth Dynasty. However, the interpretation of this 'lacuna' remains highly uncertain, and its position at the end of the line raises questions about its relation to the sequence of kings.[277]

According to the Turin Canon the next king is another Amenemhat, who may be identical to a certain king called Ameny Qemau whose small unfinished pyramid was uncovered at Dahshur in 1957.[278] The pyramid could only be identified by the name of the king inscribed on the canopic jars found inside. Without these the pyramid would be anonymous, like several other pyramids of the Thirteenth Dynasty. The two pyramids at Mazghuneh, a pyramid at Saqqara South and some pyramids at Dahshur, all unfinished and in an early stage of construction, may belong to the same period. They do not preserve the name of their owners. Ameny Qemau bears a double name, a typical feature of the late Middle Kingdom, also well known from private individuals.[279] In the Turin Canon the next king in the sequence is a certain Sehetepibre. A king with the same name appears also as eighth king of the Thirteenth Dynasty; one of these entries may perhaps be a spelling mistake for a King Hetepibre, not named in the Turin Canon. Hetepibre Qemau-Sa-Hornedjitef could therefore have been the successor of Ameny Qemau. He is only known from two monuments: a statue found in the Delta, but originally coming from Memphis ('Ptah, south of his wall' is mentioned on it), and a relief decorated block from Atawla in Middle Egypt, on which he appears as Hetepibre Qemau-Sa-Hornedtjef (Qemau's son Hornedtjef). He was possibly the son of Ameny Qemau, as his name suggests.[280] At this point in the Turin Canon comes a group of badly attested kings: Iufni, Seankhibre, Semenkare, Sehetepibre, Sewadjkare and Nedjemibre. From Seankhibre are known an offering table found at Karnak and some smaller objects, where he appears with the birth names Amenemhat Intef Ameny;[281] from each of Semenkare and (or the previous?) Sehetepibre there survives a stela found at Gebel Zeit.[282]

67

A certain King Nerikare is not attested with this name in the Turin Canon, but also seems to belong among the early Thirteenth Dynasty kings; he is known from a Nile-flood-level rock inscription and a stela.[283] There is then another small group of kings, this time a little better attested, though there is still the impression that they did not rule long: Khaankhre Sobekhotep I, who is mainly known from a small chapel or similar building at Abydos,[284] Amenemhat Renseneb, known only from a bead,[285] Auibre Hor,[286] known from his well-preserved burial at Dahshur, and finally Sedjefakare Kay-Amenemhat, who left a bark stand at Medamud.[287] They may have reigned together for only a short period, perhaps not even a few years.[288] Apart from the first kings of the Thirteenth Dynasty there are no kings with a year date higher than year 1. The early Thirteenth Dynasty may therefore have been very short.

The second phase of the Thirteenth Dynasty: stabilisation
(c. 1744-1685 BC)

After the unstable period described above a number of rulers appear in the Thirteenth Dynasty who are quite well attested from monuments all around the country; some of them reigned about ten years. It seems that Egypt was again quite stable after a period of shaky succession. King Sekhemre-khutawy Amenemhat Sobekhotep II is attested on a number of monuments. He is known from Nile-level inscriptions (called there only Sekhemre-khutawy), on one of which his fourth year is mentioned. In Medamud he added to the already existing Mont temple. He built at the Mentuhotep II mortuary temple at Deir el-Bahri, a building which under Senusret III had already received some royal attention.[289] However, the most important document of his reign seems to be papyrus Boulaq 18, an administrative record of the court at the Theban palace. It is, though, not certain that he is the ruler under whom the papyrus was written; the king's name in it is almost entirely lost.[290] The capital at this time must still have been Itj-tawy, but the king seems also to have resided at times in Thebes. In the case of King Sekhemre-khutawy Amenemhat Sobek-hotep II he may have visited the town on the occasion of building work at Medamud temple. A trip to Medamud is indeed mentioned in the document, and fits well with the known building activity of the king there. The papyrus lists the court and courtiers. At the head of it was the vizier Ankhu, and under him there are officials with the ranking title 'royal sealer' and different function titles such as the 'overseer of the field', the 'high steward', the 'overseer of the troops' and the 'personal scribe of the royal document'. Finally there is a large group of other officials under this highest circle, with titles such as 'officer of the ruler's crew'. Other people mentioned are the 'king's son' and the 'king's sisters'. Of special historical importance is the mention of the king's wife Iy because she also appears on a private stela (now in Würzburg) as a member of a family of high officials.[291] To the same family belongs the same vizier Ankhu who appears in papyrus Boulaq 18. Therefore the royal family was evidently closely related to at least one family of officials, or perhaps a family of officials managed to place one of their members on the throne. The case of the vizier Ankhu has always been taken as an example of the firm administration of this period, because he is also attested in the following reign; Ankhu has been seen as some kind of 'king-maker'.[292] However this is only a guess[293] and it can only be said for sure that the administration of the period was quite stable, with many high officials such as the vizier Ankhu or the treasurer Senebsumai, both of whom seem to be in office longer than the ruling kings, and are known from a remarkable series of monuments.

King Userkare Khendjer followed Sekhemre-khutawy Amenemhat Sobekhotep II. He is mainly known from his pyramid complex in Saqqara South, which seems to have been completed; at least its pyramidion was found. The name Khendjer is also inscribed on one of two related stelae from Abydos,[294] which report renovation work at the Abydos temple originally built by Senusret I. On the stela there is also the throne name Nimaa(t)re, which led to the conclusion that there are two kings with the birth name Khendjer. However, it seems more likely that he changed his throne name at some point in his reign, or that the throne name Nimaa(t)re was inscribed at a different time on the stela and may not relate to Khendjer. The inscription on the other of the two stelae refers to the above mentioned vizier Ankhu. The date of the renovation work mentioned on the stelae is not known for sure. Normally it is assumed that it dates to the time of Khendjer himself, but there is also the possibility that it refers to events in a previous reign.[295] From some graffiti found at the pyramid complex Khendjer is known to have reigned at least four years. The un-Egyptian sound of the name of the king has given rise to various hypotheses; it has been derived from a Semitic (maybe North-Canaanite) language word for 'boar'.[296] It was assumed accordingly that Khendjer was an Asiatic general who took over the Egyptian throne. However, there is no proof of this and it only shows how much speculation there is about this period. King Khendjer was most likely married to a women with the good Egyptian name Seneb... (rest of name not preserved).[297] In Liverpool there was a stela (destroyed in the Second World War) recording a 'king's son', Khedjer. The name appears to be just a variant of Khendjer. The 'king's son' seems to be related to the king, but it is not really known how.[298]

The successor of Khendjer is a certain king called Mermesha. His name means 'general' or 'overseer of troops' but is also known as a personal name.[299] The king is only attested on two colossal statues found at Tanis.[300] The name of the king again gave rise to speculation that a military man seized the Egyptian throne, but again there is no supporting evidence for this assumption. The following king, Sehetepkare Intef, is also only known from a statue,[301] while the next king in the Turin Canon list, called Seth, is not securely attested on contemporary monuments.[302] These three kings may have reigned only a short time.

Sekhemre-Sewadjtawy Sobekhotep III is known from a relatively high number of monuments. The king built in Medamud, Tod and Elkab and erected an altar on Sehel. A number of inscriptions mention the family of the king. Of special interest is his father, who appears as the 'god's father', Mentuhotep. The title 'god's father' was held by priests, but can also be used to refer to the non-royal father of a king, and is therefore in this context not a function title. Therefore we do not know the position of this man before his son became king. However, there are a dozen scarab seals belonging to the 'officer of the ruler's crew', Sobekhotep, begotten of the 'officer of the ruler's crew', Mentuhotep. It is tempting to believe that these scarab seals relate to King Sekhemre-Sewadjtawy Sobekhotep III before he became king.[303] 'Officer of the ruler's crew' is a military title well attested at the royal court at this time. If this identification is correct this seems to be another case (if Wegaf was the first) of a military man becoming king. However, it should be kept in mind that Egyptian titles translated as military are never exclusively military in character. The title 'overseer of the troops' refers to people overseeing other people who could be used for military actions, but also for building works. The same seems to be true for the title 'officer of the ruler's crew'. The idea of a military coup at the royal court seems to be much influenced by the history of the Roman empire, where the military was important for appointing a new emperor. Egyptian society was clearly different and not so much in the hands of soldiers.

The family of the king Sekhemre-Sewadjtawy Sobekhotep III is well known from several monuments. The king had two wives: Senebhenas and Neni. From the latter he had the two daughters Iuhetibu and Dedet-anuqet. Iuhetibu must have gained some kind of special favour and status because her name was written in a cartouche. This is only the second such occurrence for a royal woman in Egyptian history. The first case is Neferu-Ptah, daughter of Amenemhat III. The wives of kings gained this privilege only later; in the Middle Kingdom the names of royal women are always written without a cartouche. King Sekhemre-Sewadjtawy Sobek-hotep III reigned for only three years and there seem to be no family ties to his successor Khasekhemre Neferhotep I, whose family is also well known. The reign of Sekhemre-Sewadjtawy Sobekhotep III introduces the core group of kings of the Thirteenth Dynasty. The king is also the first in a group of rulers who issued a high number of scarabs with his filiation on them, naming his non-royal parents: the 'god's father', Mentuhotep, and the 'king's mother', Iuhetibu. This issue of scarab seals with his name and the name of his parents is a remarkable innovation; earlier kings of the Thirteenth Dynasty are only sporadically attested on them. The change applied to high officials too. In the late Twelfth and early Thirteenth Dynasty officials are attested only by one or two seals, whereas officials of this period often had many more. From the treasurer Senebsumai, who was most likely in office under this king, over thirty scarab seals are so far known.[304]

According to the Turin Canon the next king, Khasekhemre Neferhotep I, reigned eleven years. Monuments of the king have been found all over Egypt and seem to be the proof of a prosperous reign. His father is the 'god's father', Haankhef; his grandfather is the 'soldier of the town', Nehy. His grandmother is a certain Senebtysy. It is the first time in the Thirteenth Dynasty that we know for sure the social background of the royal family. 'Soldier of the town' seems to be a military title. The title appears often on monuments of the period and belongs to officers of a certain rank (and not to common soldiers as is sometimes assumed). The function title of Haankhef, the father of the king, is again not known, hidden behind 'god's father', the usual designation for the non-royal father of a king. The name of the father appears on many royal-name seals and on royal monuments, and is even mentioned in the Turin Canon. The mother of the king was called Kemi. The spouse of Khasekhemre Neferhotep I is the 'king's wife', Senebsen, presumably the mother of his attested children, the 'king's son', Haankhef, and the 'king's daughter', Kemi.[305] It is known that the brother of the king, the future King Khaneferre Sobekhotep IV, was born in Thebes. Therefore we may assume that the whole family comes from there. One of the most extraordinary inscriptions from his reign is a stela found at Abydos, dated to year 2; it records in unusual detail the making of an Osiris figure. The king is described as being in his palace and talking to his nobles and officials, wishing to see the writings of old of Atum in order to create an image of Osiris. The central part of the text deals with the fashioning of the image.[306] The king is also attested in Byblos; a relief shows the local ruler, 'the mayor of Byblos', Iantin, in front of a King Khasekhemre Neferhotep. There are three kings of the Thirteenth Dynasty with the name Neferhotep, but only Khasekhemre Neferhotep I is well attested and belongs to a period of political stability. Officials dating to the period support the connection to Byblos. On a stela found at Abydos there is shown a certain 'keeper of the chamber of Byblos', Sobekherhab.[307] A person called Senebtyfy with an identical title appears on a stela now in Dublin.[308] The title confirms the stable relations of Egypt to this town in the Near East. On the Dublin stela also appears an 'overseer of the production place of the Oasis', confirming that Egypt at this time was a strong state which controlled its foreign trade and some outposts such as the oasis. Nubia also seems to have been still under full control. In an undisturbed Egyptian-style tomb at Buhen was found a plaque – a jewellery part – with the gold Horus name (Menmerut) of Khasekhemre Neferhotep I.[309] At Mirgissa there was found a seal impression with the name of the king. From Sehel near Elephantine is known a series of rock carvings mentioning the name of the king, his family and some of the officials serving him, such as the treasurer Senebi, who is also well known from other sources. There is evidence that the Nubian fortresses were abandoned in the Thirteenth Dynasty, but this seems not to have taken place from the south to the north; instead, fortresses in the middle fell out of use, while the larger ones with a special strategic position such as Semna and Buhen seem to have functioned all through the Thirteenth Dynasty and even into the Second Intermediate Period (though then no longer under Egyptian rule). This is not necessarily a sign of decline or loss of control over Nubia. The smaller fortresses were simply no longer needed; it is even possible to argue that this is a sign of stabilisation.

In the Turin Canon a certain Sahathor appears as the successor of Khasekhemre Neferhotep I; a Sahathor is known as his brother, but it seems that he never ruled Egypt alone, for no monument can be attributed to him as king. There is even a posthumous statue on which he is mentioned not as king but as 'king's son' only. Sahathor therefore never ruled as king in Egypt.[310] The following king – another brother of Khasekhemre Neferhotep I – is Khaneferre Sobekhotep IV. The length of his reign in the Turin Canon is lost, but there is a stela from the Wadi Hammamat naming the king and his family, including Khasehkhemre Neferhotep I. The monument is perhaps dated to the ninth year of Khaneferre Sobekhotep IV,[311] providing evidence that his reign was about the same length as that of his brother Khasekhemre Neferhotep I. The wife of the king was a certain Tjan, and there are several children attested: Sobekhotep Miu, Sobekhotep Djadja, Haankhef Iykhernefret; their mother is not certain. Amenhotep and a daughter named Nebetiunet had Tjan as mother. Khaneferre Sobekhotep IV is again known from a quite high number of monuments. Three colossal statues, originally from Memphis, with the name of the king were found at Tanis. The statues mention 'Ptah, south of his wall'. Blocks with the name of the king were found at the Osiris temple at Abydos and at Karnak, indicating building activity at these places. There are several expedition inscriptions from the Wadi Hammamat and the Wadi el-Hudi.[312] A stela found at Karnak reports donations to the temple. On a statue of the vizier Iymeru from Karnak is mentioned the 'opening of the canal' and the 'house of millions of years', Hotepka-Sobekhotep. The 'house of millions of years' is later the name of temples directly dedicated to the cult of the reigning king.[313] It is not known where the temple stood. Khaneferre Sobekhotep IV may be the King Chenephres mentioned by the early Jewish writer Artapanus (who received his information from the works of Manetho), who believed that the Moses story took place under the king; he states that Chenephres made war against Nubia and that under him parts of the Delta were taken over by Asiatics. The stela of the 'deputy treasurer', Ibia, datable to about this time (but not providing a king's name), reports that the king sent Ibia to Nubia (Kush) to open it. The event related may refer to Nubian campaigns of the king.[314]

The Asiatic occupation of the Delta mentioned by Artapanus needs further comments. People with Semitic/Asiatic names are well attested in Middle Kingdom Egypt. At the beginning of the Thirteenth Dynasty many Asiatic people coming from south Palestine started to settle along the eastern fringes of the Delta, and already early on places such as Avaris (today Tell el-Dab'a) seem to have been largely occupied by an Asiatic population. There is evidence that these people were still under Egyptian control, but at a certain point in the Thirteenth Dynasty they seem to have declared independence. Following Artapanus this may have happened already under Khaneferre Sobekhotep IV. However, there is no proof of this in archaeological evidence or from contemporary written sources. The nature of the new Dynasty in the eastern Delta is therefore not clear. There is a king called Nehesy (the 'Nubian'), whose monuments were found in this area, and it has been proposed that he was one of these rulers. His capital may have been Avaris. However, it is not possible to connect his reign chronologically with kings of the Thirteenth Dynasty.[315]

The reigns of Khasekhemre Neferhotep I and Khaneferre Sobekhotep IV clearly mark the peak of the Thirteenth Dynasty. The country seems to have functioned well in the early Thirteenth Dynasty, particularly as regards the administration. The material culture of the early Thirteenth Dynasty is almost identical to that of the late Twelfth Dynasty. Workshops produced sculpture of the highest quality, such as the statue of King Sekhemkare Amenemhat V found at Elephantine[316] and the almost life-size wooden statue of King Hor found in his tomb at Dahshur. Not only is the number of royal monuments remarkably high, but the number of private monuments datable to their reigns is hardly surpassed in any other phase of the Middle Kingdom. The life-size statue of the 'herald of Thebes', Sobekemsaf (now in Vienna),[317] the statue of the vizier Iymeru Neferkare (now in the Louvre)[318] and the statue of a vizier, father of the vizier Ankhu (Pl. V),[319] belong among the great artworks of Egyptian sculpture and date to about this period. The statue of Sobekemsaf depicts a corpulent elderly official. It is fascinating to read older art-history comments on this work, which often strive to see an emptiness of expression or formalisation in it.[320] Evidently some authors could not believe that a work of art of such a high standard is datable to the Thirteenth Dynasty, a period which was often treated as a time of decline in all areas. More amazing is the stelae production of the period. A high proportion of Middle Kingdom stelae are precisely datable to the middle of the Thirteenth Dynasty. Many officials appear on several stelae set up in small chapels in Abydos. The quality of these monuments varies. Many of them are rather crude objects; some of them are finely carved. The stelae immortalise numerous individuals dating to these reigns. There are not many long texts on them, but some of the stelae were inscribed with long prayers to Osiris or Min.

The burial furnishings of King Hor and of the 'king's daughter', Nubhetepti-khered, found next to the king are similar to royal burials from the end of the Twelfth Dynasty. The few surviving pyramids, although most often not finished, display elaborate closing systems of corridors and chambers. At Buhen was found an undisturbed burial of a rich person datable to the Thirteenth Dynasty. A steatite plaque was discovered there providing the gold Horus name of Khasekhemre Neferhotep I and a possible dating. The body of the dead person was placed with a gilded mummy mask in a small chamber perhaps without a coffin. He or she was adorned with a beautiful set of jewellery including a necklace with amethyst and golden beads and with end pieces in the shape of a lion. There was a finger ring with a scarab on which the name of King Nimaatre (throne name of Amenemhat III) was written.[321]

In terms of court officials the period is one of the best known in all Egyptian history. The vizier Iymeru Neferkare has already been mentioned. His father was 'royal sealer' and 'controller of the broad hall', Iymeru, and was therefore also a high official. Iymeru Neferkare is known from a number of monuments, many of them set up in Karnak. His second name Neferkare (the throne name of Pepy II) may indicate that he was born in the Memphite region, perhaps even near the pyramid temple of Pepy II where this name is attested for the Middle Kingdom. Senebi was the treasurer of the king. His father was the 'soldier of the town', Neb-pu. Another famous person is the 'high steward' Nebankh, also known from several sources.

The next king in the Turin Canon is a certain Khahetepre, who is known from seals as Khahetepre Sobekhotep V.[322] Nothing more is known for sure about the king. The assumption that he was the son of Khaneferre Sobekhotep IV is nothing more than a guess. According to the Turin Canon, he reigned four years and eight months, and the following two rulers, Wahibre Ibia and Merneferre Iy, reigned respectively ten and twenty-three years. There are not many monuments belonging to these kings. They are mainly known from their high number of seals. Wahibre Ibia appears on a stela from Thebes, which belongs to a family of local officials.[323] Merneferre Iy is attested on a door lintel from Karnak and a pyramidion found in the Delta. It has been assumed that the pyramid of the king was built in the Delta, but it seems more plausible that the object was moved there in later times from the Memphite region where all royal burials and burial complexes of the periods have been found. Merneferre Iy is the last king of the Thirteenth Dynasty securely attested in both the North and South of the country.[324] All later kings appear on objects found in the South. While there are still many private objects datable to the time of Khaneferre Sobekhotep IV, there is not the same quantity attested under these two long-reigning kings. Therefore all the evidence suggests that the unity of the country came to an end. This reduced kingdom became poor. High officials are now mainly known from their large number of scarab seals. The low number of monuments dating to these kings gives the impression of a sharp decline after Khaneferre Sobekhotep IV. Kings in the Delta, either foreign or Egyptian, seem to have taken over parts of the North. At this point the Second Intermediate Period begins, which is no longer part of the history of the Middle Kingdom. Egyptian kings are still well attested in the South, but they left few monuments, and those are sometimes of the lowest quality. The Middle Kingdom ends in darkness for us.

2

Archaeology and Geography[1]

Egypt was dominated on the one side by the river Nile and on the other side by the desert. Flowing from the south to the north, the Nile was the only regular water source for most parts of the country. Every year in late summer the river flooded the lower parts of the country and left behind rich soil, which made Egypt one of the most fertile countries in the ancient world. The flood – caused by heavy rains in Ethiopia – started around August and reached its highest level in September (with slight variations depending on the location in Egypt – the flood started in the south earlier than in the north). In this period of flood only the desert and some 'islands' in the cultivated land stayed dry. Settlements were always built on these islands, making travel between them possible only by boat in the flood period. Few settlements were erected in the desert or close to the desert, although this would be a perfect place for villages and towns since it is dry throughout the year. However, the deserts, even those close to the fertile lands, may have been too difficult to supply with drinking water. The desert was instead generally used as a source for different kinds of raw materials (stones), and for hunting and burial. The desert in the west was the Libyan Desert, which is basically flat and sandy. At a few places there are larger oases which seem to have become part of Egypt already in the Old Kingdom. Not much is known about the oases in the Middle Kingdom, but references in texts and titles indicate that they lay under Egyptian administration. For the Dakhla oasis there are even attested some Egyptian governors with fully Egyptian names and titles.[2] The Wadi an-Natrun, in Egyptian texts called Sekhet-hemat ('field of the salt'), was west of the Delta. There are remains of a fortress and of a temple where the name of Amenemhat I has been found. In contrast to the western desert, the eastern is a mountainous terrain with wadis cutting the hills from east to west. Egypt is rich in good stones, and many of them come from the eastern desert.

The good preservation of organic materials afforded by the deserts had and still has the effect that archaeology too often focuses on that part of the country with its rich cemeteries. However, it should be remembered that an even higher number of burials must have taken place not in the desert but close to the settlements on their islands in the cultivated river-plain. This focus on the archaeology of the desert has also for too long given the impression that settlements were merely badly preserved; it is therefore no surprise that they have not often been researched. Nevertheless, many settlements may still lie buried under modern towns or under the fields. In this respect Egypt is no different from other parts of the world.

In the north of the country the Nile divides into several branches to form its delta. This is a flat, wet region, where settlements could only be placed on mounds not inundated by flooding in the summer. If a town became too densely populated people would be forced to move to another hill. Double cities such as Dep/Pe (Buto) are therefore not uncommon. In terms of archaeology the Delta is so far little researched. Many huge hills with ancient settlements, still visible in the nineteenth century, were later destroyed by farmers and with them doubtless many Middle Kingdom levels and remains. The tombs of the Middle Kingdom were built close to these towns and villages and often also disappeared in this destruction. It is therefore possible to provide only a patchy picture of the landscape of the Delta in the Middle Kingdom. Farming was certainly important in all parts of the Delta, but cattle-herding also seems to have been important; whereas in other parts of the country agriculture was certainly the main economic factor. In the Middle Kingdom the country was divided into provinces called *nomes* in Egyptology (from their name later in Greek, *nomos*). A list of these nomes with their main towns and their main deity is found on the 'white chapel' set up by Senusret I at Thebes. It has always been assumed that these nomes were small administrative units. For the Old Kingdom this seems certain, but for the Middle Kingdom it is not so sure. There are some people with the title 'overlord of a nome', but they do not appear as often as one would expect. The following description of Egypt in the Middle Kingdom follows the division of the country into nomes, although they may not have been political units, but rather religious ones: regions each with one important town and its main deity. If nome capitals in the following description are mentioned, they are most often the main towns named on the chapel of Senusret I. It is again uncertain whether they were capitals in our sense. The chapel states that they were the towns where the measuring cord for the nome was stored. The following description starts from the south, following Egyptian practice. For each nome the main town is described first and the others follow. Where possible, a history of the governors is provided.

2.1. Upper Egypt

The first Upper Egyptian nome: Ta-seti (Fig. 6)

The first to seventh nomes were called Khen-Nekhen ('the inside-of-Nekhen') in the early Middle Kingdom. This was the region of the small realm ruled by the kings of the early Eleventh Dynasty. In the later Middle Kingdom this part of Egypt was more often called Tep-resi ('head of

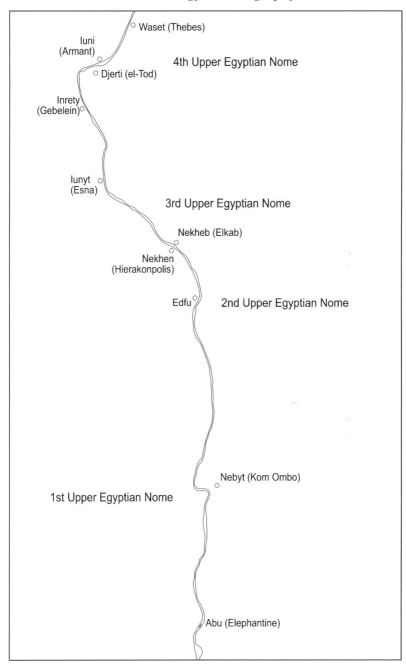

Waset (Thebes)

Iuni (Armant)

4th Upper Egyptian Nome

Djerti (el-Tod)

Inrety (Gebelein)

Iunyt (Esna)

3rd Upper Egyptian Nome

Nekheb (Elkab)

Nekhen (Hierakonpolis)

Edfu

2nd Upper Egyptian Nome

Nebyt (Kom Ombo)

1st Upper Egyptian Nome

Abu (Elephantine)

6. The first to fourth Upper Egyptian nomes.

southern Egypt') and seems to have formed a separate administrative unit. Many provinces in the other parts of Upper Egypt were ruled by local governors. In the first to seventh Upper Egyptian nomes this type of local administration seems to have been eliminated by the Theban kings of the early Eleventh Dynasty and the whole region was perhaps ruled by the central government (although this is not certain), while only single towns had their governors. This kind of local administration seems to have been introduced in the course of the Twelfth Dynasty into the rest of the country.

Ta-seti ('land of the bows') was the name of the most southerly Egyptian nome (Fig. 7). The fertile land on both sides of the Nile is not very wide in this region of Egypt. Therefore this part of the country was never densely populated. Its main towns were Abu (Elephantine) and Nebyt (Kom Ombo). The more important town in the nome was Abu ('elephant town' – Elephantine). The place seems to have been founded in the First Dynasty (or even earlier) and was at this time a place outside the main territory of Egypt proper. On the east bank of the Nile is Aswan; there are almost no Middle Kingdom remains, but the granite quarries there were certainly used in this period. South of the island there are the First Cataracts with several islands. On their rocks hundreds of inscriptions of the Middle Kingdom were found, certainly left by several expeditions to the granite quarries at Aswan. South of Aswan there is also a long Middle Kingdom fortification wall of uncertain purpose.[3] North of Elephantine at al-Kubaniya North and South were found two small Middle Kingdom cemeteries and a cemetery of about a hundred tombs belonging to the Nubian 'C-group', indicating that the region around the town was at least partly populated by Nubians, although they certainly lived under Egyptian administration. The tombs of the Nubians are totally different from those of the Egyptians. The bodies of the dead were placed in shallow holes in a contracted position. On the surface over the tomb there was most often a stone circle. As burial goods there were many Nubian vessels, and some wooden coffins – the latter surely introduced under Egyptian influence. Most of the Egyptian tombs at al-Kubaniya were found already disturbed. Common tomb types are simple holes in the ground, shafts lined with bricks and shafts with a chamber also lined with bricks. The dead were most often placed in stuccoed coffins, some of them inscribed, and there are also remains of some inscribed mummy masks. Burial goods include jewellery and pottery vessels.[4] It is hard to judge what kind of population was buried here. The tombs are richer and better built than those at other sites, but it is not known whether this is just a local custom or whether the people were quite wealthy here. It is not certain to which settlement these cemeteries belonged.

The town of Abu was on an island, opposite modern Aswan. Parts of it have been excavated and they provide perhaps the best evidence for a 'normal' non-planned Middle Kingdom town. There seem to have been

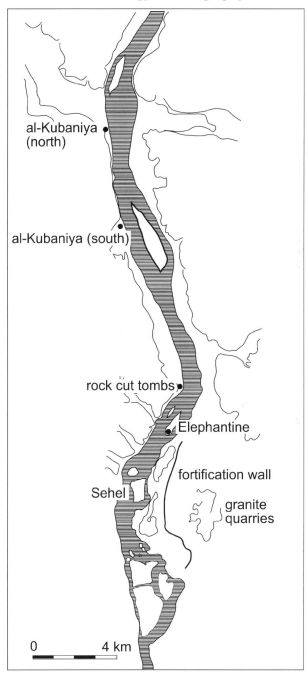

7. The First Cataract region around Elephantine.

three temples: the temple of the goddess Satet, the temple of Khnum, known only from some Middle Kingdom blocks and buried under the Ptolemaic temple, and the sanctuary of Heqaib, an official of the Old Kingdom who was worshipped as a local deity in the Middle Kingdom.

The houses excavated were in the middle of the town, next to the sanctuary of Heqaib, which is itself situated next to the other two temples: the Satet temple in the south-east and the Khnum temple[5] in the south-west. H 70 (so called by the excavators) is an example of a Middle Kingdom house (Fig. 8), datable to the end of the Twelfth or early Thirteenth Dynasty. It is quite well preserved and gives a good impression of the living conditions of the bulk of the urban population. The building is about 7 x 12 m in size; its main entrance in the east gave access to a big hall, about 6 x 8 m, with four columns in the middle to support the ceiling and a possible second floor. At the north wall of the hall there was a staircase leading to an upper level. Under the staircase there was a small chamber, perhaps just for storing vessels and other items. Behind the staircase there was a room most likely used as a kitchen, as can be seen from the burned walls and the ash found on the floor. At the west end of the big room with the columns there were two doors, one leading to a room with one column, the other to a room found filled with goat droppings. In the room with the column a storage installation was found, still containing seven vessels. In the same room there was found under the floor the burial of a new-born child, placed in a pot which was already broken in antiquity. The other room seems to have functioned at least for a while as a stable for animals. It is not known what the social status of the people living here was. The use of at least one room as a stable may indicate a family involved

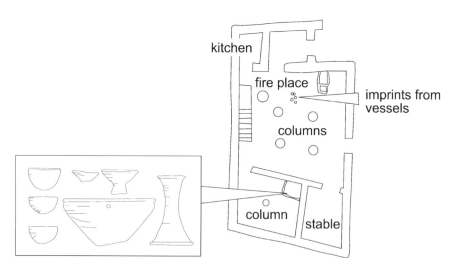

8. House H 70 at Elephantine (plan, with east at the top).

mainly in food production, but we do not have any idea how private households were organised. It seems possible that even people of status kept animals in the house for their own food supply. However, everywhere in the house are signs of economic use.[6] In the main hall there was a fireplace and next to it imprints of vessels in the ground. There is no room which could be identified as a bedroom. Certainly there was no special bedroom; it can be assumed that the people living here slept in all the rooms, or in the summer on the roof of the building.

The other houses excavated at Elephantine are of different size and arrangement. A common type is a house where the rooms are arranged around an open courtyard. Another house type, not so common, has a big central room, sometimes with columns, with the private rooms on one side and the entrance area on the other side. There are other interesting observations to make on the town of Elephantine. Houses were often inhabited for a long time, but it is often evident that no new houses were built when an old house fell out of use. The area of an empty run-down house was then utilised as a rubbish tip for the neighbourhood. There is finally a high number of burials of new-born children placed in vessels or boxes under the floors of houses. Burials of infants do not appear often in the archaeological records of cemeteries. It has often been assumed that they were buried at special places. However, at some cemeteries there have indeed been found areas reserved for the burial of the new-born. The evidence from Elephantine and from other sites shows that at least some of them were also buried inside the settlement area.

Most of the houses excavated are domestic buildings. There is also one bigger building, found full of seal impressions, indicating that it may have served for local administration. Other important finds here provide evidence for a similar function. There are small fragments of papyri and several weights. The complex was about 400 square metres in size and is therefore larger than any other house excavated at Elephantine. In the middle there was an open courtyard, which had columns on two sides. On the east there was a tower-like building with thick walls, indicating that it was several storeys high. It may have been used as a dwelling place, but also as a point from which the whole building was protected. Around the courtyard were arranged several rooms, and there were two cellars, perhaps for storing food at a cooler temperature. Several granary installations were found: the different shapes indicate that they were used for different kinds of food. The building was obviously built for storing goods for a short time, mainly or solely food. The seal impressions of the governors of Elephantine found here indicate that the highest local authorities were involved in the administration of the building. On the seal impressions appears the word *khetem*, 'enclosure'. It seems possible that the whole building is such an 'enclosure'. The building was therefore possibly a place where food was collected and stored for a short time to be given to certain people who were most likely working for the state.

We know very little about the economic system in ancient Egypt. There must have been to a certain extent a free market, at least on a local level where people exchanged goods. The best example of this seems to be the tale of the 'Eloquent Peasant'. This man, who lived at an oasis, went to Heracleopolis to sell his goods, obviously on a private level. The same kind of trade is indicated by several market scenes in Old Kingdom tombs. Similar scenes are not known from the Middle Kingdom. Besides this free market there must also have been a redistribution system for people employed by the state or involved in state projects. Goods, especially food, were collected for distribution to other people as some kind of payment. The building found at Elephantine must have been such an institution.[7]

The local history of Elephantine is better known than that of many other provinces. Here a sequence of governors is attested, who mainly seem to have controlled the town of Elephantine itself, although there are also titles referring to the whole province. In terms of population the town seems never to have been a large place, but gained its status from being the most southerly point of Egypt and 'gateway' to the south and to Africa. Old and Middle Kingdom expeditions to Nubia started here. The governors of Elephantine were buried near the west side of the Nile at a place called Qubbet el-Hawa today. At Elephantine there was the sanctuary of a local holy man (the Old Kingdom governor Heqaib), which was adorned with stelae and statues all through the Middle Kingdom. Each governor and many officials working at Elephantine or in the region set up a monument in the sanctuary. Many of the governors dedicated whole chapels in it. This sanctuary and the tombs are the main sources for reconstructing the history of the place in the Middle Kingdom.

Little can be said about Elephantine in the early Middle Kingdom. The small temple of Satet was rebuilt and renovated by several Intef kings of the Eleventh Dynasty. The first known governor at Elephantine is Sarenput (I), who left important biographical inscriptions in his tomb (Fig. 9) and on a chapel erected in the Heqaib sanctuary. Sarenput (I) lived under Senusret I, whose name appears in his tomb, and on his chapel in the sanctuary of Heqaib. Evidently the king appointed him to the position of governor of Elephantine. In his biographical inscription he mentions his duties, including that the delivery of the Medjay (Nubian) people (as servants ?) was reported to him. This is a direct reference to the task of controlling the trade between Egypt and Nubia. In further parts of the inscription Sarenput proudly reports that the king has sent craftsmen to Elephantine, who built his tomb. Of the successors of Sarenput (I) little is known. The governor Heqaib (I), who was a son of Sarenput (I) and the governor Khema are attested only from objects in the Heqaib sanctuary, but no tombs are known for sure. Better attested is Sarenput (II), who was the son of Khema. Sarenput (II) bears the second name Nubkaure-nakht ('Nubkaure is strong'). Nubkaure is the throne name of Amenemhat II, in

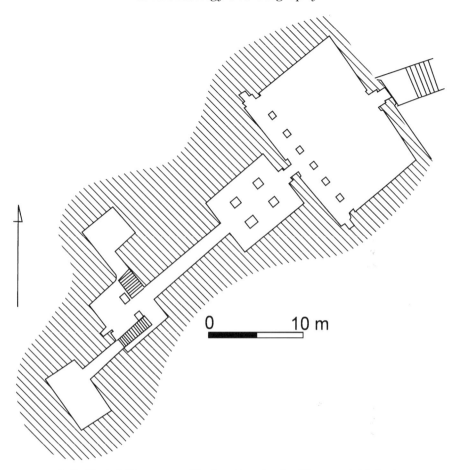

9. Qubbet el-Hawa near Elephantine: tomb of Sarenput I (plan).

whose reign he may have been born (Fig. 10). There is a stela of him in London dated to year 8 of Senusret III, reporting organisation work for the king's campaign against Nubia. His tomb is an impressive monument with a series of almost life-size mummy-shaped statues and a chapel decorated with fine paintings. In the tomb chapel is also mentioned his son Ankhu, who also bears the title governor, but who is not known from other monuments. He may have stayed in office for only a short time. Next in office was a certain Heqaib (II), who had a large tomb in Qubbet el-Hawa and a chapel in the Heqaib sanctuary. He can be dated to the end of the reign of Senusret III and the beginning of the reign of Amenemhat III. Heqaib (II) is the last governor from Elephantine with a known tomb. However, his tomb was never finished.

At many other places it is not possible to follow the succession of the

10. Qubbet el-Hawa: painting in the tomb of Sarenput II. The tomb owner
is sitting at an offering table. Before him stands his son Ankhu.

governors once the larger tombs cease to be built after the middle to late
Twelfth Dynasty. At Elephantine we know the governors up to the Thirteenth Dynasty, not because of their tombs but because they placed
monuments with their names in the sanctuary of Heqaib. A similar
situation can only be observed at Edfu, where many stelae mentioning
governors of the late Thirteenth Dynasty and Second Intermediate Period
have been discovered.

The interesting point about Elephantine, ignoring for a moment the
tombs and just looking at the surviving statues and chapels in the sanctuary of Heqaib, is that nothing really seems to have changed. The statues
of the late Twelfth Dynasty are still impressive monuments, although it
might be argued that they are no longer of the highest quality. After
Heqaib (II) Heqaib-ankh and Heqaib (III) were in office. Both seem to have
ruled for only a short period. The next governor is Ameny-seneb, known
from several statues at the sanctuary of Heqaib and seal impressions

86

found in the administrative building in Elephantine town mentioned above. He was followed by his son Khakaure-seneb. The interesting point about these two governors is that they seem to have had some kind of coregency, an institution so far only known for kings, but evidently copied by these officials. Mud seal impressions show sealings with the name of both governors together.[8] They both seem to date to the Thirteenth Dynasty, although for Ameny-seneb a dating at the end of the Twelfth Dynasty also seems possible. The next governor, who bears the name Khnumhotep, is so far known only from a stela, datable to the time of Khasekhemre Neferhotep I in the Thirteenth Dynasty.

North of Elephantine is the town of Nebyt (Kom Ombo). Horus and Sobek are mentioned in Middle Kingdom inscriptions as lords of this place. No details are known about their temples in this period, though blocks with the name of a King Senusret have been found. In the cemetery of the town there was excavated a decorated tomb chamber of a man called Sobekhotep. It most likely dates to the early Middle Kingdom.

The second Upper Egyptian nome: Wetjes-Hor (see Fig. 6)

Edfu was the main town of Wetjes-Hor ('throne of Horus') the second Upper Egyptian nome. The town – one of the main centres for the cult of Horus – appears with two names in Middle Kingdom sources: Behedet and Djeba. Behedet may be a more religious name while Djeba was the more administrative one. There are still substantial parts of the town visible, although only a little of the Middle Kingdom levels has yet been excavated. The cemetery of the town was situated right next to the settlement and its city walls and there were many tombs dating to the late Middle Kingdom and Second Intermediate Period. These tombs provide an excellent survey of burial customs in the late Middle Kingdom for common people living in an Upper Egyptian town. It is hard to decide whether these tombs are typical of Upper Egypt or whether this is an exception. Burials, including those of people belonging to the lower classes, were most often excavated in the desert at a remove from the settlement. This gives the impression that this was the rule for the whole country. However, at Elephantine and at Heracleopolis tombs have also been found close to the settlement. One wonders whether the proximity of tombs to a town was the rule rather than the exception. These cemeteries near settlements are most often not yet excavated, or were destroyed with the towns. There are basically four tomb types at Edfu: 1. small single chambers built in mud brick; 2. larger chambers reached via a shaft; 3. tombs with several chambers, also built in mud brick; 4. bodies just placed in the ground without any chamber or shaft.

Several bodies for one chamber are the rule (Fig. 11). They were sometimes placed in simple undecorated coffins, sometimes in mats; occa-

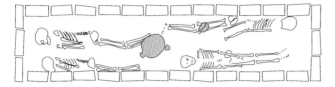

11. A burial chamber found at Edfu, very close to the town. Several bodies were found there. Some were placed in coffins (not well preserved); burial goods are pottery, jewellery and flint tools. This is a typical example of a burial for lower- or middle-class people at the end of the Middle Kingdom or the Second Intermediate Period.

sionally remains of mummy masks have been observed. Finds include pottery vessels, certainly for the eternal food supply, jewellery and tools, which seem to have symbolised the social identity of the dead, and there are sometimes simple clay figures of women. Most of these objects seem to have been taken from daily life and were not especially made for the burial. At Edfu there is also the mastaba of the Old Kingdom official Izi. Like Heqaib at Elephantine, this person seems to have had the status of a local god in the late Middle Kingdom. There are many stelae from Edfu dating to the Thirteenth Dynasty and to the Second Intermediate Period mentioning Izi in the offering formula at the point at which the name of a deity is given. It is not certain where these stelae were originally placed. Some of them may have been tomb stelae, but it is also possible that they were placed at Izi's tomb.[9]

The third Upper Egyptian nome: Nekhen

Nekhen is the name of the third Upper Egyptian nome. It contains several important Middle Kingdom sites. The capital was Nekheb (Elkab) which formed with Nekhen (Hieraconpolis, al-Kom al-Ahmar) on the opposite (west) side of the Nile a kind of double city. The main deity of Nekheb was Nekhbet, an important goddess in relation to kingship, as one of the crown deities. One of the five formal names of the king was 'the one of the two ladies', one of whom was Nekhbet. The goddess was also the vulture, a regular part of the royal headdress. In her temple were found blocks with the name of Mentuhotep II and a statue of Senusret I, and there is good evidence for building activity in the Thirteenth Dynasty. There is a large Middle Kingdom cemetery next to the town, mostly with simple shaft tombs. The decorated rock-cut tombs in the hills next to the town all seem to date to the Second Intermediate Period.

Nekhen was one of the main cult centres of Horus. It seems to have been very important in the Pre- and Early Dynastic Period, but lost importance at least as a population centre in the Old Kingdom. There are few Middle Kingdom remains from the site and it is hard to decide whether this is because of the destruction of the site or because it was not heavily populated at this period. There is the tomb of the 'first overseer of priests', Horemkhauef, and there is a statue of the 'overlord of Nekhen', Horhotep, dating to the Middle Kingdom.[10] The tomb of Horemkhauef is small but one of the few decorated examples of the period after the Twelfth Dynasty. It may belong to the very end of the Thirteenth Dynasty, when the capital of Egypt was still in the North at Itj-tawy. In the courtyard of the tomb there was found a stela reporting the journey of Horemkhauef to the capital in the North, to collect a new image of Horus from the king at Itj-tawy.

At Iunyt (modern Esna) a cemetery with many tombs dating to the late Middle Kingdom has been excavated. At Moalla, famous for the First Intermediate tomb of Ankhtyfy, some Middle Kingdom objects were found. More important was Inrety (modern Gebelein), where there was a temple of Hathor, where blocks with the name of Mentuhotep II were found. There are several stelae with names of Thirteenth Dynasty and Second Intermediate Period kings from this site and the cemetery contained several Middle Kingdom burials (Pl. X).

The fourth Upper Egyptian nome: Waset

Waset is the name of both the fourth Upper Egyptian nome and its main town, better known as Thebes. This is one of the richest provinces in Upper Egypt for Middle Kingdom finds. The Middle Kingdom cemeteries in the western desert are the best known part of Thebes, while relatively little is known about the Middle Kingdom town on the east bank of the Nile, although recent excavations now provide some idea of at least part of its residential areas. In later periods the main god of the town was Amun. In the early Middle Kingdom it was Mont, who was also worshipped at the other main towns of the nome.

The cemeteries of the early Eleventh Dynasty at el-Tarif are a huge and important burial ground for officials and the first kings of the Eleventh Dynasty. The main tomb type here is the *saff* tomb (see p. 12). However, King Mentuhotep II chose another place for his burial: Deir el-Bahri, south-west of el-Tarif. His burial complex consisted of several parts. There is a causeway with a big open courtyard in front of the mortuary temple. The temple, which consisted of two massive structures, one on top of the other, was adorned with columns. The top structure took the form either of a pyramid, as suggested by later texts which refer to the whole building as a pyramid, or perhaps of a massive square as reconstructed by Dieter Arnold.[11] The complex was richly adorned with reliefs and statues, now badly damaged, with fragments preserved in many museums all around the world. Under the temple there was some kind of ritual burial. At the end of a long gangway a small burial chamber was found containing a coffin and a statue of the king. At the back of the temple there were the tombs of the king and the 'king's wife' and 'king's mother', Tem. Not much survived of their tomb furnishings. There are remains of a canopic jar of the king, several wooden models and a fragment of the coffin. Six shrines of royal women with their burials underneath also form part of the overall building. Some of the burials were found undisturbed. The most remarkable finds are two well-preserved limestone sarcophagi, decorated on the outside with fine relief. They belonged to the 'king's wives', Aashyt and Kawit. A third sarcophagus was preserved only in fragments and belonged to the 'king's wife', Kemsit. The whole mortuary complex seems to be unique, but is clearly in the tradition of the *saff* tomb with its façade of columns. In the rocky hills around this funerary palace were the tombs of the highest court officials and of other members of the royal family (Fig. 12). One of the most important must have been the tomb of the treasurer Khety. It was adorned with fine reliefs, which included a depiction of the king. Khety's burial chamber was lined with limestone, which was decorated with friezes of objects and religious texts.

It is not certain where King Mentuhotep III was buried. South of Deir el-Bahri a large-scale building project was begun, certainly for a funerary complex similar in style to the one at Deir el-Bahri, but it is uncertain to

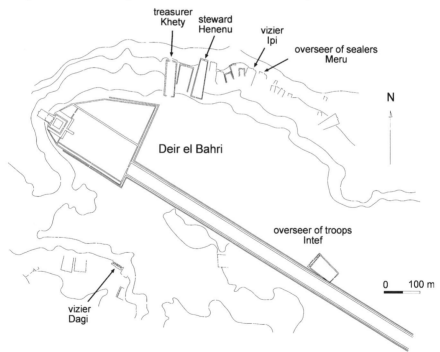

12. Deir el-Bahri, the funerary complex of Nebhepetre Mentuhotep II; the high court officials arranged their tombs around the tomb of their king.

which king it belonged: Mentuhotep III and Amenemhat I have been proposed. It was abandoned at an early stage of construction. In the hills overlooking the Theban necropolis Mentuhotep III built a chapel for Horus. This small building with three sanctuaries at the back is one of the first Egyptian temples that seems to have a pylon, two tower-like structures framing the entrance.

Under Amenemhat I the capital was moved from Thebes to the North. To the first years of his reign belongs perhaps the important Theban tomb, that of the treasurer and high steward Meketre. His rock-cut chapel was decorated with painted relief of the highest quality; sadly only small fragments survived the destruction of later centuries. An exceptional find was an undisturbed chamber filled with wooden models, so typical of many early Middle Kingdom burials. Thebes was in the Twelfth Dynasty certainly still quite important, but there are not many monumental tombs dating to that time. One exception is the tomb of Senet, mother of the vizier Intefiqer, datable to the time of Senusret I, who was depicted in the tomb. She had a tomb chapel adorned fully with paintings. The paintings display a certain provincial style, perhaps because highly trained court artists followed the king to the North and were at this time no longer available at Thebes. Under Senusret I the Amun temple at Karnak on the east bank was rebuilt (Fig. 13). There is only one column known from the temple of the Eleventh Dynasty, at least providing evidence that the temple already existed at this time. The temple of Senusret I formed the core of what later came to be one of the biggest temple complexes in Egypt.

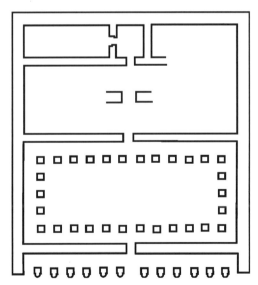

13. Reconstruction (plan) of the Amun temple of Senusret I at Thebes. In front of the temple there was a row of statues showing Senusret I as Osiris.

It was mainly built in limestone and seems to have been richly decorated with statues of the king but also with statues of his treasurer Mentuhotep, who was therefore perhaps the main person in charge of the building project. Most of the stones of the temple were in later times burnt for lime, so not has much survived. The only exceptions are a small sanctuary for a bark which could be reconstructed and the naos in granite, perhaps for the statue of the god, for which it was still used in the New Kingdom.

Not much is known about the living quarters of Thebes itself, but some excavations revealed that it may have been a planned town with blocks of houses arranged in a chess-board pattern similar to Lahun. In the late Twelfth Dynasty Senusret III set up a stela and statues in the mortuary temple of Mentuhotep II at Deir el-Bahri, and there are some shaft tombs dating to the Twelfth Dynasty. The place gained more importance only in the Thirteenth Dynasty. There are several statues of kings attested for the Amun temple. At Thebes there must also have been a royal palace. The papyrus Boulaq 18 gives an account of it. There are finally several tombs dating to the late Twelfth and Thirteenth Dynasties.[12] They provide further evidence that the city became more important in this period.

Not far to the north of Thebes, almost a suburb, is Madu (Medamud). At this site there is a temple for Mont which was already there in the Old Kingdom but was substantially rebuilt by Senusret III. There is good evidence for further building work in the Thirteenth Dynasty. It is possible to reconstruct major parts of the temple building. Many relief fragments from Sekhemre-khutawy Amenemhat Sobekhotep II were found, but other kings are also attested.

Another important town in the Waset nome is Djerti (Tod), where there was another temple for Mont. Like many temples in Upper Egypt an older building seems to have been erected in stone by the kings of the Eleventh Dynasty and totally rebuilt by Senusret I. A highly remarkable find is a set of silver vessels found in the foundation of the temple. These vessels were deposited in four boxes, two with the name of Amenemhat II, and were mostly of Aegean or Syrian provenance. At as-Salamiya not far from Tod were found several objects in burials dating to the Middle Kingdom. It seems to be the cemetery of the town.

Iuni (modern Armant), about 14 kilometres south of Thebes, is the third place in the Waset nome with a temple of Mont. Especially from the temple of the Eleventh Dynasty (mainly Mentuhotep III) many blocks with relief of the highest quality are preserved, but also from Amenemhat I, who seems to have added to the temple building.

The fifth to seventh Upper Egyptian nomes (Fig. 14)

The main town of the fifth Upper Egyptian Nome (Netjerui, the reading is uncertain) was Gebtu (Koptos, modern Qift) on the east side of the Nile, where there was an important Min temple. Essential parts of it have been

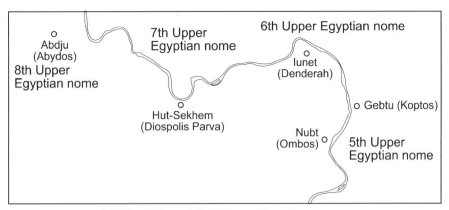

14. The fifth to eighth Upper Egyptian nomes.

discovered, although it is not possible to reconstruct a plan. Min is a god of male fertility, but he is also the god of the desert. From Gebtu started the desert route through the Wadi Hammamat (Egyptian Ra-henu) where there were important silt-stone quarries and gold mines. Gebtu is also the starting point for the shortest way to the Red Sea and it is therefore no surprise that the town had docks for building ships. These ships were constructed as sets of timber to be transported through the desert and rebuilt at small harbours on the Red Sea coast. The Wadi Hammamat is full of Middle Kingdom rock inscriptions reporting expeditions to bring stone for building projects, but there are also reports of travel to the Red Sea and to Punt. Opposite Gebtu over the river on the west bank and a little to the south there was another important town: Nubt (Ombos, modern Naqada). It was the main cult centre for the desert and chaos god Seth; blocks with the name of Mentuhotep II were found at Deir el-Ballas (north of Nubt) which may have come originally from a temple to Seth. Nubt means 'the Golden town' and refers perhaps to the gold mines in the eastern desert. The town may have been in earlier times an important point for gold work or the end point of a route bringing the gold from the desert. In the town itself only some seals and seal impressions of the Thirteenth Dynasty were found. At the northern end of the fifth Upper Egyptian nome the bed of the Nile suddenly curves from east to west. The main town of the sixth Upper Egyptian nome (Iqer) was Iunet (Denderah), where Hathor was worshipped. Only loose blocks with names of Middle Kingdom kings survived from the temple of this period.

Next to the main temple at Denderah there was a chapel built by Mentuhotep II. It survived intact till the beginning of the twentieth century and is an important example of early Middle Kingdom architecture and art. It measures only 2.3 x 1.45 m and is 2.37 m high. The inscription at the entrance tells us that it was made for his image and that it is a 'ka-chapel'. At the back the king is shown striding forwards in the

93

stance of a king smiting enemies, but instead of an enemy he is holding two plants: the lotus and the papyrus, representing Upper and Lower Egypt. It is tempting to see in this depiction a reference to the unification of Egypt under his reign. In front of him is written: 'Horus-who-subdues-the-foreign-countries'. The inscription behind the king reads: 'Clubbing the eastern lands, striking down the hill countries, trampling the deserts, making the Nubians pay tribute … the hands, uniting Upper and Lower Egypt, the Medjay, the Libyans and the marsh lands (?) by the Horus Netjeri-hedjet, king of Upper and Lower Egypt, Nebhepetre'. In a lower register the *sematawy*-sign ('uniting the two lands') is shown. On the right wall the king is shown in front of Hathor, while Harachte is standing behind him. In the lower register he is sitting on the throne while a cow and several offerings are before him. In another scene Hathor is giving him the *ankh*-sign at his nose. On the left wall the king is again sitting on the throne, while in other scenes he is shown together with different gods. The function of this chapel seems clear from its name: it contained a statue for the cult of the king. Such chapels for the king's cult are typical of the late Old Kingdom, but are no longer so common in the surviving records from the Middle Kingdom. There are also several tombs in the cemetery behind the town of Denderah dating to the Middle Kingdom, although the impression is that the more important decorated tombs date rather to the early Middle Kingdom than to the Twelfth Dynasty.

The capital of the seventh Upper Egyptian nome (Bat) was a place called Batiu or Bayt which has not yet been securely located, but may lie on the (in this case) north bank of the Nile. The only place with Middle Kingdom remains in this nome is Hut-Sekhem, which is located at modern Hiu. In the cemetery next to the town many Middle Kingdom tombs were found.

The eighth and ninth Upper Egyptian nomes

The capital of the eighth Upper Egyptian Nome (Ta-wer) was Tjeni (Thinis or This, not yet securely located but perhaps near modern Girga), and in this nome lies Abydos, one of the most important towns in the Middle Kingdom and later periods.

Abydos (Egyptian Abdju) was the main cult place for Osiris, the ruler of the underworld. Already in the late Old Kingdom he had become one of the most important Egyptian gods, and his popularity continued into the Middle Kingdom. At least since the Twelfth Dynasty, but perhaps even earlier, the tomb of this god was identified by the Egyptians in Abydos. Abydos had been the burial place for the kings of the First Dynasty and for some kings of the Second Dynasty. The tomb of the First Dynasty king Djer was treated as that of Osiris. Many offerings of the Middle Kingdom – mainly pottery – were found there, but also a sculpture showing Osiris impregnating Isis as kite and datable to the Thirteenth Dynasty. Not much has survived from the Osiris temple at Abydos, which is located in the town. Inscribed blocks mention Mentuhotep II and Mentuhotep III, who seem to have rebuilt or at least added much to an Old Kingdom temple. Senusret I seems to have erected a totally new building of which only a few remains have survived, including some colossal granite statutes depicting the king. The temple seems to have been still standing in the Thirteenth Dynasty. A journey to Abydos is mentioned in several inscriptions referring to funerary rites and at least one of the model boats found in many Middle Kingdom burials seems to have had the function of enabling the dead to travel to the town. There is evidence that some kind of festival or dramatic play (mysteries) were performed for Osiris at Abydos. Therefore it seems that many Egyptians who could afford it travelled to Abydos on a kind of pilgrimage or at least stopped there while passing the town on a mission to another place. Under Senusret I many officials seem to have started to build small chapels with stelae, statues and offering tables, to be close to Osiris. These officials were not buried here, but many of these chapels seem to have functioned as some kind of symbolic tomb. It is therefore no surprise that in some of the Thirteenth Dynasty chapels were found symbolic burials: a small mummiform figure was placed in a model coffin and buried under the floor of the chapel.

The tradition of building a chapel or at least of setting up a stela at Abydos seems to have gone on until the end of the Middle Kingdom. At this time certain areas at Abydos seem to have been fully packed with offering chapels. Their stelae (Pls. XX, XXI) and statues are one of the main sources for the history of the period. Many important officials whose tombs have not yet been discovered are known only from their monuments at Abydos. There are still many problems identifying the kind of people who went to Abydos. There are surprisingly few examples of officials known from their tombs in the residence and also known from their monuments at Abydos. It is therefore possible that mainly people passing Abydos or working there for a short time erected stelae. Finally there are also many stelae which functioned as tomb stelae; many locals were certainly buried here and it is often impossible to decide whether a particular monument belonged to a tomb or to a chapel for a person buried somewhere else.

King Senusret III had a huge corridor tomb with chambers cut into the mountain at Abydos South and it seems possible that he was even buried here and not in his pyramid at Dahshur. To this tomb belonged a valley temple (Fig. 15) and there was also a town called Wahsut functioning up to the Thirteenth Dynasty. The town, so far only partly excavated, consisted basically of two types of houses. There is one big building, which belongs, according to seals found there, to the governor, and there are a number of smaller, but still quite big houses obviously belonging to officials working at this place. The whole town must have had a similar plan to Lahun, with rectangular gridded street pattern and planned houses. The house or building complex of the governor may have contained special apartments for the wife of the house owner (Fig. 16). Some rooms in the

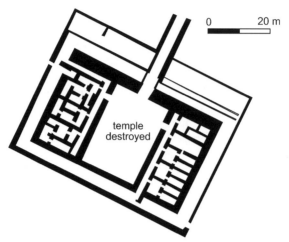

15. Valley temple of Senusret III at Abydos (South). The original stone temple is mostly destroyed. The remaining parts are granaries or storage rooms built in mud brick.

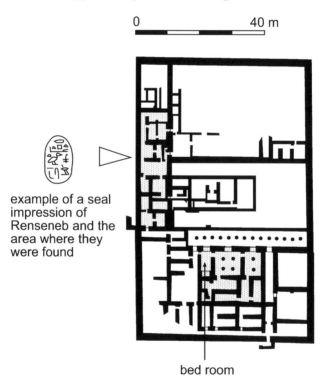

example of a seal impression of Renseneb and the area where they were found

bed room

16. The house of the governor of Wahsut (only partly excavated so far). The living quarters are highlighted by dots. The rooms for the wife of the last governor, the 'king's daughter' Renseneb, were identified by many seal impressions found there.

main house had wall paintings; the house owner had his own bedroom and there was a garden with Christ's thorn trees (small trees with yellowish flowers and ovoid fruits).

Next to the funerary complex of Senusret III in the desert smaller but still impressive tombs were found. New excavations show that they were most likely the burial place of Thirteenth Dynasty kings.

Other towns in the nome seem to have been less important. At Naga ed-Deir some Middle Kingdom tombs were found, but they are far fewer than in the Old Kingdom or in the First Intermediate Period. One of these tombs contained the famous Reisner Papyri, found placed on the coffin. These are accounts relating to some building work in this region under Senusret I.

The ninth Upper Egyptian nome (Menu) with its capital Ipu (Akhmim) was certainly an important place in the Middle Kingdom. There is a stela of the 'overlord of the nome of Menu' named Intef dating to the time of Amenemhat I, so far the only person known with this title from this place. At Ipu there are almost no finds dating to the Middle Kingdom.

The tenth Upper Egyptian nome: Wadjit and Qaw el-Kebir (Fig. 17)

The Middle Kingdom is often described as a feudal period. There is almost no other period from which so many monuments, most often tombs of local governors and their subordinates, have been found, not only in the royal residential regions, but all over the country. The origins of these local governors and their servants buried next to them are not always clear. For some places such as Asyut and Deir el-Bersheh it can be shown that there was already in the First Intermediate Period a line of local rulers. At other places such as Meir, Beni Hasan or Qaw el-Kebir the impression is that the governors were mainly installed by the kings themselves in the Middle Kingdom. It seems possible to assume that the kings appointed people in their confidence to certain positions in the country. Local governors at some places seem to have been powerful and it has even been assumed that they challenged the power of the king. There are large rock-cut tombs at several places, demonstrating the wealth of these local rulers. However, many of these local rulers refer in their inscriptions to ruling kings, pointing out their loyalty. In some of the latest tombs symbols appear that are known earlier only from royal contexts. It has been believed that the governors felt so strong that they could even assume royal attributes. However, a closer look demonstrates that many of these royal symbols became common in the whole of Egypt with the introduction of new religious beliefs in the mid-Twelfth Dynasty. The deceased was now identified more than before with Osiris. Osiris is the ruler of the under-world. Identifying the dead with Osiris resulted in their being adorned with many royal symbols. Mummy masks were sometimes adorned with a (royal) uraeus and a *nemes* headdress. The coffins were decorated more

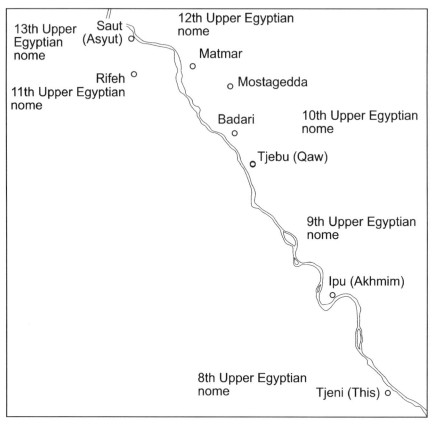

17. The eighth to twelfth Upper Egyptian nomes.

often than before with a palace façade and in the tomb of the governor Ukh-hotep (IV) at Meir the wish is expressed that Ukh-hotep may become a king.[13] In this context there is no sign that the local governors assumed royal power, they just followed new religious beliefs (see p. 58).

For the Upper Egyptian provinces 1-7 there are indications that there were indeed no such local rulers. This is the part of Egypt which was under the control of the early Eleventh Dynasty and it has been assumed that the kings of this period organised their kingdom in a different way, without using powerful local governors. This new structure was maintained after the unification in the first to seventh Upper Egyptian nomes. The Heracleopolitan kings in the North instead placed loyal local governors at certain points in the country. This is evident at Asyut, where some governors of the time before the unification refer clearly to the Heracleopolitan kings and express their loyalty. For other places it is harder to say what was going on. There are almost no larger tombs datable to the First Intermediate Period at Beni Hasan. Are these tombs just missing?

Were these people simply buried somewhere else? The same question arises for the Middle Kingdom. At some places large tombs are known, at other places none have survived. However, from inscriptional evidence it seems clear that each province north of the seventh nome had its governor. Inscriptions in the tombs of Beni Hasan refer to the governors of the neighbouring provinces, but nothing survived there. There simply seems to be a gap in the archaeological record. Therefore it can be assumed that most of the country was divided into provinces in the early Middle Kingdom, which were ruled by governors, while only in the Upper Egyptian provinces 1-7 were places ruled by local mayors with a responsibility only for towns. In the course of the Middle Kingdom this system seems to have been introduced in the whole of the country: governors of provinces were replaced by governors responsible only for towns and perhaps the surrounding region.

The governors of the Middle Kingdom are mainly known from their rock-cut tombs in Middle Egypt (Fig. 18). In the tenth Upper Egyptian nome the line of remarkable rock-cut tombs of governors begins. The tombs of this nome were located at Qaw el-Kebir, which was the cemetery of the ancient Egyptian town Tjebu, capital of the tenth Upper Egyptian province (Wadjit). Cemeteries of all periods of Egyptian history were found mainly on the east bank, stretching in a chain from the north to the south. However, there are amazingly few Middle Kingdom tombs (Fig. 19). This province was nevertheless one of the most important in this period, judging from the size of the tombs of the governors. These tombs, located at the desert edge at a distance from the ancient town, were excavated several times (by Ernesto Schiaparelli, W.M. Flinders Petrie, Georg Steindorff, Hans Steckeweh), but found already heavily damaged. Most of the finds are now in Turin, where they are one of the highlights of the collection. The fragments of almost life-size statues belong among the finest examples of Middle Kingdom sculpture. Several fragments demonstrate that at least some of the tombs were once decorated with fine relief, while the tomb of Wakha (II) had a painted decoration. The governors at Qaw el-Kebir seem to be the most important of the Middle Kingdom. However, for several reasons their sequence remains uncertain. Many of them bear the name Wahka and it is too often impossible to assign a single monument to a single person, especially because there is little information about their families. There are no royal names preserved in the tombs, so it is only possible to date the tombs and their owners on stylistic grounds.

There are four huge tombs at Qaw el-Kebir, each with a valley temple, a causeway, an upper temple and finally the burial apartments. The oldest tomb seems to be that of a certain Ibu, who ruled, according to the dating of the style of his sculpture, under Amenemhat II, but may have already been in office in the last years of Senusret I. The finest sculpture can be assigned to him. He is also the owner of a finely decorated sarcophagus, now in Turin, which is an outstanding piece without parallel in the Middle

18. Two tombs of governors at Qaw el-Kebir.

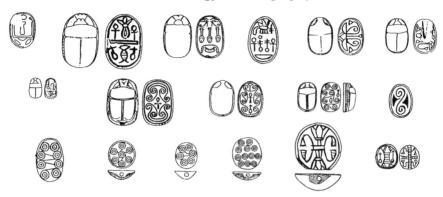

19. Scarabs found in some Middle Kingdom tombs at Qaw. Burials of people not belonging to the ruling class contained a high number of objects already used in daily life. Scarabs may have been used as amulets or status symbols.

Kingdom. Its outside is decorated in relief with a palace façade, normally known only from painted wooden coffins, whereas most of the other sarcophagi of the period are not decorated at all. His tomb was decorated with raised relief, preserved only in fragments, but also executed to the highest standard. His successor was Wahka (I) who may still date to the time of Amenemhat II or a little later. However, the succession Ibu–Wahka (I) is far from certain and they may have been in the reverse order. The next governor seems to have been a certain Nakhti, who did not have his own tomb, but was buried in the tomb of Wahka (II), whose father he may have been. Nakhti was perhaps in office for only a short period, and was therefore not able to build his own tomb. The last of the largest tombs belongs to another Wahka (II). His tomb is datable on stylistic grounds to Senusret III or Amenemhat III. In Stockholm there is a stela showing the 'governor Wahka begotten of Nakht'. The monument is dated with a cartouche to Amenemhat III and seems to confirm the dating of his tomb.[14] The decoration of this monument, although only badly preserved, is of special interest, because it shows women performing work normally done by men. The decoration and style is similar to that of the tomb of Ukh-hotep (IV) at Meir (p. 109). Interestingly, both tombs are also mainly decorated with paintings while the earlier ones were decorated with reliefs. The two tombs seem to be more or less contemporary. The next governor in Qaw el-Kebir seems to have been a certain Sobekhotep, who has the smallest of the four big rock-cut tombs. However, the tomb is still an impressive monument bigger than any tomb at Beni Hasan or Meir. It is badly damaged. Sobekhotep is placed at the end of the sequence mainly because of his name, which was popular at the end of the Middle Kingdom, though in fact the name was already common before. His position is therefore nothing more than a guess. The following governors are known only from seals or smaller objects and may date to the end of the Twelfth or beginning of the Thirteenth Dynasty: Nemty-nakht, Hetep, Hetepuy. Finally there is a further Wahka (III) known from an almost life-size statue and a stela, also dated on stylistic grounds to the end of the Twelfth or the beginning of the Thirteenth Dynasty.

The evidence from Qaw el-Kebir is of special importance. At Meir or Beni Hasan there are no signs of governors dating after Senusret III/Amenemhat III. In Qaw el-Kebir the succession seems to go well into the Thirteenth Dynasty. This is otherwise only securely attested at Elephantine, where the sanctuary of Heqaib provides further evidence. However, the evidence for governors of the Thirteenth Dynasty in Qaw el-Kebir comes not from the tombs but from other objects such as scarabs, statues and stelae. The series of big rock-cut tombs stops here under Amenemhat III, which is just a little later than at other places. The disappearance of the Middle Egyptian governors in our records seems therefore to have much more to do with the disappearance of large tombs than with the elimination of the office itself.

The eleventh and twelfth Upper Egyptian nomes: Sha and Atfet

The eleventh Upper Egyptian nome (Sha) was situated south of both the thirteenth and the twelfth. It was on both banks of the Nile. Its capital was Shas-hotep (modern ash-Shatb), where Khnum, 'lord of Shas-hotep', was worshipped. At a place now called Rifeh were found the cemeteries belonging to the town. The situation here is similar to that at other sites, with the rock-cut tombs of the governors (Fig. 20) higher up the cliff, and the tombs of their relatives and lesser officials in front of them (Pls. XI-XIII). Unlike elsewhere the cemetery of the more common people is also known, situated several hundred metres away, closer to the fertile land. Three governors are so far known from this place: Nakht-ankhu, son of Iam, Khnum-aa and Nefer-khnum. Their succession and precise dates are not clear.[15] Khnum-nefer and Nakht-ankhu[16] bear next to their titles of governor also the title 'true overseer of Upper Egypt' or 'overseer of the entire Upper Egypt'. This may indicate that these governors also had some special responsibility, not only locally, but to the whole of Upper Egypt. Khnum-aa, who is only indirectly attested in the filiation of his (grand) sons, had the biggest tomb and was perhaps the last of the governors. His tomb was reused in the New Kingdom and nothing of the original decoration seems to have survived. Some of the burials in front of the governors' tombs were found intact, and contained many important objects. One of them is the so-called Tomb of Two Brothers, which contained the undisturbed burial of two men; each had a box coffin and a finely crafted anthropoid wooden coffin. Next to the coffins were wooden statues and only one canopic box with one set of canopic jars. The tomb dates to about the time of Senusret II to Amenemhat III, when anthropoid coffins became more popular.

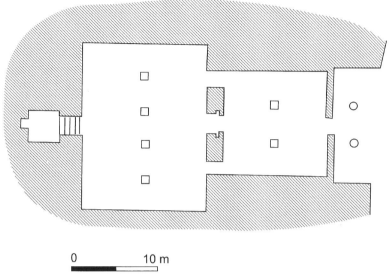

0   10 m

20. The tomb of Nakht-ankhu at Rifeh (plan).

On the east bank of the Nile a series of minor cemeteries were excavated near Matmar and Mostagedda, perhaps belonging to smaller settlements or villages in this region. Not many tombs there date to the Middle Kingdom, but nonetheless they provide crucial evidence for the burial customs of the bulk of the population. At this level, not many objects were made especially for the burial. Jewellery and some cosmetic objects are typical for burials of women; vessels, most often found empty, guaranteed the eternal food supply. These burial grounds are part of a chain of cemeteries on the east bank reaching from here to Qaw in the south. They were excavated in the 1920s to 1930s and provide a full picture of the burial grounds of a whole region.

The twelfth Upper Egyptian nome, opposite the thirteenth, was on the east bank of the Nile. Not much is known about the province from the Middle Kingdom. Its capital was Atfet (modern el-Atawla), where there were found two blocks inscribed with the name of a king – one with the name of Senusret I of the Twelfth Dynasty, the other with that of Hetepibre of the Thirteenth Dynasty. The main deity worshipped here was the ferryman god Nomty. Near the town was a cemetery; there are not many finds from the Middle Kingdom.

The thirteenth Upper Egyptian nome: Nedjfit-Khentet (Figs. 17 and 21)

The thirteenth Upper Egyptian nome was restricted to the west bank, with its capital Saut (modern Asyut), where the jackal god Wepwawet was worshipped. At Asyut the rocks of the western desert come very close to

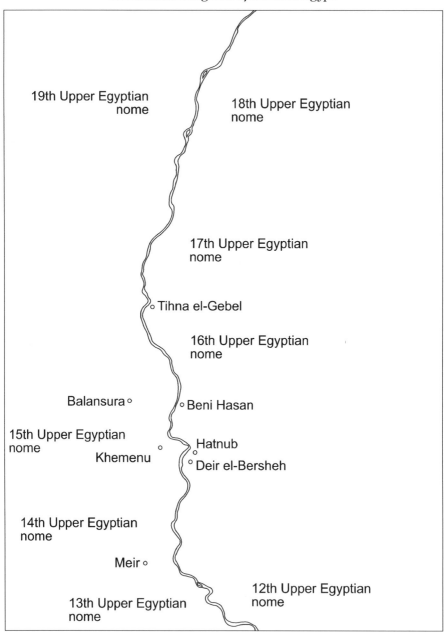

21. The thirteenth to nineteenth Upper Egyptian nomes.

the Nile. The town was therefore of special strategic importance. The ancient city is buried under the modern town, but the cemeteries next to it are well known. They suffered the same fate as many Middle Kingdom burial grounds. Many excavations were made too early and not systematically. They are often scarcely published. Another problem is that most tombs of the governors in particular are not yet fully published, unlike elsewhere.[17] The succession of the governors and the history of the place are therefore still much disputed and largely unknown.

Asyut was already in the First Intermediate Period a place of importance. The inscriptions in the tombs of the governors dating to this period are a major source for the period. The place kept its influence in the Middle Kingdom, as can be seen from the big tombs of the governors but also from the hundreds of smaller tombs for lower officials. The burial of the governor Mesehti was found undisturbed at the end of the nineteenth century but not during a scientific excavation. Beside its two large coffins the tomb contained a set of remarkable wooden figures, most notably two sets of soldiers. One set showed Egyptian and the other Nubian soldiers. These models are so far unique. However, it is uncertain whether they relate to real battles or wars fought by Mesehti, or whether they were placed in the tomb as some kind of status symbol. Another important tomb found was that of the treasurer Nakht. It dates probably to the early Twelfth Dynasty and contained a remarkable set of wooden statues, some of them almost life size. A certain Anu may have been the successor of Mesehti. In his tomb, which is dated to year 12 of an unknown king (or even to the time in office of the tomb owner?) Anu states that he was personally responsible for the decoration and inscriptions in it:[18]

In year 12, third month of the peret season, day 12, drawing this tomb of the foremost of action, royal sealer, overseer of priests of Wepwawet, lord of Asyut, the revered one before Osiris, lord of the west at all his places, the governor, the overseer of cattle (?) of Anubis, the one who endures on earth, beloved of his whole town, honoured by his whole nome; the governor Anu. I completed this tomb, because I caused to be made its inscriptions by myself, when I was still alive, never any (?) governor in Asyut made this since the time of the gods. The revered one ... the governor Anu.

The governor Hapidjefa (I) is known to date to the time of Senusret I, because the name of the king appears in his tomb (Fig. 22). He and his successors all have the name Hapidjefa and it might be argued that they come from a different family to be governors from the Eleventh and early Twelfth Dynasty; this would confirm the impression that Amenemhat I and Senusret I appointed new people at several places in the country. It seems likely that Hapidjefa (I) was not the direct successor of Anu, but there are so far no other governors at Asyut datable to the time of Amenemhat I. Hapidjefa (I), son of Idi-aat, left important inscriptions in his tomb (tomb I). There are recorded several contracts between him and

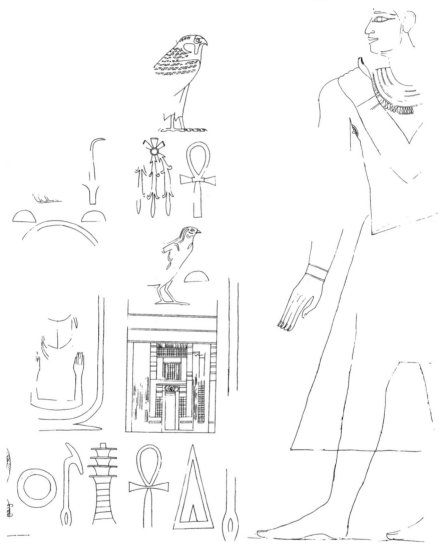

22. Depiction in the tomb of Hapidjefa (I): the tomb owner in
front of the names of Senusret I.

funerary priests, making sure that after his death the funerary cult would
last. These inscriptions are an important source for the social history of
the Middle Kingdom and they tell us that Hapidjefa had his own estate,
but also another as governor. A biographical inscription mentions the
rebuilding of a temple for Wepwawet. Hapidjefa (II), son of Idy (tomb II),
may have been his successor; nothing is really known about him, and it
has even been argued that he was in office not after but before Hapidjefa

(I). Hapidjefa (III), son of Idi (tomb VII) may be the next in the succession. There is again almost nothing known about him, but his tomb is a very impressive monument, demonstrating the wealth of this province and its rulers. It had an open court at the front with two rows of columns leading to a second hall. A T-shaped hall followed with three chapels at the back. The monument is today sadly very damaged and was never really recorded. This tomb is remarkable because 400-600 stelae dedicated to Wepwawet were found there. They belong to the New Kingdom, when the tomb must have functioned as a sanctuary. Hapidjefa (IV) (tomb VI), bears the title 'treasurer' and 'overseer of the troops' and the title 'overseer of priests'. It is not known whether he was really a governor. A final governor may be datable to the time of Amenemhat III, a certain Khety. In his tomb is a dating of year 14 or 22, where he is most often called 'deputy', making it uncertain whether he was really a 'governor'.[19]

In terms of style the coffins found at Asyut are quite different from those from further north, such as Beni Hasan, Deir el-Bersheh or Meir. The examples from Asyut often have double or even triple lines of inscriptions on the outside, while at the other places just mentioned single horizontal or vertical lines are the rule. Furthermore several coffins show certain depictions on the outside, also not known from the places just mentioned. The same stylistic elements were also found on some coffins at nearby Rifeh (Pls. XII-XIII). North of Asyut therefore began a different cultural province in terms of coffin styles; whether this also applies to other crafts or arts is not yet researched in detail.

The fourteenth Upper Egyptian nome: Nedjfit

The capital of the fourteenth Upper Egyptian nome (Nedjfit) was Qis (modern al-Qusiya). The main deity was Hathor. The ruling family of this town was buried at Meir on the west bank of the Nile. It is no surprise that many of the governors buried at Meir had titles connected to Hathor. The cemetery of Meir, so far as is known, was divided into two main areas. There are the rock-cut tombs of the governors and there is a cemetery for the middle-ranking officials working for the governors. Most of the important rock-cut tombs are well published, while the cemetery of the middle-ranking officials has never received full attention. Usually only the inscriptions found were recorded in short excavation reports. At Meir there are already several important Old Kingdom rock-cut tombs, demonstrating the importance of the place at that time. However, there is little evidence that the same area at Meir was used as a burial place in the First Intermediate Period. The history of the site starts again in the Middle Kingdom. The families and their activities are not so well known as for example in Beni Hasan, mainly because the governors did not record biographical inscriptions in their tombs. It is therefore only possible to give the names and the succession of the governors buried here. Only one tomb (that of Ukh-hotep III) is dated by a king's name. The order

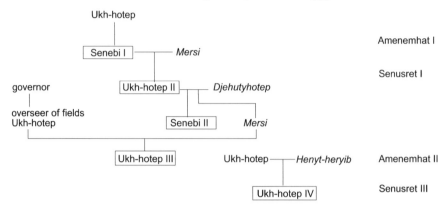

23. Family of governors at Meir (italic: women, name in box: governor).

and chronology of his predecessors and successors have been calculated by generations, and on stylistic grounds, from the study of various monuments (Fig. 23).

The first Middle Kingdom governor so far known is Senebi (I), who seems to have been put in place in the second half of the reign of Amenemhat I. This is another sign that this king installed strong and loyal governors at certain points in the country.[20] Senebi (I) may also be named in a rock inscription at the southern end of Egypt, near Aswan; this provides further evidence for the king sending local governors as well as palace officials on missions throughout the country.[21] His successor is Ukh-hotep (II). He had an important tomb decorated with reliefs, remarkable for several realistic depictions, though the technical execution is not good: the figures are often just cut in their outlines into the stone. Some figures in the scenes are well-known for their 'realism'. There is for example an emaciated, bearded herdsman or scenes with blind harpers.[22] The next governors are Senebi (II) and Ukh-hotep (III), son of Ukh-hotep and Mersi. Ukh-hotep (III) was the son of an 'overseer of fields' and 'son of a governor' called Ukh-hotep. Ukh-hotep (III) is the only securely dated governor at Meir – the name of Amenemhat II appears in his tomb.[23] His tomb is especially remarkable because it also depicts a gallery of governors of Meir and their wives, beginning perhaps already with the Fourth Dynasty. The depiction which shows the governors sitting on chairs while the women are sitting on the ground is badly damaged. It is therefore hard to tell whether the list is historically correct. However, there are indications, such as names of governors also known from monuments, that the list contains some errors but is basically correct.[24] Of Ukh-hotep (III) it is also known that he restored one tomb of a governor who perhaps dates to the Old Kingdom.[25] An ostracon found in Meir also bears a restoration inscription, indicating that he intended to restore or restored another tomb, not yet excavated or discovered, or now destroyed.[26]

His successor seems to have been Ukh-hotep (IV), whose relation to his predecessors in office is not known for sure. His father, also called Ukh-hotep, is mentioned as the 'brother' of Ukh-hotep (III), but the term 'brother' denotes in the Egyptian language not only brother in kinship, but also just 'cousin' or 'colleague'. The tomb of Ukh-hotep (IV) is remarkable.[27] It has a forecourt and a decorated main chapel. On the main walls the chapel shows only women involved in tasks normally executed by men. There are rows of female offering-bearers and women fishing in the marshes. This may have something to do with the cult of Hathor, but also with new religious beliefs at the end of the Twelfth Dynasty. In the tomb are also shown many royal symbols, previously known only from kings' temples or other buildings connected directly to the king. There are depictions of Hapy (the Nile god) along the bottom of the walls in the inner chapel, and an inscription says of Ukh-hotep (IV): 'May he appear as king of Upper Egypt, may he appear as king of Lower Egypt.' Only in the innermost chapel are men shown performing rituals in front of the dead which could perhaps only be performed by men. For stylistic reasons it can be proposed that the tomb dates to the time of Senusret III or even Amenemhat III.

The successor of Ukh-hotep (IV) seems to have been a certain Kha-kheperre-seneb Iy, who was not buried in a decorated rock-cut tomb. Inside his burial chamber were found his inscribed coffins.[28] His name, which refers to the throne name of Senusret II (Khakheperre), indicates that he was in office not much before the end of the reign of Senusret III or even later.[29] As in other places the series of big provincial tombs stops in Meir under Senusret III/Amenemhat III and there is so far no evidence for later governors.

The fifteenth Upper Egyptian nome: Wenet and Deir el-Bersheh

Going down the Nile the next Upper Egyptian nome is called Wenet ('hare'), where there are several important sites. Deir el-Bersheh is the cemetery for the highest officials working at Hermoupolis (Egyptian Khemenu), the town of Thoth and the leader of the Wenet nome. Not much survived of the Middle Kingdom town, but there are still remains of a gateway for a temple built by Amenemhat II at this site. The governors of Khemenu also controlled the alabaster quarries of Hatnub, where many inscriptions recording various events were found. Deir el-Bersheh, on the east bank of the Nile, was like many other Middle Kingdom cemeteries never systematically excavated. Our picture therefore remains patchy. Khemenu was already important in the First Intermediate Period. Unlike many other places the titulary of the governors at this place was distinctive, including the titles 'director of the double throne' and 'great one of the five'. Both titles probably refer to Thoth, the main deity at Khemenu. The titles clearly express that these governors were also the high priests of their local gods, which was also the case at the other local courts. However, people with these titles are therefore easily recognisable as being the governors of the Wenet province. The assigning of governors only known from inscriptions to a specific place is often not possible because most often they are only called 'governor' and 'overseer of priests', without a place name.

The sequence of the governors buried at Deir el-Bersheh starts early, although we do not have much information about them.[30] The first governors are Ahanakht (I), Ahanakht (II) and Neheri. Ahanakht (I) may, following the style of the reliefs in his tomb, date to the time of Mentuhotep II. He was perhaps in office for thirty years and is also attested with the titles of a vizier. From Neheri, in office at the end of the Eleventh or the beginning of the Twelfth Dynasty, several texts are known. In an inscription dated to his year 5 it is mentioned that he protected his town when an army was invading. In another inscription the king, whose name is not mentioned, appears. Many parts of the text refer to the unstable condition of the country: a 'day of plunder' and a 'day of rebellion' are cited. Neheri also had the title of vizier and seems to have been in office at least eight years. The exact dating of Neheri is problematic; initially it was assumed that he lived under Nebhetepre Mentuhotep II in the time of the unification. However, there are strong arguments that the events described in these inscriptions took place under Amenemhat I, who seems to have faced troubles in different parts of the country. Nevertheless, the interpretation of these texts is not certain. These inscriptions therefore provide a good example of the various problems in Egyptian sources. Without a secure dating it is not possible to draw any further conclusions as to whether the events refer to civil wars under Amenemhat I or to trouble at the end of the Eleventh Dynasty.

The successors of Neheri were Djehuty-nakht (VI), Neheri (II) and finally Amenemhat. Amenemhat is the first governor who is connected with a royal name. One inscription of Amenemhat in Hatnub dates to year 31 of Senusret I. Amenemhat was at this point not yet governor, but seems to have been appointed shortly after. He also bears the titles of a vizier. His successor was Djehuty-hetep. He has the best-preserved and most elaborate tomb at Deir el-Bersheh, which is famous for the depiction of a colossal statue being hauled along a quarry road by a large number of workmen. In his tomb the names of Senusret II and Senusret III appear. As in other Middle Kingdom cemeteries, the tradition of big rock-cut tombs stops under Senusret III. As in Beni Hasan there are several shaft tombs in front of the large tombs of the mayors. Some of them were found undisturbed, but sadly were excavated too early, and the short excavation reports are therefore patchy. However, from the tomb furnishings found it seems clear that Deir el-Bersheh was the burial ground of a rich community. The coffins found belong to the most beautiful of the whole Middle Kingdom. Certain religious texts, such as the 'Book of the Two Ways', are mainly known from the coffins found there. The 'Book of the Two Ways' is the earliest known pictorial or diagrammatic description of the underworld found in Egypt. The text, most often placed on the bottom of the coffin, is also richly illustrated with plans of the underworld.

Many of the governors mentioned are known from their beautiful coffins, discovered around 1900 in Deir el-Bersheh. The tombs in which these coffins were found are most often much damaged. The area was used for a long time as a quarry. Finally, seals are known which give us the names and titles of further governors. A certain Djehuty-nakht[31] could be identical with the person of the same name datable to the beginning of the Twelfth Dynasty, but seals with the names of officials are not securely attested before Senusret II/Senusret III and therefore it seems more plausible that Djehuty-nakht dates to the end of the Twelfth Dynasty. Wepwawet-hetep[32] is also only known from a seal with the title 'mayor of the Wenet-nome, director of the double throne'. He is most likely to date to the end of the Twelfth Dynasty. A final governor is attested by seal impressions found at Abydos as bearing the titles 'mayor, director of the double throne', Paenhapy.[33] He evidently dates to the Thirteenth Dynasty. As in Qaw el-Kebir it is therefore possible to show that at a certain point under Senusret III or Amenemhat III the big rock-cut tombs were no longer used, but the administration seems to have gone on without any break, at least for a while.

The sixteenth Upper Egyptian nome: Ma-Hedj and Beni Hasan

The history of the sixteenth Upper Egyptian nome is especially well known because of the well-preserved rock tombs at Beni Hasan, which seems to have formed the burial ground of the ruling class of this region. There must have been several important towns in this province, mainly known from references in the tombs of Beni Hasan, but only at Tihna el Gebel (Akoris, ancient Mernefert), Beni Hasan and Balansura (perhaps belonging to the fifteenth nome) were Middle Kingdom tombs found. The capital of the nome seems to have been Herwer, where Khnum and his wife Heqet were the main deities. Another important place was Nefrusi, where Hathor was worshipped. The exact locations of Herwer and Nefrusi are not certain. The same holds true for Menat-Khufu, whose governors were buried at Beni Hasan and which also seems to have had some importance, especially in the mid-Twelfth Dynasty.[34]

The rock-cut tombs at Beni Hasan belong – because of their good preservation – to the best-known monuments of the Middle Kingdom. Many of them are decorated with paintings and are familiar to tourists to Egypt. The order and chronological position of some of the earlier tombs and their owners is still a matter of discussion, but in general the history of Beni Hasan and its province are better known than others. The cemetery in Beni Hasan has two parts. 1. There are the rock-cut tombs of the governors and high officials and their important family members. The tomb chapels are often decorated with paintings. 2. There are over 800 shaft tombs in front of these rock-cut tombs, belonging to middle-ranking officials who served the people buried in the decorated rock-cut tombs. Some of these middle-ranking officials are indeed depicted in the bigger tombs and are shown as servants and minor officials of the local governors. For the history of the region the decorated rock-cut tombs are of the highest importance; some of them have long biographical inscriptions providing detailed information. The people buried here belong to two important groups of high officials. There are on one side the governors of the sixteenth Upper Egyptian nome with the titles 'overlord of the nome', and there are on the other side the 'overseers of the eastern desert', who were also 'governors of Menat-Khufu'. The 'overseer of the eastern desert' was an important office. He seems to have been an official in charge of the eastern deserts, responsible only directly to the king.

Because of the two lines of title holders ('overlords of the nome' and 'overseers of the eastern desert', 'governor of Menat-Khufu') buried at Beni Hasan the history of the nome seems to be a little confusing. There is some uncertainty about the date of the first decorated tombs here. Newberry, who at the end of the nineteenth century copied most of the inscriptions and decorations, believed that the first tombs date from the First Intermediate Period to the Middle Kingdom. However, there seems today to be general agreement that the earliest rock-cut tombs belong to the time after the unification of the country in the Eleventh Dynasty.[35] Of the first rulers not much more than their names and their tombs are known:

Baket (I)
Baket (II), son of Baket (I)
Ramushenty
Baket (III), son of Ramushenty
Khety, son of a Baket

They all seem to date to the Eleventh Dynasty; only the last of them may have ruled into the Twelfth Dynasty, although this is nothing more than a guess. None of them is connected with a king's name. They are all 'overlord of the nome' and seem to have been put in position by one of the Mentuhotep kings of the Eleventh Dynasty, presumably to install people loyal to the new royal line in this region. Their tombs are rather simple. There are rock-cut chapels decorated with paintings and there are the shafts leading from these chapels to the burial chambers. The paintings in these earlier tombs are still quite provincial and seem to be very much in the tradition of the First Intermediate Period. It is therefore no surprise that they were often dated to this period. The subjects depicted are sometimes unique. In most of the tombs groups of wrestlers are depicted, and in the tomb of Baket (III), son of Ramushenty, this scene is combined with the siege of a fortification also shown in some of the later tombs.

The tombs of the minor officials buried in front of the governors are much simpler but the burial chambers were sometimes found undisturbed and it is therefore possible to gain a picture of the typical burial furnishings of the early Middle Kingdom. The body was often placed in a wooden coffin. The coffins are most often decorated with single horizontal lines of inscriptions. More elaborate coffins are also decorated on the inside (Pl. IX). There are religious texts, friezes of objects and the offering list naming around a hundred items important for the dead in the underworld. Next to the coffin was a set of wooden models: a granary, a brewery and a bakery are common and important for the eternal food supply. Figures of two female offering-bearers are also typical. Two boats, one going up and one downstream, enable the dead to travel around and to visit important religious sites. Other wooden models appearing in these tombs are sandals and a head rest. The body was often adorned with a mummy mask and with jewellery especially made for the tomb, such as a broad collar.

Of the governors of the Twelfth Dynasty much more is known (Fig. 24). Most belonged to one family, as shown by the inscriptions in their tombs. Khnumhotep (I) reports that he was placed in office by King Amenemhat I. This might be taken as a sign that the king replaced the old ruling family by new, more loyal people. Khnumhotep (I) was 'overlord of the nome' but he also held the title 'overseer of the eastern desert' and 'governor of Menat-Khufu'. He therefore combined the already existing title of the governor of the province with the title of the 'overseer of the eastern desert'. The son of Khnumhotep (I) was Nakht. He also held both titles and was therefore most likely in office under Amenemhat I and Senusret I.

Of the next governor, Amenemhat, it is known that he was in office from year 18 of Senusret I till at least year 43 of the king. His relation to the other governors is uncertain. He seems not to be related to Khnumhotep (I) and Nakht. His main title was 'overlord of the nome'. He may have been

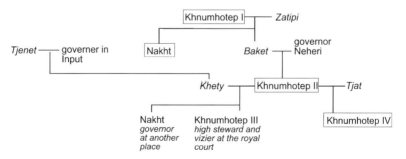

24. A governor's family of the Twelfth Dynasty at Beni Hasan
(italic: women; name in box: governor at Menat-Khufu).

113

related to the family of the Eleventh Dynasty, at least he was the last one to bear their main title 'overlord of the nome'. This office was no longer used under Amenemhat II. Amenemhat left important inscriptions in his tomb. He reports that he followed the king to Kush (Nubia), where he overthrew enemies, which may have happened in year 18 of Senusret I as in exactly this year a campaign of the king to Nubia is attested. After this he sailed upstream (i.e. south) together with the 'king's son', Ameny (the future Amenemhat II?), and 400 men to bring gold (it is not stated from where). Finally it is mentioned that he went together with the vizier Senusret to Koptos, again to collect gold. In all his actions he is always together either with the king (going to Nubia) or with high courtiers, such as the 'king's son' or the vizier. A remarkable feature seems to be that Amenemhat counted his years of rule just as the king did.[36] However, there are no legal documents known from Beni Hasan which could confirm the impression that people in the province dated their monuments to the governor rather than the king. This kind of dating might therefore be something rather personal, relating only to the governors in their tombs and not to the administration. The tomb of Amenemhat is an impressive monument consisting of a court with two columns with the main cult chamber fully painted. At the entrance is found the long biographical inscription of Amenemhat. Scenes in the tomb show workshops and food production, but also wrestlers or a desert hunt. The figures are still painted in a rather clumsy style, but prominent images such as depictions of the tomb owner or female offering-bearers are elaborate and depicted with many details, suggesting that various trained artists were involved in making the paintings.

The town of Menat-Khufu seems have become more important at this point. All the succeeding governors seem to have ruled from there. There is Netjernakht, of whom not much is known, except that he must have been related to Khnumhotep (II), his successor. He was in office under Senusret I and Amenemhat II. The tomb of Netjernakht is unfinished; he may have been in office for only a short period.

Khnumhotep (II) is the best known governor of Beni Hasan. He bears the titles 'overseer of the eastern desert' and 'mayor of Menat-Khufu'. He was the son of a man called Neheri, who seems to have been the ruler of another provincial town. His mother was a certain Baket, who was the daughter of Khnumhotep (I) and the sister of Nakht, both governors of Beni Hasan. Khnumhotep (II) was himself married to the daughter of the 'governor of the jackal nome' (Input – seventeenth Upper Egyptian nome), whose name is not recorded. The well-documented family of Khnumhotep (II) demonstrates how families at the highest levels might arrange marriage over the border of provinces. The fact that the father of Khnumhotep (II) is not the governor from Beni Hasan is also important. Father-son succession seems to have been common but is not the absolute rule. The biographical inscription of Khnumhotep (II) in his tomb is one of the longest of the whole period. It reports the installation of Khnumhotep (II) to his office as mayor of Menat-Khufu in year 19 of Amenemhat II and the repair and erection of several buildings (for example a *ka*-chapel in Merneferet). A large part of the inscription is occupied by naming the favours of the king to Khnumhotep (II), but also to his son Khnumhotep (III). The paintings in the tomb of Khnumhotep (II) are surely the best in Beni Hasan and perhaps the high point of painting in the Middle Kingdom. The scene showing Khnumhotep catching birds is famous. The birds are drawn with great detail. Another famous scene in the tomb shows a group of Palestinian people arriving. Their different look – hairstyle, beards and colourful clothes – is again painted in great detail. A scene showing Khnumhotep hunting in the desert includes fabulous animals also known from tombs at Deir el-Bersheh and from the so called 'magical wands', an object type found mainly in late Middle Kingdom burials.

Nothing has survived from the burial furnishings of the governors themselves. Only the tombs of their officials provide evidence that other objects than those common in the early Middle Kingdom were placed in the burial chambers of the mid-Twelfth Dynasty. The tomb of the 'warrior' Userhet may date to the time of Khnumhotep II or slightly later. His tomb contained an outer box coffin, which was decorated all around with a palace façade. The inside of the coffin was no longer decorated with religious texts and friezes of objects, but an inner coffin was found in the shape of a mummy. This anthropoid coffin was placed on its left side, like the contemporary mummies. The only other finds in chambers are pottery vessels. There were none of the wooden models so typical of the early Middle Kingdom.

Khnumhotep (III), a son of Khnumhotep (II), was not buried in Beni Hasan; instead he seems to have made a career at the residence, where a certain Khnumhotep appears as 'high steward' and vizier and is buried next to the pyramid of Senusret III in Dahshur.[37] In Beni Hasan was found the tomb of another Khnumhotep (IV), born of the 'mistress of the house', Tjat. Tjat seems to have been a lesser wife of Khnumhotep (II). The tomb of Khnumhotep (IV) is rather unimpressive. The series of important local tombs in Beni Hasan stops with him, perhaps under Senusret III. However, the cemetery in front of the rock-cut tombs was still used in the late Twelfth and even maybe in the Thirteenth Dynasty (and on into the New Kingdom) and it seems likely that we do not know the next mayors simply because they were no longer buried in big rock-cut tombs. Their burial places may be closer to Menat-Khufu, although this is only a guess.

The seventeenth to nineteenth Upper Egyptian nomes

Going further down the Nile there is a remarkable gap in the archaeological record. There are almost no finds from the seventeenth to the nineteenth Upper Egyptian nomes dating to the Middle Kingdom. From inscriptions it is known that there were towns and settlements. Texts from Beni Hasan refer to Input (the seventeenth Upper Egyptian nome), but actual sites of the Middle Kingdom have yet to be located here. There are various possible reasons for this. In the last 4000 years the river Nile has often shifted its course. It is possible that such a change has happened since the Middle Kingdom, destroying many important sites. Another reason may be that in these nomes most tombs were built closer to the settlements and therefore disappeared with the settlements, or lie buried under the fertile lands.

The twentieth to twenty-second Upper Egyptian nomes and the Fayum (Fig. 25)

North of the nineteenth nome there is the entrance to the Fayum, a region rich in Middle Kingdom sites and finds. This is the twentieth Upper Egyptian nome (Naret-khentet). In the First Intermediate Period the main town here was Heracleopolis (Egyptian Nen-nisut), which may even have functioned as capital of the kings ruling over Lower and Middle Egypt. There are not many Middle Kingdom remains in the town, but in the main temple of the town dedicated to Heryshef were found blocks and statues with the names of several Middle Kingdom kings. In the desert some kilometres west of the town important cemeteries of the First Intermediate Period and earliest Middle Kingdom were found. The tombs are quite simple, consisting most often of only a shaft or a shaft with a chamber. The preservation conditions for organic materials at Sedment are very good. Therefore many wooden models, typical burials of the period, and several decorated coffins were found. It seems unlikely that these burial grounds served Heracleopolis. They probably rather belong to a series of villages near the desert edge.

North of Heracleopolis there are three important Middle Kingdom sites: Lahun, Hawara and Harageh. Near the modern town of Lahun King Senusret II erected his pyramid and pyramid complex. The pyramid town of Senusret II is one of the best excavated settlements of the Middle Kingdom and of Ancient Egypt in general. Its ancient name was most probably Hetep-Senusret. Many papyri were found there, providing insight into an ancient town, its administration and its life. The town may have been started as a village for the pyramid builders, but continued as an important local centre. The valley temple of the pyramid complex of Senusret II is surely the focus of the local cult, dedicated to the king. A god mentioned quite often in the papyri is Sopdu, who may also have had a cult in the town, although no temple for him survived or could be identified. There are important administrative offices in the town, such as an office of the vizier. Building work for the pyramid complex of Amenemhat III at Hawara was organised from here. The occupation of the town seems to have lasted long into the Thirteenth Dynasty. The name of the Thirteenth

116

I. Head of a statue of Senusret I, found in his funerary temple
at his pyramid at Lisht.

II. Double statue of Amenemhat III in a naos,
found in the 'Labyrinth' at Hawara.

III. Head of a sphinx of Amenemhat III, found at Tanis. The statue was re-inscribed several times in later periods with the names of other kings. It may originally have come from the Labyrinth at Hawara.

IV. Bead with the name of Sekhemre-khutawy.

V. Statue of a vizier (name not preserved), father of the vizier Ankhu, Thirteenth Dynasty. The typical vizier's costume of a long garment partly concealing a necklace did not develop until the Thirteenth Dynasty.

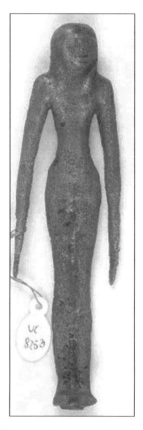

VI. Two block statues and standing figure of a woman found at Kom el-Khatein (Delta); c. 33 cm high. Block statues are an innovation of the Middle Kingdom.

VII. Bronze statuette of a woman, 10.7 cm high. Small-scale bronze figures appear in the Middle Kingdom quite often.

VIII. Life-size statue of the high steward Nakht,
found at Lisht, early Twelfth Dynasty.

IX. Coffin fragment. The decoration of the interior of a coffin from the cemetery of the lower officials (tomb 564) at Beni Hasan. The inscription, painted in green, reads: '[the revered one] of the great god, lord of heaven, the steward Henu(i)'. Under the inscription are visible traces of an offering list, naming the seven sacred oils.

X. Ini and his wife receiving offerings; paintings on Ini's coffin found at Gebelein. The coffin dates most likely to the mid-Twelfth Dynasty (c. Senusret I – Senusret II). The style of the figures is provincial. Contemporary paintings at Beni Hasan or Asyut are much more elaborate, and together these examples provide evidence for the wide range of local styles in the Middle Kingdom.

XI. The two long sides of the coffin of the lady 'Ankhet begotten of Iti' found at Rifeh. Previously unpublished excavation photograph. See Fig. 41 on p. 166 for a drawing of this photograph.

XII. Coffin fragment found at Rifeh. The fragment is decorated with a palace façade typical of coffins of the late Twelfth Dynasty. Previously unpublished excavation photograph.

XIII. Coffin fragment found at Rifeh. The fragment is decorated with a palace façade typical of coffins of the late Twelfth Dynasty, and may adjoin the other fragment from Rifeh (above). Previously unpublished excavation photograph.

XIV. Mummy mask found at Harageh, late Middle Kingdom. Mummy masks are typical of burials of the ruling class all through the First Intermediate Period and Middle Kingdom. This mask is not mentioned in the publication of the cemetery. In the background of the photograph the coffin of Senusret-ankh (Harageh tomb no. 250) is visible (next to the foot of one of the archaeologists). The mask may come from the same tomb as the coffin, although this is no more than a guess. Previously unpublished excavation photograph.

XV. The pyramid of Senusret II at Lahun.

XVI. Mastabas found next to the pyramid of Senusret II at Lahun. The mastabas are cut into the rock. There are no shafts or burial chambers next to them. However, at the opposite site of the pyramid were found several shafts for members of the royal family and one leading into the pyramid. The shafts and the mastabas may have been separated for reasons of security.

XVII. Two canopic jars of the 'lady of the house', Senebtysy, found at Harageh, tomb 92. Previously unpublished excavation photograph.

XVIII. Stela of Djari, el-Tarif, Thebes. The stela is executed in a distinctive local style as is typical of many places in the First Intermediate Period.

XIX. Stela of the treasurer Khenty-khety-em-sauef Seneb; Harageh tomb 136. The stela was found in the filling of the shaft. The tomb was rather small and it seems unlikely that such a high official was buried here. The stela was set up for the treasurer by a lower official called Sepi, who was presumably buried here. Previously unpublished excavation photograph.

XX. Relief fragment found at Abydos, showing the 'treasurer' Ameny-seneb hunting in the marshes. Previously unpublished excavation photograph.

XXI. Stela of Mentu Sahathor and his family found in a small niche in his mastaba (tomb no. 219) at Abydos. The stela belongs most likely to the late Twelfth or early Thirteenth Dynasty. It is dated to 'year 2' of an unknown king. Previously unpublished excavation photograph.

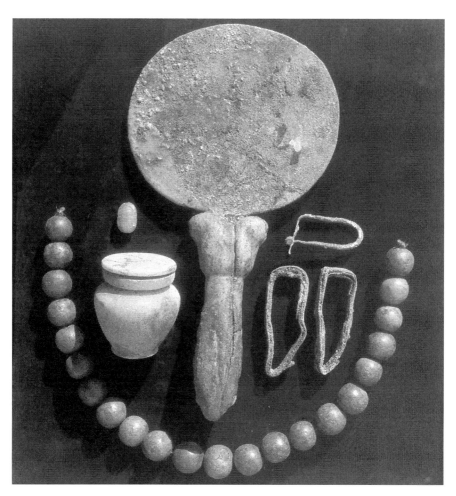

XXII. Objects found in Abydos tomb 793. Tomb 793 was found undisturbed and contained the remains of a man and a woman. There were fragments of a coffin, these photographed objects and pottery vessels. Previously unpublished excavation photograph.

XXIII. Pectoral found in the tomb of the 'king's daughter', Sathathoriunet, at Lahun. Jewellery found in the tombs of royal women of the late Twelfth Dynasty is often of higher quality than is known from any other period of Egyptian history.

25. The twentieth to twenty-second Upper Egyptian nomes, the Fayum
and the first Lower Egyptian nome.

Dynasty king Wahibre appears on the fragment of a faience cup. However,
the reading as a king's name is not certain. Fragments of a large papyrus
with accounts can be dated just a little earlier by the repeated mention of
the Thirteenth Dynasty treasurer Senebsumai.

The town consisted of several parts. There were the large houses in the
north of the town, certainly belonging to the ruling class; in the west were
many smaller houses; and there are some middle-sized houses south of the
big houses. The whole town was surrounded by a wall, which does not show
any signs of defence installations.

Around the town were the cemeteries. There were some tombs of high
officials belonging to the court of Senusret II. The most important is that
of the 'overseer of the gateway', Inpy. The tomb, erected on a small hill,
consisted of two parts. There was a relief-decorated chapel cut into the hill
and behind it on top of a small hill there was a mud-brick mastaba. Under

117

the mastaba were found the burial apartments. Inpy was certainly an important official who was still in office under Senusret III, as can be seen from a stela where he appears together with the treasurer Iykhernefret. Inpy's title 'overseer of the royal works in the whole country' indicates that he was involved in important building projects. Other mastabas at Lahun seem to have been decorated all around with a palace façade and inscriptions. There are only fragments preserved, making it often impossible to identify the tomb owners. The Middle Kingdom cemeteries at Lahun were already heavily looted in antiquity, and therefore the picture of these burials of the highest court officials is patchy. In a series of burial grounds which lie opposite ancient Lahun on a desert island surrounded by cultivation the tombs are better preserved. This series of cemeteries is called Harageh by Egyptologists, the name of a modern village in this region. These cemeteries seem to have flourished mainly in the late Twelfth and Thirteenth Dynasties and have revealed the best documented cemetery of this period so far. The tombs seem to have been quite rich (Pls. XIV, XVII, XIX). Several decorated coffins were found, although they are no longer inscribed on the insides as in the early Middle Kingdom. There were many fine statues, some stelae and several small faience figures of animals typical of burials of the late Middle Kingdom. Nothing survived from the chapels which may have been placed over these tombs.

North-west of Lahun is the Hawara pyramid of Amenemhat III, whose temple is probably identifiable as the legendary 'Labyrinth' described by Greek and Roman authors.[38] Amenemhat III had initially started a pyramid complex at an entirely different site, Dahshur, at the southern end of the Saqqara/Memphis cemeteries. Technical problems with this first building seem to have led to the construction of a second pyramid complex, the one at Hawara, right at the entrance to the Fayum. The new pyramid and its pyramid complex were on a vast scale. Today it is badly damaged and it is therefore not possible to gain a clear picture, but it seems to have been impressive because of its amazing size, its rich furnishings of extraordinary statues depicting the king and several gods, and the rich decoration with painted reliefs.

Around the pyramid was a vast cemetery for the courtiers of the king. It was already heavily damaged in antiquity and has not yet been systematically researched, so that it is hard to gain a clear picture of it. There were remains of large mastabas. One sarcophagus of the treasurer Ameny most likely comes from here, but it was found reused in Tanis and demonstrates that the tombs had already been heavily looted 3000 years ago. Two kilometres south of the pyramid complex was found the tomb of the 'king's daughter', Neferu-Ptah, who was most likely the daughter of Amenemhat III. Her tomb was found intact, but had suffered from the wet ground. All organic materials including the body were destroyed, but the burial still contained a fine set of jewellery, three silver vases, a large sarcophagus decorated at the bottom with a palace façade and the remains of several weapons and a stave, typical of burials of the ruling class in the late Middle Kingdom.

At about this point starts the Fayum (called Ta-shi, 'the land of the lake', in the Middle Kingdom) a river oasis which was connected with the Nile via a river today called Bahr Jusuf, west of the Nile. For the Old Kingdom there is not much evidence for any activity in the Fayum. Most parts of it may have been some kind of marshlands, not very suitable for agriculture or cattle farming. In the Middle Kingdom this seems to have changed. There is much evidence for royal activity here. Large tracts of the land may have been reclaimed for agriculture. The main town was Shedyt (Krokodilopolis, modern Medinet el-Fayum); the ancient city is now covered by the modern town or destroyed. Many fragments with the name of Amenemhat III were found there. However, it is not certain whether they come originally from here or were brought there in the Roman Period. The town was in the Ptolemaic or Roman Period still important, and it is known that the Romans quarried the funerary complex of Amenemhat III at Hawara. These fragments may therefore originally come from Hawara. The main deity of the Fayum and of Shedyt was the crocodile god Sobek, who certainly had a temple in this town. Sobek is one of the main deities of the late Middle Kingdom. The importance of the Fayum is certainly one reason for the importance of Sobek.

A short distance southwest of Shedyt, at a place today named Abgig, Senusret I erected a round-topped monolithic pillar. The original context of this monument is unknown. At Biahmu the bases of two colossal statues of Amenemhat III are still standing. These figures may have been part of a temple or been free-standing, overlooking Lake Fayum. Although their function is not certain they provide further evidence for the importance of the region. Three other places in the Fayum should be mentioned. To the south of Medinet Fayum there is one of the best-preserved Middle Kingdom temples: at Dja (Medinet Maadi) Amenemhat III erected a small temple with three sanctuaries mainly dedicated to Renenutet (Fig. 26). The building is richly adorned with reliefs and was finished by Amenemhat IV. In the north of the Fayum at Qasr as-Saga another Middle Kingdom temple build in limestone, but undecorated, is still standing. In the same area a workmen's settlement and a small cemetery were excavated, both belonging to about the mid-Twelfth Dynasty. The tombs are simple and most probably belong to very poor people. Most of them are just holes in the ground, about 1 m deep. The only burial goods are often just one pot placed at the head end (Fig. 27). However, some tombs contained fine examples of jewellery, and in one woman's burial a figure of a frog and one of a hippopotamus were placed as the sole burial goods.[39] Such animal figures are not common burial goods, though characteristic of late Middle Kingdom temple and town sites. These figures must have had some religious meaning. Similar statuettes have been found in temples and it seems that they were offerings to gods. Each figure may have symbolised

26. The temple at Medinet Maadi.

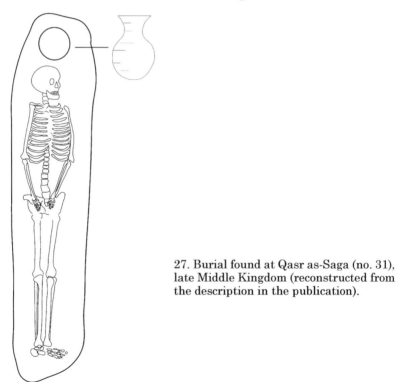

27. Burial found at Qasr as-Saga (no. 31), late Middle Kingdom (reconstructed from the description in the publication).

a particular wish, which was also important for the afterlife. At Khelua far to the south of the Fayum a large Middle Kingdom tomb in a style and size so far only known from Middle Egypt for the period was recently excavated, belonging to a governor called Wadj.[40]

Returning to the Nile valley, Riqqeh may have been the cemetery of the capital of the twenty-first Upper Egyptian nome, where Khnum was mainly worshipped. The burial ground contained some hundred Middle Kingdom tombs and rich finds of the period, including inscribed coffins. One famous burial was found only partly looted and still contained the body of the dead person while next to it was found another skeleton, clearly the human remains of the tomb robber who was looting the tomb and died when the roof of the chamber collapsed. The burial itself was typical of the late Middle Kingdom; it contained the body of the dead richly adorned with jewellery, in this case of not very high quality. At Tarkhan – an important cemetery of the First Dynasty and the Old Kingdom (north of Riqqeh) – were also found some Middle Kingdom tombs. South of Riqqeh is the Old Kingdom pyramid of King Snofru at Meydum. At this site were again found Middle Kingdom remains.

Opposite the Middle Kingdom capital, Lisht, on the east bank of the Nile valley was found a rock-cut tomb of the latest First Intermediate Period or early Middle Kingdom belonging to a man called Ip. This is the region of the twenty-second Upper Egyptian nome (Medenit), which was located on the east side of the Nile. Its capital was Tep-ihu (Atfih), where 'Hathor, mistress of Tep-ihu' was worshipped. The town seems to have been of some importance, because it is quite often mentioned in Middle Kingdom texts.

2.2. Lower Egypt

The first Lower Egyptian nome: Ineb-hedj, 'the White Wall'

At the border of Upper and Lower Egypt there is the huge Middle Kingdom cemetery of Lisht, which is most likely to be connected with Itj-tawy, the capital founded by Amenemhat I. Amenemhat I and his son Senusret I built their pyramids here. It is not known why the following kings chose other places for their funerary complexes. Itj-tawy seems to have functioned as capital till the end of the Thirteenth Dynasty and it is therefore no surprise that the cemeteries around the pyramids were in use up to the end of the Middle Kingdom, although there are no longer burials of the highest state officials after Amenemhat II. Therefore these people are most often buried next to their kings and had their burials at Dahshur, Lahun or Hawara. The pyramids and pyramid complexes of the two kings are about two kilometres apart. Around each pyramid there was a large cemetery dating from the early Middle Kingdom to the Thirteenth Dynasty. A wide range of tomb types and burial furnishings were found at this site. There are burials of rather poor people, where the body was wrapped in a mat or placed in an undecorated coffin. These burials were just placed in holes in the ground. There are only a few burial goods: a drinking cup or cosmetic jar and/or some jewellery. People of slightly higher status were buried in a coffin which was placed in a shaft tomb. Other people were buried with gilded plaster masks in uninscribed coffins, sometimes adorned with jewellery. There are other burials dating to the late Middle Kingdom where the dead are adorned and surrounded by royal insignia. In this burial type they were identified and buried like Osiris. The famous, undisturbed burial of the 'mistress of the house', Senebtysy, also called Sat-Hapy, is of this type. People placed in a wooden and then into a stone sarcophagus all belong to the earliest phase of the cemetery when Lisht was used as a burial ground for high court officials.[41] One example of a burial (for another example see Fig. 28) of a high state official is the mastaba of the treasurer Mentuhotep, who was in office in the second part of the reign of Senusret I. Mentuhotep was an outstanding official. His mastaba, next to the pyramid of Senusret I, had its own causeway. In the burial chamber were found two sarcophagi, both belonging to Mentuhotep, but one had already been smashed in antiquity while

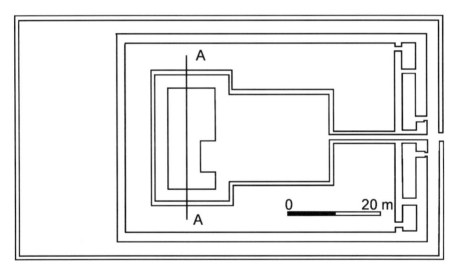

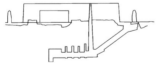

28. The mastaba of the high priest of Ptah Senusret-ankh at Lisht, datable to the time of Senusret I (plan and cut A-A); the burial chamber was decorated with religious texts.

122

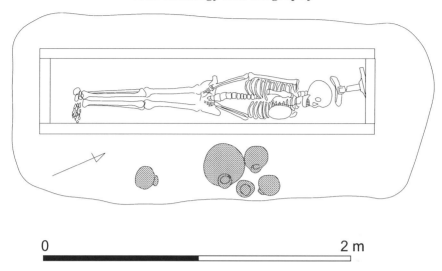

0   2 m

29. The burial of Ankhet at Lisht.

the other was well preserved and decorated on the inside in the finest lines with the so-called frieze of objects and with many religious texts.[42] The burial of the lady Ankhet, datable to the time of Senusret I, may be an example of a less wealthy person (but certainly still belonging to the ruling class) buried at Lisht (Fig. 29). Ankhet was placed in a decorated coffin in a shaft tomb about 5 m deep. Her coffin was inscribed and decorated inside and out. On the inside of the lid and on the bottom there were long religious texts. Some of them are called Pyramid Texts because they were first discovered in the pyramid chambers of the late Old Kingdom, where the walls were inscribed with religious texts. Other texts found on the coffin are called coffin texts because they are mainly known from Middle Kingdom coffins. These texts are common on richly decorated coffins especially of the early Middle Kingdom until about the time of King Senusret III. Although coffins and their text programme are often quite standardised, there are almost no two coffins with the same texts and decoration. The body of Ankhet was wrapped in linen and adorned with a mummy mask. Around her neck there were two necklaces. At her head there was a simple wooden head rest and on her chest there was a mirror and a wooden *hes*-vase. Outside the coffin were placed several pottery vessels. The burial makes a quite simple impression. There are no wooden models of servants bringing and preparing food, so common in many other burials of this period. However, most of the objects found were specially made for the tomb, such as the head rest, the *hes*-vase and of course the coffin. Ankhet was therefore certainly a woman belonging to the ruling class, who could afford craftsmen to produce funerary objects.

Next to the pyramid of Amenemhat I were found remains of a settlement belonging to about the Thirteenth Dynasty. These are perhaps the remains of a suburb of Itj-tawy. The city must have grown over time and reached the cemeteries. The houses provide a good idea of a non-planned settlement of the late Middle Kingdom (Fig. 30).

Memphis (Ineb-hedj, 'the White Wall', later Men-nefer) was the capital of the Old Kingdom and the main town in the first Lower Egyptian nome, which in the Middle Kingdom was located on the west side of the Nile. The city was certainly still important in the Middle Kingdom, but does not

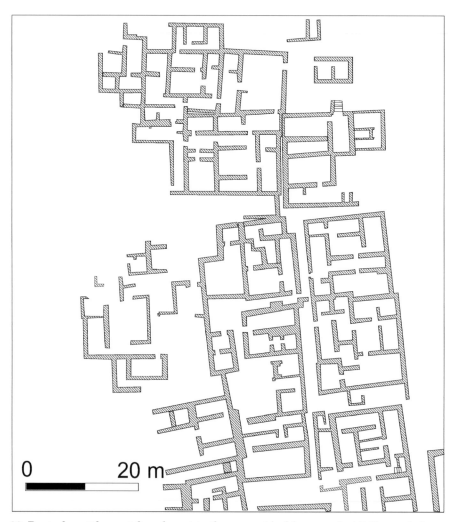

0   20 m

30. Part of a settlement found next to the pyramid of Amenemhat I. It may belong to the capital Itj-tawy, which expanded at the end of the Middle Kingdom into the area of the cemeteries.

appear with this name very often in Middle Kingdom sources, when it was probably called Djed-sut (sa-ra-Teti), which was the name of the Sixth Dynasty pyramid of King Teti. Many burials of people of high status were found around his pyramid (at Saqqara) and it might be assumed that the population centre of Memphis in the Middle Kingdom was near this pyramid. There are indications that King Amenemhat I ruled from Memphis for a short period before he founded his new capital Itj-tawy. The tombs of the 'overseer of the royal private apartments', Ihy, and the tomb of Hetep are still relatively well preserved. They both consisted of an open columned courtyard with chapels at the back. The chapels contained block statues of the tomb owners – so far the earliest examples of this statue type.

At Dahshur, Saqqara and north of it (at Abusir) were the royal pyramids of the Old Kingdom. The cults of the Old Kingdom kings went on or were reinstated in the Middle Kingdom and seem to have continued till the end of the Twelfth Dynasty. The best evidence for this comes from Abusir, were many well-preserved burials of the Middle Kingdom have been found. These burials contained coffins richly decorated with religious texts and friezes of objects. Other finds are wooden models and fine statues of the tomb owner. One burial contained an anthropoid wooden coffin and may date to the late Twelfth Dynasty. There is surprisingly little evidence for any cult activity at Gizeh, the site of the greatest Old Kingdom pyramids. The Middle Kingdom evidence may have been destroyed or the kings buried here were not worshipped on the same scale as the kings of the Fifth and Sixth Dynasties.

At Saqqara South a huge Middle Kingdom cemetery begins, stretching south to Mazghuneh (including Dahshur). Here stand the remains of the pyramid and pyramid complex of Pepy II; objects such as stelae found here show that this king was still worshipped in Middle Kingdom times, as were most Old Kingdom kings. At Saqqara South also begins the series of Middle Kingdom pyramids. The Thirteenth Dynasty king Khendjer built his pyramid complex here. The building may have been finished, for fragments of the pyramidion were found. Next to his pyramid was an even bigger pyramid, which was never completed and which is so far not connected with a royal name.

Dahshur (Fig. 31) seems to have been the main cemetery of the royal court in the late Twelfth and Thirteenth Dynasties. The Middle Kingdom activity in this region started on a larger scale under Amenemhat II, who built his pyramid and pyramid complex at Dahshur quite close to the fertile land (the Old Kingdom pyramids are often sited considerably further into the desert). Around the pyramid was the cemetery of his courtiers. The most important tomb was that of the treasurer Siese: its chapel was decorated with four slabs showing Siese in front of an offering table. His face is realistically modelled, showing a not very young man. His tomb chamber was inscribed with religious texts. Next to the pyramid of

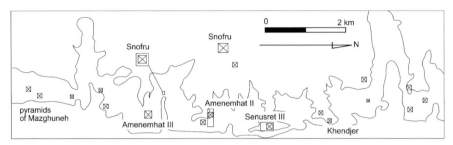

31. Saqqara South and Dahshur in the Middle Kingdom:
the main royal necropolis in the late Middle Kingdom.

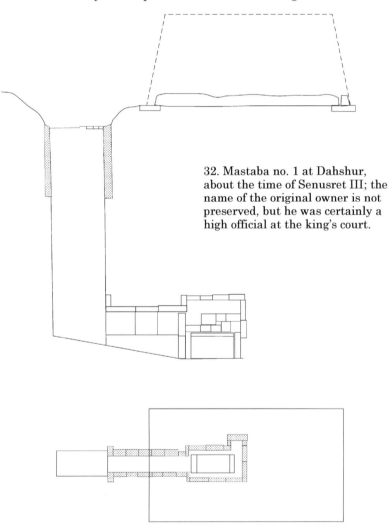

32. Mastaba no. 1 at Dahshur,
about the time of Senusret III; the
name of the original owner is not
preserved, but he was certainly a
high official at the king's court.

the king, still inside the enclosure wall, were found three galleries, each with two burials. The next pyramid at Dahshur belongs to Senusret III and is situated a little to the north of that of Amenemhat II. The pyramid and its complex[43] were surrounded by the smaller pyramids of wives and daughters of the king. In the north was found a gallery with several burials. Two of these still contained valuable treasures, belonging perhaps to the 'king's daughter', Sathathor, and to the 'king's daughter', Mereret. Their names appear on scarabs found there. This underground gallery is a unique feature in terms of size and number of burials. At both sides of a gangway about 30 metres long were cut niches for the sarcophagi and canopic chests of eight royal women. Some of the sarcophagi are inscribed and they provide the name of their owners: the 'king's daughters', Senet-senebtysy and Menet. This gallery was connected via a long underground corridor with the burial chambers of four pyramids placed at the north side of the royal pyramid. Only for two of these pyramids are the owners known for sure. There is the 'royal wife', Nefer-henut, and the 'king's daughter', Itakayet. At the south side of the pyramid were found three more satellite pyramids. One belongs to the 'king's wife', Khenmet-nefer-hedjet-Weret (II), and one to the 'king's mother', Khenmet-nefer-hedjet-Weret (I). None of these pyramids was ever used as burial place. The burial chamber of the 'king's wife', Khenmet-nefer-hedjet-Weret (II), was found in the king's pyramid. The burial apartments of the 'king's mother', Khenmet-nefer-hedjet-Weret (I), were simply too small for a real burial; she too must have been buried somewhere else. The last of the three pyramids was the satellite pyramid of the king, known from most of the Old and from many of the Middle Kingdom pyramid complexes. The whole complex of Senusret III was surrounded by a palace façade wall, imitating most probably the wall of the Djoser complex at Saqqara. Later, perhaps at the time of the coregency with Amenemhat III, a huge temple was added to the south of the complex, which was again surrounded by a wall. The temple was badly damaged but many relief fragments were found, showing that it was once richly decorated. The reliefs mention the first *sed* festival of the king; other reliefs show different gods or Nubians certainly once belonging to some kind of war or battle scene. The pyramid also had its own separate pyramid temple; it is much damaged, so it is hard to gain a clear picture of its original appearance.

The royal pyramid itself contained two burials. One belonged, as already mentioned, to the 'king's wife', Khenmet-nefer-hedjet-Weret (II). This tomb was reached via the small pyramid south of the pyramid of the king. From it a corridor led under the large pyramid into a chamber, where further remains of treasures were found. The entrance to the burial chambers of the king was found at the west side of the pyramid. The burial apartments consisted of three rooms, as in many Old Kingdom pyramids. The burial chamber of the king in the pyramid was found empty with only a few fragments of pottery perhaps left by the tomb robbers and it raises the question whether the king was ever buried here (see above on Abydos). North of the pyramid complex the burials of the royal court were found (Fig. 32). There are the mastabas of the treasurer and later vizier Sobekemhat and the mastaba of the vizier Nebit. Of special interest is the mastaba of the vizier Khnumhotep, which was decorated with a palace façade all around and on one side a long biographical inscription providing important information on the history of the Middle Kingdom.

The pyramid of Amenemhat III was erected in Dahshur South. This monument was also never used for the burial of the king but as a tomb for the 'king's wife', Aat, and the 'king's wife', Khenmet-nefer-hedjet, and some other members of the royal family.[44] Next to the pyramid were found the well-preserved tombs of the Thirteenth Dynasty king Auibre Hor and of the 'king's daughter', Nubhetepti-khered, perhaps a daughter of this king. The burial of the princess is a typical example of the tomb of a member of the highest ruling class at the end of the Twelfth and beginning of the Thirteenth Dynasty. It is a shaft tomb with two chambers one on top of the other. In the first chamber were found several types of pottery – many small plates mainly attested in Middle Kingdom burials and offering deposits. There were also two boxes. One contained a set of vessels for different kinds of ointment, the other contained a set of weapons and staves typical for such burials. In the burial chamber was found the sarcophagus (stone coffin) of the princess; in it there was a wooden coffin with gilded bands bearing hieroglyphic inscriptions, and finally there was an innermost gilded anthropoid coffin, almost totally decayed when found. On the body of the princess were found fine examples of jewellery and next to her there were again staves and weapons.

The funerary complex of Amenemhat III was therefore still used in the Thirteenth Dynasty; this is indeed supported by the pottery found in the structures (houses and temples) around it. A highly exceptional find is the model of the innermost chamber system of a pyramid found here. Other important buildings at Dahshur were the two pyramids of the Fourth Dynasty king Snofru. At the valley temple at the so-called bent pyramid (the more southerly of his two pyramids at Dahshur) many monuments of the Middle Kingdom were found, indicating continuing cult activity in this period. Right at the south end of the area labelled Dahshur by modern Egyptologists was found the small Thirteenth Dynasty pyramid of King Ameny Qemau. The building was never finished but still contained in the burial chamber the inscribed canopic jars of the king. South of Dahshur at Mahzguneh there were two further – most likely Thirteenth Dynasty – pyramids. Neither monument provides the name of their builders. Some Middle Kingdom tombs were also excavated in this area, but the great cemetery region connected with Memphis seems to have ended here.

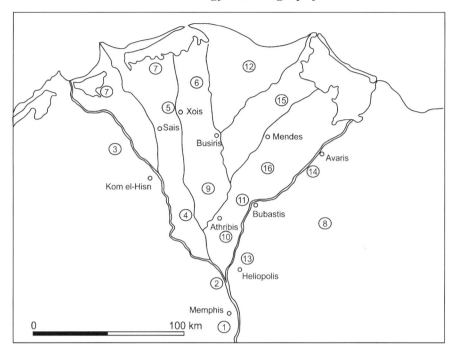

33. The Delta and its nomes (the numbers of the nomes are given).

The Delta (Fig. 33)

North of Memphis begins the Delta, where the Nile divides into several branches flowing into the Mediterranean Sea.

At the western side of the Delta in the second Lower Egyptian nome (Khepesh; capital Khem) are two further important Middle Kingdom sites. At Abu Ghalib substantial parts of an early Twelfth Dynasty settlement with large houses were excavated.[45] At Qattah there was an important Middle Kingdom cemetery. Some of the tombs were decorated with false doors and longer religious texts. The cemetery may have belonged to a town called But. Imau is the ancient name of modern Kom el-Hisn, an important town in the third Lower Egyptian nome (Imentet, 'the west'). It is the site of a First Intermediate Period and Middle Kingdom cemetery, including the relief-decorated tomb of the 'overseer of singers', Khesu-wer. Other remains indicate that the town had a temple of Hathor from which blocks with the name of Amenemhat III have survived, as well as a statue of that king with two royal women, and a unique vulture statue of the same reign. The capital of the third Lower Egyptian nome was Hut-Ihyt ('house-of-the-cattle'). The location of this town is still disputed but it may be close to Kom el-Hisn or even part of it. The name 'house-of-the-cattle' demonstrates the importance of cattle-herding in this region.

129

Not much is known about the fourth Lower Egyptian nome (Naret-resyt, the 'southern Neith nome'), whose capital seems to have been Djeqaper, attested only from the New Kingdom on and not yet located. An important religious centre in the fifth Lower Egyptian nome (Net-mehyt, the 'northern Neith nome') was Sau (Greek Sais), whose main deity was the goddess Neith. Several temples and chapels of the town are named in Middle Kingdom texts but nothing of that date from the site itself has survived. In the sixth Lower Egyptian nome (Khasuu) was the double city Pe and Dep, also known as Buto. It was an important religious centre with the sanctuary of one of the crown goddesses Wadjit (also called Uto). Although the names of the towns often appear in religious texts and in titles it is not possible to decide whether they were important centres of population in the Middle Kingdom. Nothing survives there from this period. Not much is known about the seventh Lower Egyptian nome (Huy-imenti) in the Middle Kingdom. The region was known for its wine. The eighth Lower Egyptian nome is again fairly unknown. Djedu (Busiris) was the capital of the ninth Lower Egyptian nome (Andjeti) in the middle of the Delta. From the Old Kingdom onwards the town was an important centre for the cult of Osiris, and still in the Middle Kingdom Osiris is most often called 'Lord of Djedu'. There are almost no remains of the Middle Kingdom at Djedu, although some tombs found at al-Kom al-Ahdar may belong to the cemetery of the town. Another important Middle Kingdom town in the Delta was Kem-wer (Athribis), whose main deity was Khenty-Khety and which was the capital of the tenth Lower Egyptian nome (Kem-wer). Not much survives from the Middle Kingdom town, but personal names formed with Khenty-khety are popular in the Middle Kingdom, indicating the importance of the cult and the town. The eleventh Lower Egyptian nome was Hesebu. The name is not attested in Middle Kingdom sources. Its capital was Ter-remu (or Ti-remu), not yet securely located. At Tall al-Muqdam in this nome were found some Middle Kingdom remains; it is uncertain whether they originally come from here. The name of the twelfth Lower Egyptian nome Tjeb-netjeret is again not attested in Middle Kingdom sources. Behedet was an important town there. The name is identical to those of Edfu and in both towns Horus was worshipped. There are no Middle Kingdom remains from this place.

In the south of the Delta on the east side of the Nile was Iunu (Greek Heliopolis, now a suburb of Cairo), belonging to the thirteenth Lower Egyptian nome (Heqa-andju; the capital of the nome, Su, is not yet located); this was one of the most important religious centres of ancient Egypt, including during the Middle Kingdom. Here there was the temple of the sun god Re and of the creator god Atum. The importance of Re can be seen in the title for Egyptian kings, 'son of Re'. The throne name, the name received on becoming king, also always referred to Re. The Middle Kingdom temple of Re at Heliopolis is badly damaged, and has not yet been systematically excavated. An impressive feature still standing is the obelisk of Senusret I; a building inscription of the same king, known only from a New Kingdom copy, indicates the scale of his building activity (p. 40). Scattered inscriptions from here were found at Heliopolis and at Cairo, where they had been reused in the Middle Ages. From here too comes the great limestone stela of the governor Khety-ankh, dating to the early Twelfth Dynasty. Further south at Helwan (now a suburb of Cairo) a huge cemetery of the first dynasties was excavated; some tombs there date to the Middle Kingdom. Of special importance is that of the 'overseer of sealers', Sokarhotep, who may have been a member of the royal court; Memphis lies just opposite Helwan.

One of the most important, if not the most important site in the Delta was Baset (Bubastis) in its eastern half. The city was also part of the thirteenth Lower Egyptian nome at this time. Baset was already of some standing in the Old Kingdom and maintained its role in the Middle Kingdom. It was the cult centre of the lion/cat goddess Bastet. From her Middle Kingdom temple only loose blocks survive. A huge palace building datable to the time of Amenemhat III was excavated at the site. Next to the palace a funerary complex was found, consisting of one large building with several chambers, most of them reserved for one burial. Some objects with names and titles of the local governors were found here, perhaps indicating that the nearby palace was erected for the governors. However, the place differs clearly in its plan from other architectural structures found at Abydos and Tell el-Dab'a which served without doubt as mayoral residences. A statue found here belongs to the governor of Baset, but a lintel shows Amenemhat III celebrating his *sed* festival. The lintel points very much to a royal use for the building.

The entrance of the complex was at the north and led directly into an open courtyard with six columns. From there, there was access to another courtyard with twenty-six columns. The private rooms seem to have been to the east. There are then two more courtyards with columns, and four smaller rooms, one perhaps the bedroom of the king or governor.[46]

North-east of Baset was Imet (today Nebesheh/Tell Farun). Already in the Old Kingdom the town was famous for its wine. 'Wadjit, mistress of Imet' was its main deity, and she seems to have gained special importance in the late Middle Kingdom and Second Intermediate Period; she is mentioned on several monuments of this period from this region. Several Middle Kingdom sculptures were found but it is not certain whether they were brought here in the New Kingdom from somewhere else or whether they where erected here originally. Not far away, about 10 km to the west at Tell Ibrahim Awad, remains of a large Middle Kingdom temple were recently excavated, about 20 m wide and over 20 m long. The ancient name of this place is not known nor is it known which god was worshipped here.[47]

The fourteenth Lower Egyptian nome, which was called Iabti ('the east') or Khenty-Iabti ('first east') had Benu as capital, not yet located for certain. In the nome was situated Hut-waret (modern Tell el-Dab'a). The site, situated at the edge of the Delta, seems to have been without special importance in the Old Kingdom. Perhaps at the end of the Eleventh or at the beginning of the Twelfth Dynasty a substantial settlement was founded here, a planned town with small houses arranged in blocks of about twelve or more units. This place was only occupied for a short period. In the Twelfth Dynasty a little further north a town developed around a temple at modern Ezbet Rushdi (Fig. 34). The town seems to have become increasingly important at the end of the Twelfth Dynasty and in the Thirteenth Dynasty, when many people from Palestine settled here. The town seems to have been the starting point of the Hyksos kingdom, which ruled parts of Egypt in the Second Intermediate Period. The development is still unclear. It has been assumed that one of the governors of Hut-waret

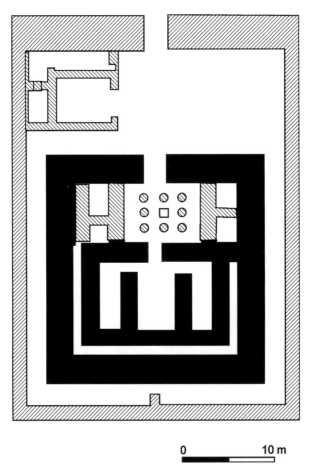

0 _____ 10 m

34. The Middle Kingdom temple at Ezbet Rushdi (black: temple of the early Middle Kingdom; hatched: additions of Senusret III).

declared independence, perhaps under the Thirteenth Dynasty king Khaneferre Sobekhotep IV, but this is still no more than a guess. Although many parts of the town have been excavated the overall structure is still not very clear. Most parts of the town seem to have been only loosely occupied with houses.

The dead were buried within the settlement area, and at special sites small Egyptian style temples were also found. In the Thirteenth Dynasty a palatial house was erected in a totally Egyptian style, but with burials in Palestinian style in the palace garden behind it. Here were found the fragments of a statue of Egyptian workmanship showing an official with Near Eastern hairstyle and dress. The name of only one governor of Hut-waret is known: Ameny-seneb is attested on a seal impression and calls himself 'governor of Hut-waret'.[48] His name and title are unequivocally Egyptian.

The region east and north-east of Hut-waret seems to have formed some kind of border land between Egypt and Asia. The area was perhaps some kind of marshland (the modern Menzala lake and the region south of it) and is perhaps identical with a region called Sekhet-ad, 'field of the storm', in a literary composition of the Middle Kingdom and in later sources. The so called Way-of-Horus was the route starting here and passing through some small settlements on the way to Raffah and south Palestine. This north-east frontier of Egypt was in the Middle Kingdom protected by the Walls-of-the-Ruler, which were built by Amenemhat I against invading people from Palestine. The Walls-of-the-Ruler seem to have been a chain of fortresses on the eastern Delta. However, especially in the late Middle Kingdom the whole region at the edge of the eastern Delta seems to have been a settlement ground for people coming from Asia. On the evidence of Tell el-Dab'a too, this defence system does not seem to have been very effective at keeping Asiatics out, although many settlers may have received official permission to come to Egypt.

Capital of the sixteenth Lower Egyptian nome (Hat-mehit, the 'first-of-the-fishes') was Djedet (Mendes, modern Tall ar-Ruba), which was the site of the temple of Ba, lord of Djedet. The town was already important in the Old Kingdom, and several decorated tombs of that period have been found, as well as inscribed remains of the Middle Kingdom from a cemetery of the period.

2.3. The neighbouring lands (Fig. 35)

Contacts between Egypt and its neighbours are only sporadically attested for the Old Kingdom. This changed dramatically in the Middle Kingdom, when there are many contacts on several levels. Middle Kingdom culture was now more open to foreign influences than that of the Old Kingdom, and this paved the way for the New Kingdom, when Egypt conquered parts of Nubia and the Near East.

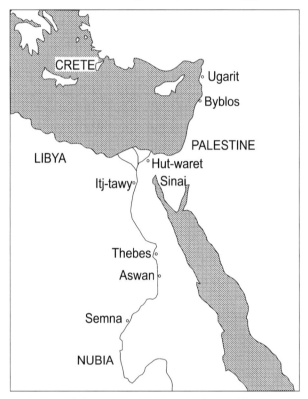

35. Egypt and the Near East during the Middle Kingdom.

South of Egypt, Nubia was of special importance. There were many raw materials, especially gold, which were not so abundantly available in Egypt itself. It is therefore no surprise that the kings of the Middle Kingdom tried to gain control over this country. Lower Nubia was not very fertile; there are only small portions of agricultural land on either side of the Nile. There is evidence for military actions in the Eleventh Dynasty, but it is doubtful whether the country was already fully occupied. Lower Nubia seems to have been conquered in the Twelfth Dynasty under Senusret I and then again under Senusret III. Buhen and Mirgissa are important fortresses controlling parts of Lower Nubia and perhaps also the trade with Nubians and incoming raw materials. It seems that in the Twelfth Dynasty soldiers only lived in Nubia for shorter periods (and were buried in Egypt), while in the Thirteenth Dynasty there is also evidence for an Egyptian population living here together with the soldiers who stayed here constantly. The cemeteries where these people were buried have been found.[49]

There is a remarkable chain of fortresses from the north to the south. Some of them were already built under Senusret I, others mainly under

134

Senusret III. The most northerly is Kuban at the entrance to the Wadi Allaqi; it may have had the function of controlling copper mines in this region; not far away is the fortress of Ikkur; it was most likely built by Senusret I. At Aniba there was a town which was obviously controlled by the fortress there. It also dates most likely to Senusret I. The fortresses at Faras and Serra East are badly preserved but also seem to have had the function of suppressing the local Nubians. One of the most important fortresses was at Buhen, where there had already been an Egyptian settlement in the Old Kingdom. The Middle Kingdom fortress was built by Senusret I. The place seems to have functioned as a trading point and administrative centre for the Nubian provinces in the early Twelfth Dynasty. Extensive cemeteries next to the town provide evidence for an important civilian population. At Kor, a town about 5 km south of Buhen, a building complex about 100 x 100 m in size was excavated. It seems likely that it was a royal palace. Like a similar building at Uronarti it is oriented strictly north-south. The complex seems basically to consist of two parts. In the west was a long building with a courtyard in the middle while on the east there were two buildings with many smaller rooms. The courtyard in the west building had columns. To its north were some smaller rooms, some also with columns. It seems possible that these were the private rooms of the king. The arrangement of the rooms with a courtyard in front seems similar to parts of the previously mentioned building in Uronarti. The fortress at Mayanarti was on an island. Mirgissa (Iqen) is the largest of the Nubian fortresses, perhaps founded by Senusret I and heavily rebuilt by Senusret III, after whose reign the fortress became the main trading point for Lower Nubia. Askut was a fortress on an island and seems to have had the function of controlling gold mines in that region. On seals found here an institution called 'enclosure' (*khenret*) is mentioned, which seems to have been an organisation for labour, where Egyptians were obliged to work. It also seems possible that Nubians were employed in these gold mines. Shalfak is a small fortress perhaps for controlling the Nubian population. Uronarti was a fortress on an island next to a royal palace.

Semna (west/south) and Kumma are the most southern fortresses of Nubia sited on either side of the Nile. They certainly functioned as border posts of the southern part of the Egyptian-controlled world. At both places many rock inscriptions were found. At Semna Senusret III set up two stelae, which seem to have functioned as boundary stelae but also as a demonstration of the power of the king.[50]

South of Lower Nubia, in Upper Nubia, was the Kerma culture, with its capital Kerma. Its rulers became powerful in the Second Intermediate Period, conquering parts or all of Lower Nubia, and even raiding Upper Egypt.

In the North the desert peninsula of Sinai east of the Delta was already in the Old Kingdom the target of several expeditions, mainly for collecting turquoise and copper. At Serabit el-Khadim, a site on Sinai, turquoise was found; several expeditions mainly of the Twelfth Dynasty are attested to that place. They left many inscriptions, providing important historical information, and there was also a temple for Hathor.

There is much evidence for several kinds of contact between Egypt and Palestine and Syria. The story of Sinuhe is one example, describing the adventures of an Egyptian official in south Palestine. There is evidence for military action by Egypt against the east; on the annal stone of Amenemhat II the conquest of two cities is mentioned, and there is the report of the official Khusobek, who describes an attack against sites in Palestine under Senusret III. There is rich evidence for people from Palestine living in Middle Kingdom Egypt.[51] They seem to have been represented at almost all levels of society, although there is little evidence that they reached the highest administrative positions; there is no vizier or treasurer known to come from a foreign background.[52] It is not certain how they came to Egypt. However, the annal inscription of Amenemhat II mentions about 1500 captives from Palestine. The evidence from the east Delta, where there is at Hut-waret (Tell el-Dab'a) a town with a large Palestinian population, may indicate immigration on a wide scale over a period of time. The execration texts are lists of Egyptian enemies compiled for magical reasons. Several of them were found listing names of Palestinian rulers. They seem to display a good knowledge of this region.

Byblos was an important trading point in modern Lebanon. Contact between this town and Egypt was already strong in the Old Kingdom, but in the Middle Kingdom their rulers even took over the Egyptian title 'mayor' or 'governor' in Egyptian hieroglyphic script; the Egyptian language was used there. Some of them were buried in Egyptian style and there is even a relief dating to the Thirteenth Dynasty showing a ruler from Byblos in front of King Khasekemre Neferhotep I. The town was an important trading post for wood. In Egypt there was little high-quality timber, so that cedar wood was imported from the Lebanon. Another town with many Egyptian finds is Ugarit, north of Byblos. Many Egyptian statues were found there, but it is not certain when they reached the site, or whether there were many Egyptians there.

There is some evidence for contact between Egypt and Crete. A small quantity of Minoan palace pottery has been found at several places in Egypt, and some Middle Kingdom objects on Crete. In both countries scarabs appeared about the same time and the motif of spirals so typical of Minoan art becomes quite popular in the Middle Kingdom.[53] The nature of contact between the two lands is not known. There is plenty of evidence for Asiatics living in Egypt and Egyptians visiting Palestine and Lebanon. For such direct contact with Crete there is so far little evidence and it might be argued that the objects were traded via a third country such as the coastal towns in Lebanon.

The states of the Near East had already developed intensive diplomatic

136

contacts in the first half of the second millennium. At several places, Mari being the most important, archives of the correspondence between individual rulers have been found. Egypt does not appear in these texts and it seems doubtful whether Egyptian kings had any diplomatic contacts with other states. Although there are many contacts attested on various levels, Egypt was still to some extent isolated from the rest of the Near East.

3

Society

Like most societies today ancient Egyptian society was a class society.[1] At
the top was the representative of a closed ruling class, an inaccessible
political ruler, and at the bottom were the much poorer farm workers,
craftsmen and, under or outside these groups, beggars. A child born as son
of a king or high official had dramatically different expectations of life and
career as compared with the son of a farm worker. As today, personal
abilities would have played only an insignificant role in such a system.
Indeed in this respect ancient Egyptian society is not so different from
modern societies. Statistics on social mobility in industrialised and post-
industrial nations indicate that a child of average intelligence born as the
son of a factory worker has a high chance of becoming a factory worker,
while a less intelligent child born in an academic family is highly likely
to become an academic. A son of an Egyptian farmer would most likely
also become a farmer; the son of an ancient Egyptian official was most
likely to become an official.[2] This observation is not only true in terms
of social stratification but also in terms of sex. The most talented girl
born in ancient Egypt had no chance of becoming a high official in the
administration of the country. Ancient Egyptian society was not only a
class society but also a sexist society, from a twenty-first-century
European perspective.

It is hard to gain a clear picture of Middle Kingdom society as a whole.
Texts and monuments are set up by and for the ruling class and reflect
their views. Archaeology seems more helpful since remains of almost all
social levels have been found. However, archaeological remains are often
difficult to interpret and it can be a complicated matter to relate archaeological evidence to written sources. To give just one example: at the
pyramid town Lahun there are the palatial town houses of the ruling class,
and also small houses most probably of the poorer population (Fig. 36).
However, a social reading of these house arrangements is open to varying
interpretations. Did the servants of the rich live in the large houses
together with their masters or did they have their own small houses? Was
there a part of the population (for example beggars) not living in houses at
all but living on the streets or even outside the town enclosure? What kind
of people lived in the small houses? Were they farmers, or craftsmen, or
were they on a higher social level, such as scribes? What kind of people
lived in the big palaces? There are many written sources from Lahun, and

36. Plan of the excavated Middle Kingdom town at Lahun.

many titles and names of officials are known, but who precisely among the people mentioned in the written sources lived in the big houses?

Archaeological data from Middle Kingdom cemeteries are even more complicated to interpret. Tomb-size statistics are useful for gaining some information, but in the Middle Kingdom the custom of placing more than one body in one tomb is quite common and it is therefore difficult to compare tombs, when in one tomb only one body was found and in another more than one. There are also tombs with few but well-made objects, while there are other tombs well furnished with many objects, but of lower quality. A high number of objects in a tomb is therefore certainly not always a reliable index of social status.

As in all other periods, Egyptian society in the Middle Kingdom was rigidly hierarchical. This is evident from several titles, such as the ranking titles which announced a high status at the royal court and placed certain officials above others. Hierarchy is visible everywhere in ancient Egypt and it is always clearly expressed in both words and images. In art the most important person is generally shown much larger than his servants, and often even depicted on a bigger scale than his wife and children. On stelae, where there is sometimes no space to depict certain people as larger

140

than others, the more important people are shown with different attributes of status. They may be represented standing while everybody else is sitting, or sitting on a chair while everybody else sits on the ground.[3] In letters there are specific formulae when a person of low rank is addressing somebody of higher rank. In contrast, if a person of higher status addresses somebody of lower status there are almost no special greeting formulae.[4] More than once art and writing illustrate how lower officials or other people came in obeisance to a higher official.

Most of these examples expressing the relationship between members of society of different status relate to people belonging to the ruling class. It can be assumed that the differences between simple farmers and officials must have been even greater, but these differences are often known only from art, where, for example, a tomb owner is shown in front of his servants. Surviving examples of this relationship elsewhere are not so common. The story of the 'Eloquent Peasant' is surely one case. In this story a person of quite modest social position is confronted with one of the highest state officials. However, it is not certain how his behaviour can be interpreted. Was the way the peasant talked to a high state official normal or (more likely) exceptional? This is, after all, a literary composition, in which one might expect the creator of the composition to play with living experience to literary effect for his audience.

Social differences were certainly also expressed in particular behaviour. The 'Teaching of Ptahhotep' gives several examples of this:

> If you are a man at a sitting
> at the table place of one greater than you,
> take whatever he causes to be set before you,
> do not stare at what is before him,
> do not pierce it with many glances.
> Pressing it is an offence to the *ka*.
> Do not speak to him until he has requested:
> you never know what may displease.
> Speak when he questions you
> and your speech will please.[5]

In general terms the question arises of how Egyptian society was organised. There are two opposing views on this:

1. Egypt was a fully controlled society, in which almost everything was planned by the state.[6] The Middle Kingdom town sites might be taken as evidence. Many of them display a planned pattern, as at Lahun with the houses of the ruling class on one side and the smaller houses of the poorer classes on the other side. Such planned patterns are not only visible at 'artificial' settlements; even Thebes – a town which certainly goes back to the Old Kingdom – seems to have been laid out on an orthogonal grid by the state at some point in the Middle Kingdom.[7] The uniformity of material

culture in the Middle Kingdom, especially in the mid-Twelfth Dynasty, might be taken as further proof that more or less everything was intensively controlled by the state. Finally, major building projects seem possible only in a strong state which does not allow great personal freedom. In such a society personal wealth can only be gained by working as part of the administrative upper class.

2. Egypt was a relatively free society in which only certain things were planned by the state and where there was a certain economic freedom.[8] In particular wealthy tombs of people without titles might indicate such a society.[9] The literature which seems at some point relatively critical of institutions ('The Eloquent Peasant' – an attack on high state officials?) might be taken as further evidence that a middle class was able to express its own ideas almost in opposition to the state. The Heqanakht papyri might provide yet another indication of a certain economic freedom. Heqanakht always speaks of 'my land' or 'all my land'[10] giving the impression that he was the private owner of it. In all his transactions there seems to be little involvement of the state or any higher institution, also providing the impression that he was an independent landowner. The same impression is given when Hapidjefa from Asyut mentions that he inherited his house from his father.

From the sparse and difficult evidence it might seem that Egyptian society in the Middle Kingdom was tightly controlled. However, it should be kept in mind that the Bronze Age technology of Middle Kingdom Egypt did not give the rulers the same possibilities of restriction as a modern state. An ancient prescriptive state might be freer than many modern western societies in practical terms.

The following rough outline of Egyptian society tries to combine archaeology, the visual arts and written sources. It is never easy to describe a society, especially an ancient society four thousand years ago. Social status may have been expressed and gained by personal wealth but also by knowledge, which was not necessarily expressed in wealth. However, wealth is for us mostly visible in tombs, sometimes in house size and to a lesser extent in burial furnishings. Although ancient Egypt was clearly a class society, classes were certainly not as monolithic as it might seem, and the classes were perhaps not so fixed as the caste system in India. Within the ruling class there is visible a certain degree of social mobility. However, there is little evidence for social mobility between the lower and the upper ends of society. Possible exceptions will be discussed. Social borders may not have been closed in a legal manner, but there is little evidence for anyone crossing class borders from the bottom to the top of society.

The following description of society is basically divided in two blocks (see sections 3.1 and 3.2), based on the sources.

The first group consists of individuals outside the ruling class, known

142

from their tombs, from their houses at some excavated settlement sites and from depictions on monuments of the ruling class. These people seem not to have had (or at least not often) their own inscribed monuments and they often do not bear titles. However, they are sometimes shown on the monuments of the ruling class and there they appear with certain titles or job descriptions: 'servant', 'nurse', 'fowler' or 'backer', just to give some examples. This social level is certainly not as homogeneous a group of people as it might appear at first. Different tomb sizes or tomb furnishings already indicate differences in status and wealth. These variations are most often hard to pinpoint. The majority of these people – the foundation of Egyptian society – certainly could not write, and had no or little access to any education other than training in their manual livelihood. A high percentage must have been involved in food production. They are the farm workers and herdsmen. However, we have little knowledge whether they owned their land or whether most of them were serfs. A smaller number were workers (for example in quarries and mines) or craftsmen. Some of the latter may even have been able to write and to gain some wealth. Finally, there may have been a group of people such as traders or people with other professions (for example barbers, healers or physicians in communities), who had a different source of income. These people are hard to locate in our sources.

The other group of people is the ruling class, including the king's family, which formed perhaps only a few percent of the whole population. These people are known from their own monuments, many of them were able to write, and they ran the country. However, there are many questions still open, even for this much more visible group. To what extent were women able to write? To what extent was everyone in this group literate? What were the relations of this class to their servants? Were particular servants able to follow a career in a household of a high state official, and so be able to cross class borders? The evidence for this is not conclusive, but it exists.

3.1. Outside the ruling classes

Marginalised groups

Most societies include numbers of people not living in organised structures. From both archaeology and written sources there is little known about such people. They are hard to identify in the archaeological record, and do not appear often in writings, other than in literary settings. The 'Eloquent Peasant' relates the injustice that such a group might suffer: its main character lived in the marginal territory of the Wadi an-Natrun, west of the Delta, and is robbed of his belongings on his way to market. He is called a marshland-dweller. He did not belong to the poorest as he was the owner of donkeys and of products which he could sell. Such individuals, collecting goods at the desert edge and living from small-scale trading, are otherwise almost invisible in our sources. Marshland-dwellers also appear in other monuments, and at the royal court there was a high official with the title 'overseer of the marshland-dwellers', indicating that these people, although living at the edge of society, were put under the charge of an official and were therefore under the Egyptian administration. Other groups of people are also hardly visible in the archaeological records, such as beggars (appearing for example in the 'Laments of Ipuwer'). These people appear as *shuau, tuau, maru* or *huru* in texts; the meanings of these expressions, not very often mentioned, are still very vague.

Peasants, herdsmen and craftsmen: the working population

From comparable societies it seems clear that a very high percentage of the Egyptian population must have been farm workers or herdsmen, people directly involved in food production. It is hard – more so than for the ruling classes – to gain a clear picture of this foundation of society. Texts relating to farmers present the view of the literate ruling class. Depictions in tomb chapels or wooden models placed in tombs also reflect the view of the ruling class and show farmers in specialised functions, as providers of agricultural products. No farmhouse has yet been identified for sure and archaeological remains are often hard to interpret. There are certainly many graves and burials of farmers and poor people excavated and published, but it is often impossible to say to what precise social level a 'poor' burial belongs. In the archaeological record of burials of poor people, it seems impossible to distinguish between slaves, poor craftsmen and farm labourers.

Egyptians rarely if ever placed objects relating to their profession in their tombs.[11] Therefore the archaeological record of these poorer tombs should be treated as one group, belonging to people with similar resources. For the Middle Kingdom there is a further problem that no large cemetery has been excavated and published where all social levels are attested. For the Old Kingdom there are the cemeteries of Naga ed-Deir or Gurob with tombs certainly belonging to people at the lower end of society. For the First Intermediate Period there are the extensive cemeteries at Qaw/Badari/Matmar and Mostagedda excavated by Guy Brunton in the 1920s and certainly belonging mainly to people living at the lower end of society, most likely the farming population in this region. However, Brunton deliberately avoided excavating tombs without burial goods; these would certainly have belonged to the lowest end of the social scale. As a result it is now hard to gain a full picture of the society from these otherwise well-excavated and published cemeteries.[12] The problems are worse for the Middle Kingdom. There are not many burials in this region dating to the Middle Kingdom, and other sites excavated and published have so far provided only burials belonging to a higher social level. By comparison, at the New Kingdom cemetery of about 600 tombs at Fadrus in Nubia all social classes, perhaps with the exception of the ruling class of the country or province, seem to be represented. In this context it is interesting to note that about 20 per cent of the tombs found are without any preserved burial goods. These burials evidently belonged to the poorest and may indicate that at the bottom of society there was a large number of people with few resources. However, these make up only 20 per cent and while other burials are also quite poor, they contained various objects, showing that most people even at the lower end of the social ladder had at least some resources.[13] Such statistical observations are for the moment not possible for the Middle Kingdom. The total number of tombs excavated at several Middle Kingdom cemeteries is for each of them relatively small. At al-Kubanieh, about 10 km north of Elephantine, were found several hundred tombs of the Middle Kingdom.[14] All were published, and offer an idea of the resources and customs of the rural population in this region. Interestingly, there are almost no tombs without any burial goods; many tombs are simple shafts, but cut to a certain depth into the ground, indicating that these people, even the poorest, had some kind of supporting family or other social structure to arrange a proper burial, however simple. The living conditions of the lower classes in Middle Kingdom Egypt were certainly quite horrible – especially in comparison with modern life in western European societies. However, this does not mean that these people did not have any resources: simple coffins and at least one pottery vessel are the regular goods for most of the burials at al-Kubanieh.

A large planned settlement excavated at Tell el-Dab'a certainly belonged to a working population, providing for one place a good idea of the living conditions of these people. Each house here was only about 5 x 5 m and contained an entrance room, a minuscule kitchen, a courtyard and two other small rooms, perhaps for sleeping (Fig. 37). The houses seem to be

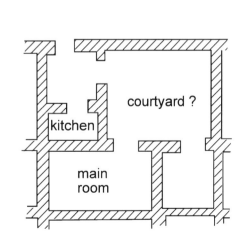

37. A typical house found at Tell el-Dab'a; early Twelfth Dynasty.

very small even for people of lower status and one wonders whether they were just built for a short period of use, more barracks than houses. The site may be connected with royal building work, for which a large number of workmen were needed. The finds in the settlement consisted mainly of pottery. Almost all tools found were made of stone, demonstrating that even in the Middle Kingdom metal tools were not yet common. Animal bones found show that cattle, sheep and pig seem to have been the main meat sources, though fish was also consumed. Wheat was ground with stones not especially prepared for that task but collected when suitable in size and shape. Several artefacts have been identified as loom weights, which would demonstrate that linen was produced here, although it is not impossible that they were net sinkers.[15] The whole settlement creates an impression of a rather poor life for its inhabitants; there are only two fragments of stone vessels, a few faience beads and some scarabs. Doubtless all valuable objects were taken away when the town was abandoned; nevertheless, this is clearly a place where people at the lower end of society lived and worked.

Depictions of farm workers or herdsmen in tombs are also often hard to interpret. In a tomb at Meir there is a type of man depicted dramatically differently from the canonical norms of ancient Egyptian art, with wizened body, elderly-looking face and disordered hair. One might expect such depictions to present persons living at the bottom of society. However, the wizened old man brings fattened cattle, and it might be argued that this is not a poor man, but simply an elderly herdsman or farmer. By contrast it might be argued that these are the poorest people working on the estate of the tomb owner. In that case the cattle would not belong to them.[16]

In the Egyptian language of the Middle Kingdom there was no word exclusively used for a status which could be translated as 'slave'.[17] There are several indications of slavery in Middle Kingdom Egypt, but they are open to different interpretations. Amenemhat II captured 1554 people in Asia and brought them to Egypt.[18] It is not known for what kind of labour or for what kind of purpose they were used, but it is tempting to think that they became slaves, simply by comparison with similar situations in the Roman Empire. However, it is also possible that they were placed in sparsely populated parts of the country to become farm workers on estates.

The following legal document from Lahun illustrates these problems:

Year 29, month 3 of flood season, day 7
Made in the office of the vizier in the presence of the 'overseer of the city' and 'vizier' Khety by the scribe in charge of the seal of the bureau for issuing people, Amenemhat's son Ameny. Transfer deed of the 'deputy treasurer' Shepset's son Ihyseneb, northern sector together with the 'pure-priest' in charge of the protection (?) of Sopdu, lord of the east, Shepset's son Ihyseneb. Assent by the scribe of this town, Ptahwenenef's son Sehetepibre

Asiatic woman   Akhiatef/Kemeteni
                                 Kemeni/Sopdummeri
                                 Meshy/Senen (?)
                                 [...]-am/[...]-benu (?)[19]

In this document four Asiatic women were given by the 'deputy treasurer', Ihyseneb, to his brother, a 'pure-priest' also called Ihyseneb. Each woman bears a double name, common in this period – perhaps in these cases one Asiatic and one Egyptian. The legal transaction was recorded in the office of the vizier. Are we dealing here with slavery? Perhaps these four Asiatic women were 'only' serfs, with at least some degree of personal freedom. It is at present not possible to give an answer.

There are several inscriptions that refer to transfers of larger numbers of individuals to an official. The governor Sarenput (I), in office at Elephantine under Senusret I, states that he received 300 'head' from Lower Egypt.[20] On a stela dated to the time of Senusret III, Khusobek proudly describes his military success. As reward he received from the king sixty 'head'.[21] Another important document is a list of servants on a papyrus most likely from Thebes, which contained a list of ninety-five servants – many with foreign names – who were given to a woman called Senebtysy, perhaps related to the family of the vizier Ankhu.[22] Although the scale of the allocations is informative, in none of these three cases can much be said about the real status of these servants.

Several terms referring to the working population are known, but it is again hard to distinguish the precise meaning of each and it is impossible to decide how much they were dependent on a person or an institution (Fig. 38). There are other documents that record a transfer of people in these categories, but it does not mean that the people transferred were slaves. Besides being attached to a certain person, an estate or an office, they may

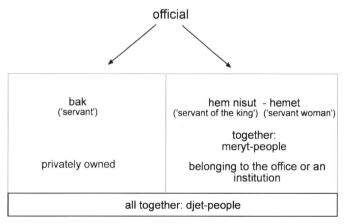

38. Expression and status of servants of an official.

147

have enjoyed rights which were not given to slaves in classical Greek and Roman or more recent societies. One term relating to working people is *bak*, often translated rather neutrally as 'servant'. From the sources it seems clear that *bak* servants were not connected to a title or an office. It seems instead that they were privately owned. In contrast, the terms *hem-nisut* ('servant of the king')[23] and *hemet* ('servant woman'), were people attached to an office or title. Together the 'servants of the king' and 'servant women' were called *meryt*-people. If, for example, an official such as a governor died, his *bak* servants would be given to his heir, whereas the *meryt* people had to work for the next governor, whether or not that was, as often, the son of the governor. All these people together, those attached to a title (*hem-nesut/hemet*) and those attached to an individual in some other way (*bak*), were called the *djet*-people, the entire working staff of an official. It has been proposed that the whole working population belonged to one or other of these dependent categories, with a status comparable to that of serfs. However, it is also possible that there were 'free farmers' or other working people not categorised in such ways.[24] This remains one of the great unsolved questions in our histories of ancient Egypt.

That the working population did not have an easy life is no surprise. The way in which the ruling classes looked down on them is sharply expressed in the 'Satire of Trades'. This is a literary composition demonstrating to a pupil the low quality of life of all professions other than that of 'scribe':

> The field labourer complains for eternity,
> his voice rises higher than the birds,
> with his fingers turned into sores
> from carrying overloads of produce (?).
> He is too exhausted to report for marsh work,
> and has to exist in rags.
> His health is the health [of a man forced to work] on new lands;
> sickness is his reward.
> His labour-duty there is whatever they have forgotten.
> If he can ever escape there from the order (?),
> he reaches his home in utter poverty,
> downtrodden too much to walk.[25]

Most of the professions listed in this work involved manual labour. Some of them may have been of relatively high status, such as that of goldsmith.

The 'great enclosure'

In the late Middle Kingdom the titles 'overseer of the enclosure' and 'scribe of the great enclosure' appear together with the institutions called 'enclosure' and 'great enclosure'. The few references in texts suggest that these were institutions where people were sent to work for the state, at least for a certain period. The exact nature of this institution is still under discussion, but it seems certain that several of these 'enclosures' existed in Egypt in this period, each perhaps responsible for a certain region. The 'enclosure' at Thebes seems to have held people mainly from the first to the ninth Upper Egyptian nomes and to have organised them as a temporary work force. It seems likely that it was an institution organising work rather than a specific building. There seems to be no evidence that this work was done as punishment, as is sometimes argued. The 'enclosure' was therefore most likely no prison, but the work there must have been extremely arduous, because a papyrus now preserved in the Brooklyn Museum lists people who ran away from the 'enclosure'. The runaways are most often described as belonging to specific places, such as towns, or to specific kinds of land, or to particular people with titles. It is therefore possible to argue that they were serfs, belonging to estates, towns or officials, who were forced by the state to work in the 'enclosure'. Therefore it might be argued that this was an institution where some kind of corvée was conducted. The men in charge of these enclosures were the 'scribes of the great enclosure', while the 'overseer of the enclosure' was a high state official, perhaps in charge of all enclosures in the country.[26] This institution raises several questions. Were all Egyptians – at least those not belonging to the ruling classes – forced to work there for a certain period, or were people just sent there when they were needed? Which class of people worked there?

Wealthy people without administrative titles: remarks on the problem of the 'middle class' in Middle Kingdom Egypt

In recent years there have been several approaches to identifying some kind of 'middle class' in Middle Kingdom society.[27] They were first made on philological grounds, in an attempt to interpret certain general expressions for people[28] or to prove that there was some kind of 'free-thinking' population with an education and some income, not belonging to the administrative ruling class. These people were regarded as responsible for the rise of literature which was critical of the system in the Middle Kingdom.[29] However, all these approaches are vague, and not based on contextual analysis of the written sources. There are also archaeological approaches to the subject, which note that next to rich and poor tombs there are many burials which certainly do not belong to the ruling class but are still quite well furnished with precious objects, indicating that there was a certain class of people able to accumulate some wealth, without belonging to the ruling class.[30] The problem is difficult. Many tombs at the cemeteries at Qaw/Badari/Matmar and Mostagedda are already in the late Old Kingdom quite well furnished. There was therefore without doubt already in the Sixth Dynasty some kind of middle class in the sense of a significant social stratum of people not belonging to the administrative class but with a certain level of wealth. Going back in time, it is harder to gain a picture from the classical Old Kingdom. In Fourth and Fifth Dynasty tombs, even in the burials of the highest state officials, often only a few objects were placed. If there was already a middle class in the Old Kingdom it is difficult to recognise it in the tomb furnishings because of the burial customs of that period. The 'middle-class' problem is therefore not confined to study of the Middle Kingdom, at least from the point of view of archaeology.

However, there are also other possible ways to explain the archaeology and the written sources. It is for example possible to interpret wealthy tombs of people without titles in different ways:

1. Administrative titles simply were not placed, or did not survive, on the monuments related to these burials.
2. The people buried in them were family members of the ruling class, but these members did not bear titles; in this way many rich burials of women could be explained.

One specific instance is the burial of a person called Senusret-ankh at the cemetery of Harageh, quite close to Lahun.[31] His tomb was plundered but still contained a wooden coffin with blue painted inscriptions on it, a canopic box and perhaps a mummy mask (Pl. XIV). Senusret-ankh does not bear any titles on the coffin and canopic box and therefore it might be argued that he belonged to a non-administrative elite. The position of the tomb in the cemetery is also revealing. The cemeteries of Harageh, so called by the excavator Reginald Engelbach, consist in reality of a series of several separate burial grounds. Senusret-ankh was interred several kilometres from the main cemeteries at the desert edge overlooking the fertile land. The main cemetery must have been the burial place of a wealthy community, but for some reason he was buried separately from his contemporaries. It is tempting to see in Senusret-ankh a rich farmer, who chose to be laid to rest close to his own farming estate. However, this is only a guess.

At the cemeteries at Asyut were found hundreds of coffins without owners' titles. On coffins found at Meir, Deir el-Bersheh or Beni Hasan, titles always appear, showing that the people buried here served the governors of their town. The same must hold true for the people buried in Asyut. The coffin owners at this place presumably belonged to the same class of people. It remains unknown why they did not record their administrative titles on their coffins. People not mentioned with titles on monuments may therefore have had a position in the administration, which is not mentioned on one monument, but which may have appeared on other monuments or documents that have not survived.

There are some examples in writing of people who may have belonged to a 'middle class'. One of them is perhaps the letter London UC 32203 found at Lahun.[32] It is written by (or written for) the 'mistress of the house', Irer. After a formal introduction, different from that used for most letters from Lahun, she says:

> This is a communication to the lord about the servant-women who are here without getting down to weaving ... on the guiding threads. The servant there could hardly have come himself, since the fact is that the servant there entered into the temple on day 20 to purify for the month.

'Mistress of the house' is not an administrative title relating to weavers, but Irer was clearly in charge of female weavers. She possibly had a certain standing and income from her work, and it might be argued that she had some kind of economic freedom. However, certain questions remain open in her case. Was she in charge of the weavers only because her husband (who perhaps had a title) or son was not there at that moment, or was she really the main person in charge? It would be interesting to see her burial place or her house, but neither has been identified.

As a preliminary conclusion it may be stated that there was certainly some kind of middle class in the Middle Kingdom, as in other periods, but at the moment our sources do not reveal from where these people obtained their income/wealth. A middle class in the sense of people having some kind of wealth does not necessarily mean that the Egyptian state was not prescriptive. It is only possible to guess how these people gained their small wealth. Are these well-trained craftsmen, traders or rich farmers with some servants? For the Middle Kingdom it seems at the moment impossible to give a definitive answer.

3.2. The ruling classes: people with administrative titles

The local bureaucrats

The early Middle Kingdom sources for the local ruling class are different from those of the late Middle Kingdom. For the early Middle Kingdom there is abundant evidence from the provinces. The tombs of the local governors are often extensively inscribed. Their family relations are therefore often well known. There are also many sources relating to the lower bureaucrats. They appear in the tombs of their masters and their own burials provide further information. In the late Middle Kingdom these sources disappear. There are no longer decorated tombs of the governors or burials of the people working for them. These people are now sometimes found on stelae, but it is often impossible to specify from stelae whether they come from regional centres rather than from the royal court. In the early Middle Kingdom all important towns were ruled by governors who had the title 'governor' and very often 'overseer of priests' or 'overseer of temples', but never all three titles together. At certain places the governors had additional titles. Especially in the early Middle Kingdom there are several governors with the title 'great overlord of a nome', which implies some control over a whole nome and not only over a town. 'Great overlord of a nome' disappears in the first half of the Twelfth Dynasty, which may indicate some kind of reorganisation of the provincial administration. Several of the governors also had high-ranking titles, showing that they were on the same level as people with ranking titles at the royal court. There is good evidence for father-son succession in the office of governors and there are also attestations that families of different governors were connected by marriage. This is surprising, as it is rarely attested for the highest officials at the royal court, as will be shown. There is no doubt that the local governors were responsible to the king. A rock inscription in the Wadi Hammamat dated to the time of Senusret I mentions twenty 'governors' who joined the expedition, working for the king.

Under the governors were people working for them. They bear different administrative titles. So far there is little evidence that these people were related to the governor's family. The sons of the governors are shown in the tombs of governors or on their stelae,[33] but not very often with specific titles, though religious and military titles sometimes appear. These sons (and daughters) are also known from their own monuments, being identified by their title 'son/daughter of a governor', but again they do not often bear administrative titles. An exception is the 'son of a governor' and 'overseer of fields', Ukh-hotep, at Meir. One other example is that of the two brothers whose burial was found in the courtyard of the tomb of a governor at Rifeh. The brothers have the title 'son of a governor', but the only other title attested there is 'great *wab*-priest', which seems not to be an administrative post.[34] The families of the governors therefore seem be rather isolated from the rest of their subjects, rather like the royal family, which also seems to have been isolated from the rest of the population.[35]

Next to the tombs of most of the governors buried in the provinces were found the tombs and graves of people who served them. These people bear similar titles to the bureaucrats at the residence. Each local court seems therefore to have been a small copy of the royal court, with only a few titles missing (such as the vizier or 'overseer of marshland dwellers'). The local officials are often depicted in the tombs of the governors. There was a 'treasurer', who is described in the tomb of Khnumhotep (II) at Beni Hasan as responsible for building the tomb of his master. There are 'stewards', 'overseers of the troops', 'overseers of the gateway', 'overseers of cattle' and a 'scribe of the royal document'. An official of special importance was the 'herald', who was most probably a person directly responsible to the king and the residence, inspecting and controlling the work of the local governors.

It is not certain how these people were related. They are most often known only from their coffins and from depictions in the tombs of the governors. Neither type of source provides much information on the families of the people mentioned. On a stela found at Abydos belonging to 'deputy governor from Tjebu [Qaw]', Heny, his family is listed.[36] Heny himself was the son of a certain Ibu, who had the same title. His children bear the titles 'follower' and 'steward'. They clearly had administrative titles similar to those found at places in the provinces. From the title 'deputy governor from Tjebu' it is clear that this family is from a provincial town; there are certainly many more examples with families of local towns, but they are often not easy to identify if no specific place is mentioned on a monument. There is so far no evidence that the lower local bureaucrats had any specific connection to the royal residence. They seem rather to have had a client status to their governors, as can be seen by the position of their tombs close to the tombs of their masters.

The sources for the local bureaucrats for the late Middle Kingdom are more difficult. The big provincial cemeteries with their rich inscribed material on coffins and decorated tombs are no longer found. However, there are the many papyri found at Lahun, and they give the impression that the administrative structures went on. Still attested are a local 'treasurer', an 'overseer of the gateway', an 'overseer of the field' and an 'overseer of the troops'.[37]

The ruling class: the bureaucrats at the royal residence

The evidence for the ruling class at the royal residence is more balanced than the evidence for the local ruling class. There are many stelae, statues and some tombs from both the early and the late Middle Kingdom. However, especially in the late Middle Kingdom stelae provide more details on the families of this class and the relation between different title holders. There are also several important papyri known from that period with further information. The new range of sources provides us with greater insight into the social relations of the late Middle Kingdom ruling class than we have for the early Middle Kingdom. This discussion of the ruling class at the residence is divided into two parts: (1) the bureaucrats and (2) the restricted group of ministers next to the king.

At the top of society were the men with titles, known from their monuments all around Egypt, which identify them as the bureaucrats running the country. At least some of them seem to have been called *ser*, 'official', in Egyptian texts,[38] but a group name for them as a class is less easy to identify. Other expressions for people of the ruling class are *pat* and *henmemet*. It is hard to discern the real meaning of these words, found mainly in religious contexts.

It is almost impossible to decide what proportion of society the ruling class formed, but it was doubtless not a high percentage. At the court these people are most visible in papyrus Boulaq 18 (a Thirteenth Dynasty administrative document of the Theban palace), where many people with different titles appear as a distinct group of high officials. They have titles belonging clearly to various branches of the administration. People with military titles such 'officer of the ruler's crew' or 'great officer of a town regiment' are mentioned there; another frequent title is 'great one of the tens of Upper Egypt' whose function is still under discussion. The same holds true for the common late Middle Kingdom titles 'eldest of the hall' or 'mouth of Nekhen', which also appear relatively often at the royal court and whose functions are also unclear. People with these and similar titles are known from many monuments, and there is good evidence for father-son succession in their offices. Each new stela found provides new data on these people, and the impression is that they formed an upper class where a number of families held all key positions of the country in their hands. These people seem to have been quite mobile, as they are often attested at several sites, perhaps on a mission for the king. They are best attested in their own monuments on the Abydos stelae, where it is sometimes possible to reconstruct families over several generations.

On these stelae from Abydos and other sites there appear several groups of titles relating to these people: 1. administrative titles relating to land and food production; 2. military titles; 3. priestly titles. In the late Middle Kingdom the following groups of titles appeared in addition: 4. non-specific titles ('great one of the tens of Upper Egypt', 'eldest of the hall', 'mouth of Nekhen'); and 5. titles connected with the organisation of labour ('scribe of the great enclosure') and scribal offices. Different members of one family could bear titles from these different groups. However, more often is seems that various family members tended to work in the same part of the administration.[39] These people did not, of course, form a totally homogeneous group; some of them certainly had higher positions than others. Within this social level as a whole there seems to have been a degree of social mobility. Several careers are attested for officials who seem to have started at quite a low level and reached a high position in the state.[40] This gives the impression of high social mobility. However, it should be stated clearly that even the people at the lowest end of this class are, in terms of the society as a whole, high in the social hierarchy. They could afford inscribed objects and were most probably able to write. The social mobility of these people operated only inside the narrow parameters of a social group.

There is little evidence that people from the lower end of society entered this group. Nobody ever states that his father was a simple farmer. Even titles such as 'soldier of a town regiment' – the title of the grandfather of two kings and of a treasurer of the Thirteenth Dynasty – seem to belong to a higher command level. It is certainly not the title of a common soldier.[41] On the other hand, many foreigners lived in Middle Kingdom Egypt and some of them belonged to the bureaucrats at the royal residence.[42] Although little can be said about their social background it seems likely that they come from the lower end of society as they appear first (in

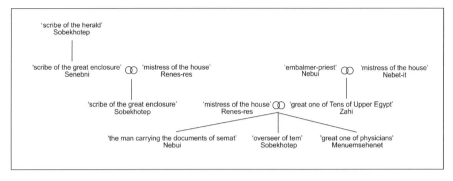

39. The families of Sobekhotep and Zahi.

the Twelfth Dynasty) most often in lists of servants and only later (in the Thirteenth Dynasty) in higher positions. Their social mobility seems a surprising indication of a more open society. However, their social movement upwards may relate to their special status as outsiders. In other societies[43] slaves could cross social borders through their close relations to their masters (a well-known example from ancient history would be the 'freed-man' of imperial Rome[44]). Assuming that many foreigners came to Egypt as slaves or as people with a slave-like status, they may have been promoted by their masters to a higher social status, and even gained important positions in the administration, perhaps not in the first, but in a succeeding generation.

One example of family of bureaucrats from the Thirteenth Dynasty may be described (Fig. 39). 'The scribe of the great enclosure', Sobekhotep, is known from several stelae.[45] All can be dated on stylistic grounds to the time of Kings Khasekhemre Neferhotep I and Khaneferre Sobekhotep IV. The father of Sobekhotep, named Senebni, had the same title of 'scribe of the great enclosure'. The mother of Sobekhotep was the 'mistress of the house', Renes-res. The grandfather of Sobekhotep was the 'scribe of the herald', Sobekhotep. The latter title seems to be less important than 'scribe of the great enclosure', or at least is less common. The family therefore attained a slightly higher position over one generation.

There is another stela in Cairo[46] where a 'scribe of the great enclosure', Sobekhotep, appears, but without further references. This is possibly the same man. The stela belongs to the 'great one of tens of Upper Egypt', Zahi. It is not known for sure how these two people are connected. There may have been family ties not shown on the monuments which have survived, but it is also possible that they were just colleagues or friends. Zahi[47] was member of another important family. Zahi's father had a quite different title from Zahi. He was the 'embalmer-priest', Nebui. This sounds like a rather menial position, but it is possible that he worked at the royal palace, in which case he would have been quite important. The sons of Zahi had several administrative positions in the country. One of them was physi-

155

cian, one held the probably military (but not yet fully comprehensible) position of *hery-en-tem*, 'overseer of *tem*', and one worked in a scribal office as 'the man carrying the documents of *semat* [literally 'unity' or 'collection', significance uncertain]'. No member of either of these families had a very high position: nobody was a minister with ranking titles. Nevertheless, it seems obvious that this family was able to place all their men in administrative positions. The picture for the bureaucrats in the late Middle Kingdom is therefore clear. These people formed a network of families with key positions in their hands.

The picture is not so certain for the early Middle Kingdom, as on most monuments only the core family is depicted and it is therefore hard to make links between families. There is also no good evidence for father-son succession in office. The main reason for that may simply be that fathers on monuments are often not mentioned with specific titles.

It is surprisingly hard to gain any detailed picture of the living conditions of this class, but funerary and settlement archaeology provide a certain basic level of information. At Thebes was found the undisturbed burial of the 'great one of the tens of Upper Egypt', Renseneb. He was placed in a decorated coffin; over his head there was a gilded mask and he was adorned with a necklace partly of gold. Other finds in his coffin included one figure of a hippopotamus and a nicely crafted and inscribed mirror. The coffin itself was found in a tomb with two chambers, where several other people had been buried. Other finds from this tomb are a box with a picture showing King Amenemhat IV and a gaming board.[48] The tomb is datable to the early Thirteenth Dynasty. It is certainly smaller and less richly furnished than the mastabas around the king's pyramid at Dahshur or Lisht, but the objects found are all of high quality, showing that Renseneb had access to well-trained craftsmen.

While there is at least some evidence from the cemeteries about the ruling class, the evidence from settlement sites is hard to interpret. First of all it should be said that there are not many excavated settlements where we can expect to find houses of bureaucrats, and only small outlying parts of the residence are known. Lahun is the only settlement which may give us an idea. At one side of the town were palatial houses certainly belonging to the bureaucrats, but it is an open question whether people with ranking titles lived in these houses, perhaps only at a time when Lahun was some kind of residence under Senusret II, or whether bureaucrats lived in them. At Abydos at the town called Wahsut were found houses most probably belonging to officials of some standing but not of the highest level, as their houses are significantly smaller than the largest one found at the site (Fig. 40). They had a columned courtyard or garden, a main hall also with columns and some rooms, presumably for living and sleeping, arranged around it. The essential living quarters of these houses are not much smaller than in the largest house in the town belonging to

156

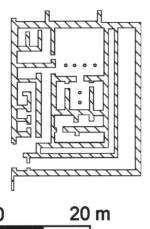

40. Building B, Wahsut (Abydos).

0   20 m

the local governor. The big difference seems to be that the economic part of the house is rather small and there were perhaps no special rooms for the wife of the house owner. Seals were found next to the houses belonging to certain women, most of them with the title 'mistress of the house'.[49]

The people of this social level doubtless had estates with servants working for them. Such servants are often shown in the tombs and on the stelae of the ruling class. However, in many cases it is not easy to decide whether the lower officials shown are servants working in the private estate of an official or whether these servants were working in the administration under the officials. The Heqa-nakht papers found at Thebes belong to a person of this social level. Heqa-nakht appears in his letters with the rather low title '*ka*-priest'. He was responsible for the cult of a statue and for the funerary cult of a high official. Despite his modest rank he had his own estate with different people working for him. His household included several family members but also two maidservants, a household scribe and a household steward. It is not known how many people worked for him on the fields.[50]

There was certainly some kind of client system, not yet fully understood but clearly visible within this class. Archaeology has uncovered many cases where lower officials were buried next to the tomb of the highest officials. The most famous example is perhaps the 'overseer of the storeroom', Wah, whose tomb was directly next to the tomb of the 'high steward' and 'treasurer', Meketre, at Thebes. The name Meketre appears on a seal found in Wah's tomb, proving that Wah's burial is not much later. Interestingly, there are many stelae from the late Middle Kingdom where an 'overseer of the storeroom' is shown in front of a treasurer, again apparently demonstrating this client relationship between the highest and lower officials.

157

The ministers

We have more information about the highest social stratum of the country in the Middle Kingdom than for any other group of people, although there are still big gaps in our knowledge; the tombs of many of these people are still missing, a principal source for this category of people in the Old and New Kingdom. However, the evidence from the numerous stelae, the few excavated tombs and statues and other sources should suffice to provide an outline of the Middle Kingdom's highest section of the ruling class. At the royal court the top level of officials consisted of a number of people with the classical ranking titles *iry-pat*, 'member of the elite', *hati-a*, 'foremost in action', *khetemti-biti*, 'royal sealer', and *semer-wati*, 'sole friend [of the king]'. These titles announced the social status of a person at the royal court and hence the number of people with these titles in the Middle Kingdom is not very high. The four ranking titles mentioned were most often written in that sequence, but in the few cases when they appear alone they seem to indicate a special position. *Iry-pat* alone announced a higher position than the title *iry-pat* and *hati-a* together. An official who had the honour to bear the title *iry-pat* was almost second only to the king. Officials with ranking titles in general occupied the highest administrative positions in the country and it does not seem wrong to call them ministers, rather then just officials or bureaucrats. They clearly ruled the country, comprising a small group of perhaps five to six people at the royal court. In the Eleventh and early Twelfth Dynasty these high titles were borne regularly by the vizier, the treasurer and the high steward and the overseer of the troops. Other officials, such as the 'scribe of the royal document', the 'overseer of the gateway' or the 'overseer of the troops' were given high-ranking titles sporadically as needed. On gaining these titles they were in effect promoted to the inner circle around the king. They seem to be the officials called 'friends' in royal and other inscriptions,[51] though whether the term *ser* also applies to them is not certain.[52] The most senior of them was the vizier, in charge of the administration of the provinces, the scribal offices and the supreme juridical authority. Next to the vizier there was the treasurer, responsible for the palace as an economic institution. The high steward was responsible for the fields and the agricultural belongings of the king and the country and ranked below the treasurer.

Little is known about the families of these ministers, but succession in office seems to have been less common than in other periods of Egyptian history. The remarkable exception is the office of the vizier, which was held in the early Thirteenth Dynasty by four members of the same family. The famous vizier Ankhu was the son of a vizier, whose name is not known, and Ankhu was the father of two other viziers, who must have been in office after him. However, such a family of highest court officials seems exceptional. This may be an accident of the surviving sources, but it appears more likely that many of these officials came from important families, whose members had titles and positions just under these highest state officials. The highest officials were perhaps chosen by the king from that wider group of people. Therefore most ministers were appointed from the class of bureaucrats, as can be seen from their families and their careers.[53] The names of some parents of ministers are known, but they do not often bear titles. This certainly does not mean that the highest officials came from a non-administrative background and that this is a sign of high social mobility. It seems more likely that the title of the father is simply not mentioned in a filiation. A parallel comes from the Nineteenth Dynasty. In this period there are several of the highest state officials (viziers) who identified their fathers in filiations simply as '*zab*-official'. This also creates the impression that they came from a quite modest background. However, from other sources some of the fathers are known in reality to have held quite important positions, not mentioned in the filiations of their children.[54] Several officials describe in their biographies how they were appointed by the king because of their abilities and their character.[55] This also gives the impression that they came from a not particularly exalted background. However, as it never sounds good to say 'I obtained this position because my father promoted me', these references do not amount to a convincing indicator of any kind of greater social mobility.

Many of the bureaucrats must have lived at the royal residence or were at least connected with the royal court. This is evident in the Thirteenth Dynasty papyrus Boulaq 18: under the vizier there are the officials with ranking titles, followed by a group of many other officials. The early Twelfth Dynasty vizier Intefiqer bears the title 'foster son of the king', indicating that he was brought up at the royal court. The treasurer Iykhernefert also reports that he 'grew up as foster son of my majesty'.[56]

In the late Middle Kingdom (after Senusret II) the picture changed slightly. The ranking titles 'member of the elite' and 'foremost in action' lost their importance and were only occasionally given to officials. The title 'royal sealer' now became the main designation for a high court official. The number of offices regularly combined with this ranking title was now extended on a regular basis. In addition to the treasurer, high steward and the 'overseer of the troops', there were now the 'overseer of the sealers', the 'overseer of the fields' and the 'scribe of the royal document' just to name the most important of these offices. These offices seem to have formed a certain group, attested from the late Twelfth Dynasty to the Seventeenth Dynasty. There is again little evidence for father to son succession in the offices. Each king seems to have chosen his ministers from the ruling families of the country, for an amazingly large number of these officials is known from the Thirteenth Dynasty, when many kings ruled for a short time; presumably each chose new high officials on their accession to the throne. For some officials, though, such as the vizier Ankhu and the treasurer Senebsumai, it seems likely that they stayed in office under several kings. In titularies the vizier is in the late Middle Kingdom again an exception. The vizier did not often bear the ranking title 'royal sealer', but had a special titulary instead, including 'overseer of the city' and 'overseer of the six great mansions'.

The picture we gain from the provincial courts is slightly different. The governors or mayors at the local courts belong to the same high social level. They often bear the same high-ranking titles. However, especially from the inscriptions in Beni Hasan we have the impression that the whole country was ruled by several families, all connected by marriage. It is not known whether they were also connected with the ruling families at the royal court and whether it was common for these people to make a career at the royal court or whether they normally stayed in the provinces. There is the case of Khnumhotep (III) at Beni Hasan who made a career at the royal court, leading an expedition, and becoming high steward and finally vizier. We do not know whether this career was normal or exceptional.[57]

Loyalty to the king was the most important aspect of ruling-class life and is expressed on many monuments. Biographical inscriptions and biographical phrases often refer directly to the king. Phrases like 'he who fills the heart of the king', or 'the great one for the king' are relatively common on private stelae of high officials. In biographical inscriptions the promotion of an official by the king seems very important and is often stated. A certain number of monuments – stelae and tombs – are dated with a king's name, sometimes with a year of his reign, and this also appears to be a demonstration of loyalty.

This loyalty of an official to the king receives its clearest exposition in the so-called 'Loyalist Teaching'. The text seems to be in part almost an introduction to how to relate to the ruler:

> Praise the king within your bodies,
> embrace his majesty in your hearts.
> Spread awe of him every day.
> Create rejoicing for him at every time.
> He is the insight into what is in the hearts,
> his eyes probe every body.
> He is the sun in whose leadership [people] live.
> Whoever is under his light will be great in wealth.
> He is the sun by whose rays [people] see.
> He brightens the Two Lands, more than the sun-disk.[58]

Significantly, references to kings are more often found under strong rulers of the Eleventh and Twelfth Dynasties than under the weaker kings of the Thirteenth Dynasty. There are still some stelae dated to the time of Amenemhat IV with the name of the king, but only a few dated to the time of a king of the Thirteenth Dynasty. Even the people at the top of society seem to have lost their faith in the king during this period. The only exception might be the time of Khasekhemre Neferhotep I and Khaneferre Sobekhotep IV, when there are some private monuments naming the kings, but these monuments are few. There is no impression of a real restoration of royal power. The ruling upper class seems to have gone its own way. However, especially from the Thirteenth Dynasty many statues exist with the formula 'given by the favour of the king'. They seem to be a direct expression of loyalty, although strangely the name of the king is most often not mentioned.

The importance of people with ranking titles is also evident from their monuments. There are not many mastabas known from the royal cemeteries, but the few bigger ones all belong to them. The best evidence available comes from Dahshur where, next to the pyramid of Senusret III, there was a cemetery for his officials. There are three big mastabas north of the pyramid. Two belong to viziers of the king; the owner of the third is so far not identified, but was also most probably a vizier or a high official. Another mastaba smaller in scale was built for the high steward and (later?) vizier Khnumhotep. All other mastabas excavated here are rather small and did not belong to people with ranking titles. Houses of the highest state officials belonging to the royal court have not yet been certainly identified in the archaeological record. At Lahun were excavated several palatial houses, which may belong to this class of people, assuming that the town of Lahun functioned at least for a certain period as a royal residence. These houses are similar to another found at Abydos South and belonging to a governor, and to a house found at Tell el-Dab'a, perhaps also belonging to a local governor. These houses centred on a core comprising the main living quarters, with a great columned hall and, beyond it, the bedroom of the house owner. Around this core were several buildings for economic functions, most importantly the granaries, and it has been assumed that the people living here were much involved in redistributing food and other goods to the local population. These highest state officials certainly had their own estates with many people working for them. Many lower officials are shown on monuments of the high officials, and some of these were wealthy enough to leave their own monuments. In the client system the ministers certainly had several clients coming from the level of bureaucrats. These people are often buried next to them.

3.3. The king and his family

There is amazingly little information about the royal family in the Twelfth Dynasty.[59] Several 'king's wives', 'king's daughters' and a few 'king's sons' are known, but there is no evidence that the sons of the kings played any important part in the administration of the country. Furthermore, there is in the Twelfth Dynasty no evidence that the 'king's daughters' or the 'king's sons' were married to non-royal people, such as high officials or members of their families. For the 'king's daughters' this is strongly supported by their tombs, found around the king's pyramids. These 'king's daughters' are also known from several statues and other monuments, but there is never a reference to a husband. The evidence implies that they had a special, probably religious, status. The situation for the 'king's sons' is slightly different. They are not very well attested and nothing is known about their families. Their tombs are not known.[60] A certain 'king's son', Amenemhat-ankh, is known to bear certain religious titles, which are not regularly attested in the administration. The 'king's son', Ameny, perhaps the future Amenemhat II, was sent on a mission to Koptos but is known only from being mentioned in a biographical inscription at Beni Hasan. In general the title 'king's son' does not appear often in the sources, and one may wonder what happened to men after their brothers became king. The mothers and the wives of the Twelfth Dynasty kings do not often have the title 'king's daughter'. The title is so far only attested for Neferu, the mother of Intef III, and for Neferu, the mother of Amenemhat II.[61] It is therefore possible that many kings married a woman from a non-royal family. Here, 'non-royal' means most likely a family of one of the highest state officials, but again this is not stated anywhere and is therefore only a guess.

Whereas there is little information on the king's family in the Twelfth Dynasty the sources for the Thirteenth Dynasty are richer. In only a few instances can a succession from father to son or brother to brother be proved, as in the case of the brother kings Khasekhemre Neferhotep I and Khaneferre Sobekhotep IV. The only clear example of a father-son succession is indirect and comes from the seal of the 'king's wife' and 'king's mother', Nubhetepti, showing that she was the wife of one king and the mother of another king. Her royal husband and royal son are not known, but scarabs with names of the royal family are especially common in the time of Khasekhemre Neferhotep I and Khaneferre Sobekhotep IV and shortly before and after, so Nubhetepti must belong to about this period. Many kings of the Thirteenth Dynasty seem to have come from important families of officials.[62] The best-known example is the family of queen Nubkhaes, who appears on a stela now in the Louvre. On the monument the queen is shown with her family. Her father is the 'chief scribe of the vizier' and 'great one of the tens of Upper Egypt', Dedusobek, who was the brother of the 'high steward', Nebankh, an important official under Khasekhemre Neferhotep I and Khaneferre Sobekhotep IV. The husband of the queen – the king – is not known for sure.[63] On a stela in Berlin[64] appears the 'king's sister', Senebsimai. She is the wife of the 'seal-bearer of the king' and 'personal king's scribe of the royal document', Iymeru. Several 'king's sisters' also appear in the papyrus Boulaq 18. On another stela in Würzburg[65] appears the 'king's wife', Iy, together with some officials known from other monuments. The family is known to be related to the family of the vizier Ankhu, while the queen also appears in papyrus Boulaq 18. This papyrus most likely dates to King Sekhemre-khutawy

Amenemhat Sobekhotep II. On stela Cairo CG 20394 appears the 'king's wife', Nefret; her daughter, the 'king's daughter', Hatshepsut, was married to a military man called Nedjesankh/Iew. The mother of the 'royal sealer' and 'overseer of fields', Ankhu, had the title 'king's sister'. There is the case of the 'king's daughter', Dedetamen, who was married to the 'seal-bearer of the king', 'governor' and 'sealer of the god', Nebsenet.[66] Finally there are at least two kings who may have been high officials before they became kings: King Wegaf, who was perhaps 'overseer of the troops' (p. 66), and Sekhemre-Sewadjtawy Sobekhotep III, who may be identical with the 'officer of the ruler's table', Sobekhotep, known from several seals (p. 70).

The general picture gained from this information is that in the Twelfth Dynasty the royal family was relatively isolated from the officials and the rest of the people. The kings of the Twelfth Dynasty married daughters of non-royal people, but their own daughters were not married to officials. 'King's sons' seem to have been 'hidden' in the palace, perhaps until the succession was clear and one of the sons became king, but this is pure speculation. In the Thirteenth Dynasty there are several links between the royal families and the ruling class of the country, notably in the two cases where the career path from official to king seems quite likely.

The king stood at the head of Egyptian society. The king was treated as a god with a special titulary consisting by the Middle Kingdom of five parts and often announcing the programme of the reign.[67] 1. the Horus name; 2. the *nebty* (Two Ladies); 3. the gold Horus name; 4. the throne name; 5. the birth name. The first, fourth and fifth of these names are distinguished by being written in a special frame. At least since the First Dynasty the Horus name was the most important. It was written in a *serekh* (a representation of a palace façade and enclosed space) with a Horus bird (a falcon) on top of it. The king was identified as the Horus on earth and Horus himself was the main deity of kingship.

The Horus name had already in the Old Kingdom lost its solitary pre-eminence in the royal titulary but in the Middle Kingdom, after the throne and birth name, was still the most important part of it. It seems typical that the Intef kings of the early Eleventh Dynasty had only their birth name and a Horus name. They did not have all the royal names, but chose the Horus and not the throne name as the main epithet of royalty in inscriptions.

The birth and throne names are always written inside a cartouche; an oval frame – the *shen* sign – symbolised duration. It is attested for sure since the Third Dynasty. The birth name was often connected with the title 'son of Re'. It has been assumed that it was the name given to a king's son (or another person who later became king) at birth. There are several cases where this is demonstrable (mainly from other periods). However, there must also have been cases where a king chose a new 'birth name' on becoming king. One example of the late Middle Kingdom is perhaps King Semenkare Nebnun. Nebnun, which is the so-called birth name of the king, does not sound like such a name and is otherwise not attested as such, and was perhaps taken by this person on accession to the throne, or by a foreigner who wanted to have an Egyptian name.

The throne name was given to a new king on accession to the throne. It is the name most often mentioned in official documents, while Manetho and Egyptologists prefer to refer to the birth names of the kings. The Horus and birth name do not often appear alone, but are usually connected with the throne name. By contrast the throne name often appears alone. In many examples it is introduced with the title *netjer-nefer*, 'the good god'. While several kings have the same birth name, there are almost no kings with the same Horus or throne name. A king was therefore easier to recognise from his throne name and this is presumably the reason why this name appears on monuments referring to a king. The *nebty* and the gold Horus name are in the Old and early Middle Kingdom pure royal titles; the names following these royal titles are always identical with one of the other names mentioned. Only under Senusret II do the *nebty* and the gold Horus become independent and are each connected with a different name. Neither appears frequently on monuments, and we do not know them for many of the less well-known rulers of the Thirteenth Dynasty.

Kingship was not only expressed by a different titulary. In all parts of life the special position of the king was reflected in distinctive attributes. His house (the palace), tomb and even clothing (for example the crowns) are different from those of all other people. In theory the tomb of the poorest man and that of the highest official are constructed along the same lines. This observation is clearest with the pyramid building. The pyramid is a form of monument reserved for the king himself and the royal women, who also occupied a special position. Only in the New Kingdom, when the pyramid was no longer the form used for the cult of kingship, did private people erect pyramids over or next to their tomb complex. Little is known about Middle Kingdom palaces, but they are also certainly totally different from the houses of the rest of the population. Houses of private individuals found at several places are not only smaller, but follow a different design. They have normally only one courtyard with a main hall and the bedroom of the house owner. The palace found on Uronarti has many different courtyards and is strictly orientated north-south. Several rooms, halls and apartments in the Egyptian palace have certain names not attested for private houses, even ones that were very large. The words *kap* and *ipat* are two such examples, referring to special rooms or institutions in the palace. In this case they refer to the innermost part and its private chambers. These expressions are not used for private houses. These are only a few examples of differences between the king and the rest of the population, but there are certainly many more and it seems that the life and work of a king was differently organised in every respect.

The concept of kingship in the Middle Kingdom is certainly different from the concept of kingship in the Old Kingdom. The clearest example may be seen in the 'Instruction of Amenemhat', where the king describes himself as victim of an assassination. However, the assault is known from a work of literature. Similar texts are not known from the Old Kingdom and it seems wise only to compare analogous sources

In the hymn to Senusret III found on a papyrus at Lahun the Egyptian idea of kingship is expressed. The king is responsible for protecting the country and extending its borders. He is protector of the people in all situations, 'the sunshade at flood, cool in the summer':

> Horus [divine] of forms, he of the Two Ladies, divine of births,
> Gold Horus who has come into being
> Dual King (throne name) Khakaura
> Son of Re (birth name) Senusret.
> He has taken up the two lands as the one true of voice.
> Hail Khakaura,
> our Horus, divine of forms,
> protector of the land, extender of its boundaries.
> He who defeats foreign lands by his Great Crown,
> he who embraces the two lands with his action.
> He who [...] the foreign lands with his two arms,
> who slaughters the bowmen without a blow of a weapon,
> who fires the arrow without the string being drawn,
> whose dread has smitten the nomads in their land,
> whose fear slaughters the nine bows,
> whose massacre causes the death of thousands of bowmen,
> those who [had dared?] to reach his border.

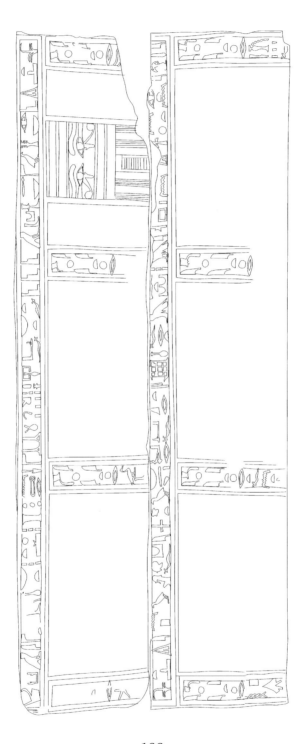

41. Drawing of Plate XI.

166

Chronology

Naqada Culture	*c.* 4000-3000 BC
Early Dynastic Period (1st-2nd Dynasty)	*c.* 3000-2700 BC
Old Kingdom (3rd-6th Dynasty)	*c.* 2700-2150 BC
First Intermediate Period (7th-first half of 11th Dynasty)	*c.* 2150-2008 BC
Middle Kingdom (11th-13th Dynasty)	*c.* 2008-1685 BC
Second Intermediate Period (14th-17th Dynasty)	*c.* 1685-1550 BC
New Kingdom (18th-20th Dynasty)	*c.* 1550-1069 BC
Third Intermediate Period (21st-25th Dynasty)	*c.* 1069-664 BC
Late Period (26th Dynasty)	664-525 BC
First Persian Period (27th Dynasty)	525-404 BC
Late Dynastic Period (28th-30th Dynasty)	404-343 BC
Second Persian Period (31st Dynasty)	343-332 BC
Ptolemaic Period	332-30 BC
Roman and Byzantine Period	30 BC – AD 640
Islamic Egypt	AD 640 – today

Appendix

A. Kings of the Middle Kingdom

Table 1. The Eleventh Dynasty

Horus name	*nebty* name	gold Horus name	throne name	birth name	years attested
Tep-aa				Mentuhotep (I)	
Sehertawy				Intef (I)	
Wahankh				Intef (II)	49 years
Nakhtnebtepnefer				Intef (III)	8 years
1. Seankhibtawy					
2. Netjeri-hedjet	Netjeri-hedjet		Nebhepetre	Mentuhotep (II)	51 years
3. Sematawy	Sematawy	Qaishuti	Nebhepetre		
Seankhtawyef	Seankhtawyef	Hetep	Sankhkare	Mentuhotep (III)	12 years
Nebtawy	Nebtawy	Netjerunebu	Nebtawyre	Mentuhotep (IV)	2 years

Table 2. The 'Nubian kings'

Horus name	*nebty* name	gold Horus name	throne name	birth name
Ankhkhnumre		Bik-nebu-ankh	Wadjkare	Zegerzenti
Geregtawyf			Iy-ib-khenty-re	Intef
Senefertawyf	Senefertawyf	Bik-nebu-nefer	Qakare	In

Table 3. The Twelfth Dynasty

Horus name	*nebty* name	gold Horus name	throne name	birth name	years of a sole reign attested[1]
Wehem-mesut (Seheteptawy)	Wehemmesut (Seheteptawy)	Wehemmesut (Zema)	Sehetepibre	Amenemhat (I)	20 (30)
Ankhmesut	Ankhmesut	Ankhmesut	Kheperkare	Senusret (I)	42 (45)
Hekenmaat	Hekenmaat	Maakheru	Nubkaure	Amenemhat (II)	32 (35)
Seshemtawy	Sekhamaat	Hetepnetjeru	Khakheperre	Senusret (II)	5/6 (8/9)
Netjerkheperu	Netjermesut	Kheper	Khakaure	Senusret (III)	19 (39)
Aabau	Itjijautawy	Wahankh	Nimaatre	Amenemhat (III)	45
Kheperkheperu	Sehebtawy	Sekhemnetjeru	Maakherure	Amenemhat (IV)	9 years, 3 months, 25 days
Merytre	Satsekhem-nebettawy	Djedetkha	Sobekkare	Sobekneferu	3 years, 10 months, 24 days

169

Table 4. The early Thirteenth Dynasty in the Turin Canon[2]

name in Turin Canon	remarks and years in Turin Canon
Khutawyre	2 years, 3 months, 24 days
Sekhemkare	
Amenemhat(Re)	2 (?) years
Sehetepibre	
Iufni	
Seankhibre	
Semenkare	
Sehetepibre	
Sewadjkare	
Nedjemibre	
Sobekhotep(Re)	
Renseneb	4 months
Autibre	
Sedjefakare	
Sekhemre-Khutawy Sobekhotep	
User ... re Khendjer	
... kare Mermesha	
... ka Intef	
... ib Seth	
Sekhemkare Sobekhotep	4 years, 2 (?) months
Kha ... sekhemre Neferhotep	son of Haankhef, 11 years
Sahathor	
Khaneferre Sobekhotep	
Khahotepre	4 years, 8 months, 29 days
Wahibre Ibjau	10 years, 9 months, 28 days
Merneferre	23 years, 8 months, 18 days

Note

The kings listed below are known from contemporary inscriptions, but their exact position within the sequence of Thirteenth Dynasty kings is not known. However, they most probably date to the first part of the Dynasty. They do not appear with the names attested on their surviving monuments in the Turin Canon:

Nerikare (known from two monuments, both dated to a year 1).[4]
Horus Djedkheperu[5] (mainly known from seal impressions found in Lower Nubia).
Horus Khabau, *nebty* name: Wehemdjed, gold Horus: Ankhrenput, throne name:
    Sekhemre-Khutawy (known from several monuments).[6]
Hetepkare (known from a cylinder seal).[7]

Table 5. The first part of the Thirteenth Dynasty, following the Turin Canon and contemporary sources

Horus name	*nebty* name	gold Horus name	throne name	birth name	years attested
Sekhemnetjeru	Khabau	Mery ...	Khutawyre	Wegaf	2
Mehibtawy	Itjsekhemef		Sekhemkare	Amenemhat (V) Senebef	4
				Ameny Qemau	
			Hetepibre	Qemau Sa-Hornedtjef	
				Iufni	
no contemporary sources					
Seankhibtawy (Sehertawy)	Sekhemkhau	Hekamaat	Seankhibre	Amenemhat Intef Ameny	
				Nebnun	
Sewesekhtawy			Semenkare		
no contemporary sources			Sehetepibre		
no contemporary sources			Sewadjkare		
			Nedjemibre		
Sematawy	Djedkhau	Kaunetjeru	Khaankhre	Sobekhotep (I)	
				Amenemhat Renseneb	
Hetepibtawy	Neferkhau	Nefernetjeru	Auibre	Hor	
Heriteptawy	Netjerbau	Aapehti	Sedjefakare	Amenemhat Kay	
Menkh ...		Ankhnetjeru	Sekhemre-Khutawy	Amenemhat Sobekhotep (II)	4
... ankh	Wahmesut		Userkare (Nimaatre)	Khendjer	5
			Semenkhkare	Mermesha	
			Sehetepkare	Intef	
			Meribre (?)[3]	Seth	
no secure contemporary sources					
Khutawy	Khaemsekhemef	Hetephermaat	Sekhemre	Sobekhotep III	3
			Sewadjtawy		
Geregtawy	Wepmaat	Menmerut	Khasekhemre	Neferhotep (I)	11
not attestested as king of Egypt				Sahathor	
Ankhibtawy	Wadjkhau	Weserbau	Khaneferre	Sobekhotep (IV)	9
			Khahotepre	Sobekhotep (V)	4
			Wahibre	Ibiau	10
			Merneferre	Iy	23

B. Viziers of the Middle Kingdom[8]
The Eleventh and Twelfth Dynasties

Bebi (Mentuhotep II)
  relief fragment from Deir el-Bahri
Ahanakht (Mentuhotep II?)
  governor of Khemenu buried at Deir el-Bersheh; the title of vizier is mentioned only once in his tomb
Dagi (Mentuhotep II and later)
  relief fragments from Deir el-Bahri, tomb
Amenemhat (Mentuhotep IV)
  rock inscriptions at the Wadi Hammamat
Ipi (end of Eleventh or early Twelfth Dynasty)
  tomb at Thebes
Neheri (Amenemhat I)
  governor of Khemenu known from rock inscriptions at Hatnub, once appearing with the title vizier
Kay (Amenemhat I)
  known from rock inscriptions at Hatnub, once appearing with the title vizier; son of Neheri
Intefiqer (end of reign Amenemhat I – Senusret I)
  tomb at Lisht, tomb of his mother Senet at Thebes, several rock inscriptions, Reisner papyri
Amenemhat (Senusret I)
  governor of Khemenu buried at Deir el-Bersheh also bearing the title vizier
Senusret (Senusret I – Amenemhat II)
  mentioned in a tomb at Beni Hasan, stela
Ameny (Amenemhat II)
  mentioned on the annal fragment of Amenemhat II
Ameny (Senusret II? identical with the former one?)
  offering table
Sobekemhat (Senusret III)
  tomb at Dahshur
Nebit (Senusret III)
  tomb at Dahshur
Khnumhotep (Senusret III – Amenemhat III)
  tomb at Dahshur
Ameny (Amenemhat III)
  rock inscriptions at Aswan
Khety (Amenemhat III, year 29)
  Lahun papyrus
Samont (end of Twelfth or beginning of Thirteenth Dynasty)
  two stelae
Qemeny (end of Twelfth or beginning of Thirteenth Dynasty)
  bronze ship mast-finial
Senusret-ankh (end of Twelfth or beginning of Thirteenth Dynasty)
  statue (found at Ugarit), stela

The Thirteenth Dynasty

Khenmes (Sekhemkare Amenemhat (V))
  rock inscription, statue with the name of the king (now in London, BM)
Ankhu (son of a vizier, perhaps of Samont; date: Sobekhotep II)
  several stelae, papyrus Boulaq 18, papyrus in Brooklyn, statues
Iymeru (son of Ankhu)
  stela, statue
Resseneb (son of Ankhu)
  stela
Iymeru Neferkare (Sobekhotep IV)
  several statues, stelae, rock inscription
Djed-ptah/Dedtuseneb (Horus Khabau and Horus Djedkheperu)
  seal impressions from Uronarti
Ibia (Wahibre Ibia?)
  stelae, only mentioned in the filiations of his sons

The Late Twelfth or Thirteenth Dynasty
(not more precisely datable)

Ameny
  statue (London, BM)
Iwy
  known only from a seal
Menu-hotep
  known only from a seal
[Neb-su]menu
  known only from a seal impression
Hori
  known only from a seal
Sobek-aa Bebi
  known only from seals
Dedumont Senebtyfy
  stela, statue

C. Treasurers of the Middle Kingdom[9]

The Eleventh and Twelfth Dynasties

Khety (Mentuhotep II)
  tomb at Thebes, rock inscriptions, mentioned in the mortuary temple of King
  Mentuhotep II
Meketre (Mentuhotep II – early Twelfth Dynasty)[10]
  tomb at Thebes, mentioned in the morturay temple of King Mentuhotep II
Intef (early Twelfth Dynasty)
  tomb at Thebes
Ipi (Amenemhat I)[11]
  rock inscription, coffin fragments
Sobekhotep (year 22 of Senusret I)
  rock inscription

Mentuhotep (Senusret I)
    tomb at Lisht, statues from Karnak, stela at Abydos; he also bears the title
    vizier, but this may be merely honorific
Rehuerdjersen (Amenemhat II)
    tomb at Lisht, stela
Merykau (Amenemhat II)
    stela from the eastern desert
Siese (Amenemhat II)
    tomb at Dahshur; he also bears the vizier's title
Sen-ankh (year 8 of Senusret III)
    rock inscription
Sobekemhat (Senusret III)
    tomb at Dahshur (identical with the vizier of the same name)
Iykhernefret (Senusret III – Amenemhat III)
    several stelae
Ameny (son of the steward Iy)[12]
    statue
Ameny (son of Iti)
    statue
Senusret (dated to a year 10)
    papyrus fragment from Lahun

The Thirteenth Dynasty

Ameny-seneb
    relief from Abydos (Pl. XX), seal impression from Mirgissa[13]
Herfu
    seals, weight, statue (Brooklyn)
Khenty-khety-em-sauef Seneb
    statue, stela found at Harageh (Pl. XIX)
Kheperka
    statue (Turin)
Seneb
    stela
Senebef
    seal, stela
Senebsumai (Sobekhotep II – Neferhotep I)
    seals, stelae, bronze statue, papyrus fragments from Lahun
Senebi (Nefehotep I – Sobekhotep IV)
    seals, stelae, rock inscription
Amenhotep (after Sobekhotep IV)
    seals, tomb at Dahshur, faience vase

The Late Twelfth or Thirteenth Dynasty (known only from seals)

Ibt
Izi
Adj-zehui
Wepemhab
Nebsumenu
Redienptah

Notes

For abbreviations used in the Notes, see the start of
the Bibliography, p. 193 below.

Introduction

1. D. Wildung, *Sesostris und Amenemhet* (Munich, 1984), 17, fig. 7.

2. S.J. Seidlmayer, in J. Assmann, G. Burkard, V. Davies (eds), *Problems and Priorities in Egyptian Archaeology* (London 1987), 201-6; B.J. Kemp, *Ancient Egypt, Anatomy of a Civilisation* (London/ New York, 1989), 239.

3. Translation after M. Lichtheim, *Ancient Egyptian Literature, A Book of Readings*, I: *The Old and the Middle Kingdoms* (Berkeley, Los Angeles/ London, 1975), 142.

4. W. Wolf, *Kulturgeschichte des Alten Ägypten*, Stuttgart 1977, 238-9.

5. Translation follows *Manetho*, with an English translation by W.G. Waddell (London, 1940), 63-73.

6. A.H. Gardiner, *The Royal Canon of Turin* (Oxford, 1959; reprint 1987); further literature: S.B. Ryholt, *The Political Situation in Egypt during the Second Intermediate Period c. 1800-1550 BC*, Carsten Niebuhr Institute Publications 20 (Copenhagen, 1997), 9, n. 9.

7. D.B. Redford, *Pharaonic King-lists, Annals and Day-Books* (Mississauga, 1986), 29-34.

1. History

1. A.B. Kamal, *ASAE* XII (1912), 132, fig. 9.

2. The chronology of the Twelfth Dynasty is according to D. Franke, *Orientalia* 57 (1988), 133-8, 267-74.

3. Cairo CG 20009.

4. L. Habachi, *ASAE* LV (1958), 179.

5. L. Habachi, *Elephantine IV, The Sanctuary of Heqaib*, AV 33 (Mainz am Rhein, 1985), 109-10, no. 97; D. Franke, *Das Heiligtum des Heqaib auf Elephantine*, SAGA 9 (Heidelberg, 1994), 32-3 dates the statue under Senusret I.

6. Cf. W. Schenkel, in *Gräber des Alten und Mittleren Reiches in El-Tarif*, AV 17 (Mainz am Rhein, 1976), 50.

7. L. Habachi, *MDAIK* 19 (1963), 46, fig. 22; Wildung, *Sesostris und Amenemhet*, 40, fig 32.

8. Arnold, *El-Tarif*, 19-22.

9. S. Roth, *Die Königsmütter des Alten Ägypten*, Ägypten und Altes Testament 46 (Wiesbaden 2001),182-5.

10. Cairo CG 20512.

11. G. Gabra, *MDAIK* 32 (1976), 45-56.

12. J.J Clère, J. Vandier, *Textes de la première période intermédiaire et de la XIème dynastie*, Bibliotheca Aegyptiaca (Brussels, 1948), 14, no. 18.

13. Stela BM 614; Lichtheim, *Egyptian Literature* I, 90-3.

175

14. Clère, Vandier, *Textes de la première période intermédiaire*, 9-11, no. 15; cf., for a reconstruction of the whole stela, G. Wenzel, *GM* 193 (2003), 71-85.

15. Kemp, *Ancient Egypt*, 65-6.

16. W. Kaiser, G. Dreyer, G. Grimm, G. Haeny, H. Jaritz, C. Müller, *MDAIK* 31 (1975), 46, pls 19-20.

17. T. Zimmer, in F. le Saout, A.H. Ma'arouf, T. Zimmer, *Karnak* VIII (1982-1985), (Paris, 1987), 293-323, pl. I, p. 314.

18. Arnold, *El-Tarif*, 25-32.

19. Lichtheim, *Egyptian Literature* I, 92.

20. Roth, *Königsmütter*, 185-9, 425-6; the stela: Cairo CG 20543.

21. Translation after Lichtheim, *Ancient Egyptian Autobiographies*, 42-3.

22. W. Schenkel, in Arnold, *El-Tarif*, 47, 57-8, see also pl. 41g.

23. W. Kaiser, G. Dreyer, G. Grimm, G. Haeny, H. Jaritz, C. Müller, *MDAIK* 31 (1975), 46, pl. 20d, e.

24. Habachi, *Elephantine IV*, 111, no. 100, pl. 190; Franke, *Heqaib*, 31.

25. Arnold, *El-Tarif*, 33-8.

26. Arnold, *El-Tarif*, 45, 48-9.

27. Mentuhotep II changed his names twice in his reign. In references to the king in general, he is called Mentuhotep II in this book, at points where a specific name is given on a monument discussed, the other distinguishing names are mentioned.

28. Roth, *Königsmütter*, 189-98 (on Tem); L.K. Sabbahy, *JARCE* XXXIV (1997), 163-6 (on Neferu). The other women are: Sadeh, Kawit, Henhent, Aashyt, Kemsit; Roth, *Königsmütter*, 428-32. A sixth women buried here (Mayt) does not bear any of the titles mentioned; see T.G.H. James, *Corpus of Hieroglyphic Inscriptions in the Brooklyn Museum I* (Brooklyn, 1974), 37-8, no. 85, pl. XXXII.

29. H. Willems, *Chests of Life* (Leiden, 1988), 110-11 (Amenet).

30. E. Naville, *The XIth Dynasty Temple at Deir el-Bahari* I, EEF Memoir 13 (London, 1907, pl. XIIB (the reconstruction of 'king's son' Mentuhotep is not certain; only '[…] son Mentuhotep' survived).

31. LD III, 163.

32. Stela: London BM 1203, *Hieroglyphic Texts 1*, 1, pl. 53.

33. W.C. Hayes, *JEA* 35 (1949), 45.

34. Stela: London BM 1203; *Hieroglyphic Texts 1*, 1, pl. 53.

35. B. Jaroš-Deckert, *Das Grab des Jnj-jtj-f*, AV 12 (Mainz am Rhein, 1984), 37-44, pl. 17.

36. Naville, *XIth Dynasty Temple* I, pl. XIV-XV.

37. J.C. Darnell, *ZÄS* 130 (2003), 37.

38. G. Roeder, *Debod bis Bab Kalabsche*, 2 vols: *Les temples immergés de la Nubie VI* 1+2 (Cairo, 1911), 103-11, § 281, pl. 107f.; G. Meurer, *Nubier in Ägypten*, Abhandlungen des Deutschen Archäologischen Instituts (ADAIK) 13 (Berlin, 1996), 78, 101 (XIII); translation follows J.C. Darnell, *ZÄS* 130 (2003), 34.

39. Habachi, *MDAIK* 19 (1963), 29-30, fig. 10 (the block found at Ballas); Habachi, *MDAIK* 19 (1963), 39, fig. 17 (Gebelein)

40. W.M. Flinders Petrie, *A Season in Egypt 1887* (London, 1888), pl. VIII, 213.

41. Habachi, *MDAIK* 19 (1963), 21-3, fig. 6, pl. 5.

42. W.M. Flinders Petrie, *Abydos II* (London, 1903), pls XXIV, LIV.

43. Habachi, *MDAIK* 19 (1963), 28-9, figs 9-10.

44. P. Newberry, *PSBA* 25 (1903), pl. 1 after p. 358 and 362.

45. Habachi, *MDAIK* 19 (1963), 36-8, figs 15-17; Wildung, *Sesostris und Amenemhet*, 40, fig. 33; G. Robins (ed.), *Beyond the Pyramids, Egyptian Regional Art from the Museo Egizio* (Turin/ Atlanta, 1990), 24, 68-75, nos 3-23.

46. *Fouilles d'El-Kab*, Foundation Ég. Reine Elisabeth (Brussels 1940), pl. 30a, b.

47. W. Kaiser, G. Dreyer, G. Grimm, G. Haeny, H. Jaritz, C. Müller, *MDAIK* 31 (1975), 46-7, pls 20f, 21, 22.

48. M.F.B. de la Roque, *Tôd (1934 à 1936)*, FIFAO 17 (Cairo, 1937), 67-79.

49. Naville, *XIth Dynasty Temple I*; E. Naville, *XIth Dynasty Temple at Deir el-Bahari II*, EEF Memoir 14 (London, 1910); D. Arnold, *Der Tempel des Königs Mentuhotep von Deir el-Bahari I, Architektur and Deutung*, AV 8 (Mainz, 1974); D. Arnold, *The Temple of Mentuhotep at Deir el-Bahari* (New York, 1979).

50. A. Gardiner, *JEA* 4 (1917), 35-8; cf. W. Schenkel, *Memphis, Herakleopolis, Theben, Die epigraphischen Zeugnisse der 7.-11. Dynastie*, Ägyptologische Abhandlungen (ÄA) 12 (Wiesbaden, 1965), 238, n. D (he believes that the word 'North' – Egyptian: mehti – is a personal name).

51. Jaroš-Deckert, *Das Grab des Jnj-jtj-f*, 131; J.P. Allen in *Studies in Honor of W.K. Simpson* (Boston, 1996), 22.

52. London BM 724; *Hieroglyphic Texts VI*, pl. 24.

53. W.Grajetzki, *Die höchsten Beamten der ägyptischen Zentralverwaltung zur Zeit des Mittleren Reiches*, Achet A 2 (Berlin, 2000), 10-11 (I.2).

54. J.P. Allen in *Studies in Honor of W.K. Simpson* (Boston, 1996), 20.

55. Grajetzki, *Die höchsten Beamten*, 10-11 (I.1).

56. W.C. Hayes, *The Scepter of Egypt I* (New York, 1953), 163-4, figs 100-1; Franke, *Heqaib*, 13, n. 31.

57. Jaroš-Deckert, *Das Grab des Jnj-jtj-f*, 131.

58. D. Franke, in Polz D., und A. Seiler, *Die Pyramidenanlage des Königs Nub-Cheper-Re Intef in Dra' Abu el-Naga: ein Vorbericht* (Mainz, 2003), 80 (with further references).

59. Roth, *Königsmütter*, 194-8.

60. D. Arnold, *MMJ* 26 (1991), 5-14.

61. J. Couyat and P. Montet, *Les inscriptions hieroglyphiques et hieratiques du Ouadi Hammamat* (Cairo, 1912), 81-4, no. 114.

62. W.M. Flinders Petrie, *Abydos II* (London, 1903), XXV (bottom), XXIII.

63. Petrie, *Abydos II*, pl. XXIII, 5.

64. W. Kaiser, G. Dreyer, G. Grimm, G. Haeny, H. Jaritz, C. Müller, *MDAIK* 31 (1975), 47, pls 22-3.

65. PM V, 157.

66. De la Roque, *Tôd (1934 à 1936)*, FIFAO 7 (Cairo, 1937), 79-97; D. Arnold, *MDAIK* 31 (1975), 181, fig. 3; cf. Wildung, *Sesostris und Amenemhet*, figs 47-51, which provides good photographs of the reliefs found.

67. G. Vörös, *Temple on the Pyramid of Thebes* (Budapest, 1998).

68. L. Habachi, *Tell el-Dab'a I* (Vienna, 2001), 170, no. 14, fig. 23 (London UC 15516).

69. A. Gardiner, *JEA* 4 (1917), 30, 35-8, pl. IX.

70. Hayes, *Scepter I*, 167, fig. 102; Arnold, *MMJ* 26 (1991), figs 15-17.

71. A.H. Gardiner, T.E. Peet and J. Ěerny, *The Inscriptions of Sinai* II (London, 1955), 86, no. 70.

72. Couyat, Montet, *Les inscriptions hieroglyphiques et hieratiques du Ouadi Hammamat*, 77-8, no. 110; Breasted, *Records* I 211-12.

73. Couyat, Montet, *Les inscriptions hieroglyphiques et hieratiques du Ouadi Hammamat*, 98-100, no. 192; Breasted, *Records* I, 213.

74. A.I. Sadek, *The Amethyst Mining Inscriptions of Wadi el-Hudi I, Text* (Warminster, 1980), 4-15, nos 1-5.

75. M. Abd el-Raziq, G. Castel, P. Tallet, V. Ghica, *Les inscriptions d'Ayn Soukhna*, MIFAO 122 (Cairo, 2002), 40-1, no. 4.

76. W.C. Hayes, *BMMA, November 1933, Egyptian Expedition 1932-33*, 26, fig. 38 on p. 31.

77. Roeder, *Debod bis Bab Kalabsche*, 115, pl. 108c.

78. R. Morkot, *The Black Pharaohs* (London, 2000), 54-5.

79. Roth, *Königsmütter*, 217-20.

80. Hayes, *Scepter I*, 167, fig. 102; Arnold, *MMJ* 26 (1991), figs 15-17.

81. R.J. Leprohon, *JARCE* XXXIII (1996), 167.

82. Abd el-Raziq et al., *Les inscriptions d'Ayn Soukhna*, 42, no. 5, fig. 12.

83. W. Helck, *Die Prophezeiung des Nfr.tj* (Wiesbaden, 1970).

84. Arnold, *MMJ* 26 (1991), 5-48.

85. Grajetzki, *Die höchsten Beamten*, 241-3.

86. Arnold, *MMJ* 26 (1991), 20.

87. Grajetzki, *Die höchsten Beamten*, 191 (XII.15), 195-6 (XII.28).

88. Arnold, *MMJ* 26 (1991), 15-16.

89. Arnold, *MMJ* 26 (1991), 16.

90. Cairo CG 20516, cf. W.K. Simpson, *JARCE* II (1963), 53-9.

91. Z. Žaba, *The Rock Inscriptions of Lower Nubia* (Prague, 1974), 31-5, no. 4.

92. Žaba, *The Rock Inscriptions of Lower Nubia*, 98-9, no. 73.

93. Lichtheim, *Egyptian Literature* I, 137.

94. Lichtheim, *Egyptian Literature* I, 143; Helck, *Die Prophezeiung des Nfr.tj*.

95. W.A. Ward, *JEA* 55 (1969), 215-16.

96. F. Gomaà, *Die Besiedlung Ägyptens während des Mittleren Reiches II. Unterägypten und die angrenzenden Gebiete* (Wiesbaden, 1987), 129-30.

97. Willems, *Chests of Life*, 84.

98. Arnold, *MMJ* 26 (1991), 18-19.

99. London UC 14785 – Stewart, *Egyptian Stelae, Reliefs and Paintings from the Petrie Collection* II, 13-14, no. 55, pl. 12.

100. De la Roque, *Tôd (1934 à 1936)*, 104-5.

101. A.E. Mariette, *Catalogue général des monuments d'Abydos* (Paris, 1880), 511, no. 1338.

102. PM V, 157.

103. L. Habachi, *ASAE* LII (1952), 448-58; P. Jánosi, *Ägypten und Levante* 4 (1994), 20-7, cf. S. Grallert, *Bauen – Stiften – Weihen* (Berlin, 2001), 553-4.

104. E. Naville, *Bubastis (1887-1889)* (London, 1891), pl. XXXIIIa.

105. Gardiner, Peet, Černy, *The Inscriptions of Sinai II*, 36, 84, no. 63.

106. Lichtheim, *Egyptian Literature I*, 136.

107. Lichtheim, *Egyptian Literature I*, 137.

108. K. Jansen-Winkeln, *SAK* 18 (1991), 241-64.

109. Žaba, *The Rock Inscriptions of Lower Nubia* (Prague, 1974), nos 11, 55, 57, 58, 59, 65.

110. Žaba, *The Rock Inscriptions of Lower Nubia*, nos 4 (dated to the time of Amenemhat I), 64.

111. Simpson, *JARCE* II (1963), 60-1.

112. Grajetzki, *Die höchsten Beamten*, 12 (I.4).

113. Grajetzki, *Die höchsten Beamten*, 12-15 (I.6). However, it is debatable whether Intefiqer started his time in office already under Amenemhat I (D. Franke, *Personendaten aus dem Mittleren Reich (20.-16. Jahrhundert v. Chr.)*, Ägyptologische Abhandlungen 41 (Wiesbaden, 1984), 146.

114. Grajetzki, *Die höchsten Beamten*, 45-6 (II.2).

115. Grajetzki, *Die höchsten Beamten*, 46 (II.3).

116. P. Tallet, *GM* 193 (2003), 59-64.

117. R.E. Freed, in W.K. Simpson, W.M. Davis (eds), *Studies in Ancient Egypt, the Aegean, and the Sudan, Essays in honor of Dows Dunham on the occasion of his 90th birthday, June 1, 1980* (Boston, 1981), 68-76.

118. Roth, *Königsmütter*, 220-4, fig. 94a, b; the statue might be posthumous. It is also possible that the inscription refers to Senusret II. His father was also a king named Amenemhat (II) and the wife of Amenemhat II is not yet known.

119. Roth, *Königsmütter*, 224-8.

120. B. Fay, *The Louvre Sphinx and Royal Sculpture from the Reign of Amenemhat II* (Mainz am Rhein, 1996), 47, no. 10.

121. Fay, *Louvre Sphinx*, 50-2.

122. L. Habachi, *MDAIK* 31 (1975), 27-31.

123. W. Schenkel, *MDAIK* 31 (1975), 109-25, pls 33-9; see also PM II (2), 61-3.

124. W.K. Simpson, *MDAIK* 47 (1991), 335-6.

125. M. Gabolde, 'Blocs de la porte monumentale de Sésostris Ier à Coptos. Règne de Sésostris Ier (circa 1990 av. J.C.)', in *Bulletin des musées et monuments lyonnais* (1990), nn. 1-2; A. Reinach, *Catalogue des antiquités égyptiennes* (Chalon-sur-Saone, 1913), 23-32.

126. C. Obsomer, *Sésostris Ier, Étude chronologique et historique du règne* (Brussels, 1995), 314-19, 100-2.

127. Petrie, *Abydos II*, 16-17, pl. XXIII (the foundation deposits), XXVI (a door jamb).

128. Simpson, *MDAIK* 47 (1991), 331-40.

129. A. Awadalla, *GM* 115 (1990), 7-14.

130. G. Daressy, *ASAE* IV (1903), 101-2 (nos 1-2).

131. Compare R.B. Parkinson, *Voices from Ancient Egypt* (London, 1991), 40-3.

132. PM V, 200.

133. PM V, 191.

134. PM V, 157-8, 160.

135. F. Gomaà, *Die Besiedlung Ägyptens während des Mittleren Reiches, I. Oberägypten und das Fayyûm* (Wiesbaden, 1986), 259.

136. E. Naville, *Bubastis (1887-1889)* (London, 1891), pl. XXXIV, d.

137. De la Roque, *Tôd (1934 à 1936)*, FIFAO 17 (1937), 106-12; Arnold, *MDAIK* 31 (1975), 175-86, fig. 4.

138. C. Barbotin, J.-J. Clère, *BIFAO* 91 (1991), 1-32.

139. LD II, Bl. 119; Kemp, *Ancient Egypt*, fig. 30.6; Gomaà, *Besiedlung I*, 429.

140. Gomaà, *Besiedlung I*, 39.

141. Gomaà, *Besiedlung I*, 50.

142. Gomaà, *Besiedlung I*, 86.

143. Gomaà, *Besiedlung I*, 369.

144. D. Arnold, *The Pyramid of Senwosret I, The South Cemeteries of Lisht I* (New York, 1988); D. Arnold, *The Pyramid Complex of Senwosret I, The South Cemeteries of Lisht III* (New York, 1992).

145. F. Arnold, *The Control Notes and Team Marks, The South Cemeteries of Lisht II* (New York, 1990), 31.

146. D. Arnold, *The Pyramid of Senwosret I, The South Cemeteries of Lisht I* (New York, 1988), 17.

147. R. Müller-Wollermann, *Chronique d'Égypte* 71 (1996), 5-16.

148. Habachi, *MDAIK* 31 (1975), 27-37.

149. Franke, *Heqaib*, 12-13.

150. O. Berlev, *BiOr* 38 (1981), 318-19; D. Franke, *BiOr* 45 (1988), 101; W.K. Simpson, *JARCE* XXXVIII (2001), 8.

151. Obsomer, *Sésostris Ier*, 311-59 (on the campaigns of the king).

152. Sadek, *Wadi el-Hudi I*, 16-36, nos 6-15; 84-8, no. 143; A.I. Sadek, *The Amethyst Mining Inscriptions of Wadi el-Hudi II, Additional Text, Plates* (Warminster, 1980), 1-4, nos 153-4.

153. K.-J. Seyfried, *Beiträge zu den Expeditionen des Mittleren Reiches in die Ost-Wüste*, HÄB 15 (Hildesheim, 1981), 247-53.

154. D. Farout, *BIFAO* 94 (1994), 145-8.

155. Grallert, *Bauen – Stiften – Weihen*, 487.

156. R. Anthes, *Die Felseninschriften von Hatnub* (Leipzig, 1928), 76-8, no. 49.

157. W.K. Simpson, *JARCE* II (1963), 61-2.

158. J. de Morgan, *Fouilles à Dahchour, Mars-Juin 1894* (Vienne, 1895), fig. 83bis; W.C. Hayes, *The Scepter of Egypt II* (New York, 1959), 50, fig. 24 (shown together with Amenhotep I); cf. K. el-Enany, *Memnonia* XIV (2003), 129-34.

159. C. von Pilgrim, *Elephantine XVIII, Untersuchungen in der Stadt des Mittleren Reiches und der Zweiten Zwischenzeit*, AV 91 (Mainz am Rhein, 1996), 286. On the bowl, which was found in a late Twelfth Dynasty context, appears a date 'year 46' and the month 'third peret', which is the seventh month in the year. Von Pilgrim argues for a dating to the time of Amenemhat III. However, the palaeography and the names on the bowl are typical of the early Middle Kingdom. Year 46 fits perfectly to the last year of Senusret I, who reigned for 45 years and an unknown number of months and days. The exact length of the reign of Amenemhat III is not preserved in the Turin Canon. His highest attested year is so far year 46, 1st akhet, day 22; see F. Ll. Griffith, *Hieratic Papyri from Kahun and Gurob* (London, 1898), 40, pl. XIV.

160. D. Franke, *Orientalia* 57 (1988), 117.

161. W.S. Smith, *The Art and Architecture of Ancient Egypt*, revised with additions by William Kelly Simpson (Harmondsworth/ New York/ Ringwood/ Markham/ Auckland, 1981), 170.

162. Smith, *Art and Architecture*, 177.

163. Roth, *Königsmütter*, 224-8.

164. Cf., for a different view, Fay, *Louvre Sphinx*, 43-7.

165. H. Altenmüller, *SAK* 18 (1991), 1-48.

166. BM 569, *Hieroglyphic Texts* 2, pls 19-20.

167. For a list of monuments in the country, see Fay, *Louvre Sphinx*, 39-42.

168. Seyfried, *Beiträge zu den Expeditionen*, 107-8; Sadek, *Wadi el-Hudi I*, 92-5, no. 148.

169. A. Nibbi, *JEA* 62 (1976), pl. IX.

170. Fay, *Louvre Sphinx*, 40-1, pls 65b, c.

171. Fay, *Louvre Sphinx*, 27, 29-30, 40, esp. 57.

172. H. Altenmüller, *Stationen, Beiträge zur Kulturgeschichte Ägyptens, Rainer Stadelmann gewidmet* (Mainz, 1998), 153-63.

173. W.M. Flinders Petrie, *The Palace of Apries (Memphis II)* (London, 1909), pl. XXIII.

174. F. Bisson de la Roque, *Trésor de Tôd, Catalogue général des antiquités égyptiennes du Musée du Caire, Nos 70501-70541* (Cairo, 1950); F. Bisson de la Roque, G. Contenau, F. Chapouthier, *Le trésor de Tôd*, Cairo 1953.

175. W.K. Simpson, *The Terrace of the Great God at Abydos: the Offering Chapels of Dynasties 12 and 13* (New Haven/ Philadelphia, 1974), 27-8 lists 28 stelae with the name of the king.

176. Stela London BM 256, *Hieroglyphic Texts* 3, pl. 38.

177. Stela London BM 576, *Hieroglyphic Texts* 2, pl. 10.

178. Stela London BM 828, *Hieroglyphic Texts* 2, pl. 21.

179. D. Franke, *Orientalia* 57 (1988), 117.

180. J. de Morgan, *Catalogue des monuments et inscriptions de l'Égypte antique I* (Vienna, 1894), 25, no. 178.

181. D. Arnold, *The Pyramid Complex of Senwosret III at Dahshur, Architectural Studies* (New York, 2002), 117-18.

182. L. Borchardt, *ZÄS* 37 (1899), 91.

183. L. Borchardt, *ZÄS* 37 (1899), 91; Arnold, *The Pyramid Complex of Senwosret III at Dahshur*, 64.

184. L. Borchardt, *ZÄS* 37 (1899), 91; she is also known from two statues found at Tanis, Cairo CG 381-2, Roth, *Königsmütter*, 437.

185. M.W. Blackden, G. Willoughly Fraser, *Collection of Hieratic Graffiti from the Alabaster Quarry of Hat-nub* (London, 1892), pl. XV, no. 12.

186. Petrie et al., *Lahun II*, 16-18.

187. R. Stadelmann, *Die ägyptischen Pyramiden*, 2nd edn (Mainz am Rhein, 1991), 239-41.

188. W. Guglielmi, 'Insel' in *Lexikon der Ägyptologie* III, ed. W. Helck (Wiesbaden, 1980), 164.

189. G. Brunton, *Lahun II, The Treasure* (London, 1920).

190. Stela London BM 257; *Hieroglyphic Texts* 4, pl. 7.

191. R. Engelbach, *ASAE* 33 (1933), 71, no. 7, pl. II, no. 4.

192. R.J. Leprohon, *JARCE* XXXIII (1996), 168.

193. Cf. Arnold, *The Pyramid Complex of Senwosret III at Dahshur*, 117 (Senusret III was perhaps the brother of Senusret II).

194. Arnold, *The Pyramid Complex of Senwosret III at Dahshur*, 82-4, 118.

195. Arnold, *The Pyramid Complex of Senwosret III at Dahshur*, 75-82, 118.

196. Papyrus Berlin 10003, Borchardt, *ZÄS* 37 (1899), 71; Roth, *Königsmütter*, 437-8 (called Khered); Arnold, *The Pyramid Complex of Senwosret III at Dahshur*, 118 (on the possibility that Sherit is identical with Khenmet-nefer-hedjet-Weret (II)).

197. Arnold, *The Pyramid Complex of Senwosret III at Dahshur*, 63, pl. 119; she was in her mid-forties when she died; de Morgan, *Dahchour I*, 151.

198. Arnold, *The Pyramid Complex of Senwosret III at Dahshur*, 71-2, pl. 119.

199. Arnold, *The Pyramid Complex of Senwosret III at Dahshur*, 72, pl. 119.

200. De Morgan, *Dahchour I*, 62, fig. 133 (only on a scarab).

201. De Morgan, *Dahchour I*, 69, figs 147, 150, 152, 153 (the name 'Mereret' or 'Meryt' appears on several scarabs found in the second treasure at Dahshur. On other scarabs appears the title 'king's wife' (op. cit., figs 146, 151). However, there is no proof that the king's wife and Mereret or Meryt are identical. The scarabs of the king's wife (without name) might be a present of a queen).

202. De Morgan, *Catalogue*, 86, no. 20.

203. R.D. Delia, *KMT* 6 (2) (1995), 21.

204. Grallert, *Bauen – Stiften – Weihen*, 184; London BM 852.

205. Translation follows Delia, *KMT* 6, 2 (1995), 22.

206. J. Vercoutter, *CRIPEL* 4 (1976), 154-5; Delia, *KMT* 6, 2 (1995), 23.

207. H. Schlögl (ed.) *Geschenk des Nils* (Basel, 1978), 48-9, no. 154; ANOC 1.9.

208. D. Duham, *Uronarti, Shalfak, Mirgissa* (Boston, 1967), 33-4, pl. XXV.

209. J. Garstang, *El Arábah* (London, 1901), pl. V.

210. M.F. Bisson de la Roque, *Rapport sur les fouilles des Médamoud (1926)* (Cairo, 1927), 67, iv. no. 2051.

211. C. Obsomer, *Les campagnes de Sésostris dans Hérodote* (Brussels, 1989), 115-22.

212. Herodotus, *Book II*, 102-3; translation follows A. de Sélincourt (*Herodotus, the Histories*, translated by A. de Sélincourt, revised, with an introduction and notes by A.R. Burn (London, 1972), 166-7).

213. J.W. Wegner, *JNES* 55 (1996), 249-79.

214. Wegner, *JNES* 55 (1996), 262-4.

215. Rio de Janeiro 627 (2419); Kitchen, *Catalogue of the Egyptian Collection in the National Museum, Rio de Janeiro*, pls 1-2

216. Arnold, *The Pyramid Complex of Senwosret III at Dahshur*, 44-5.

217. D. Randall-Maciver, A.C. Mace, *El Amrah and Abydos* (London, 1902), 57-60, pls XX, XXI; J.W. Wegner, *KMT* 6/2 (1995), 58-71.

218. Lichtheim, *Ancient Egyptian Autobiographies*, 98-100, no. 42.

219. PM V, 137-50 (Medamud), PM V, 119 (Armant).

220. De la Roque, *Tôd (1934 à 1936)*, FIFAO 17 (1937), 113.

221. PM IV, 119.

222. PM V, 199-200, Cairo CG 422.

223. Cairo CG 42011-42013.

224. PM II (2), 384-5.

225. Sadek, *Wadi el-Hudi I*, 37-41, nos 16-18.

226. Seyfried, *Beiträge zu den Expeditionen*, 253-4, no. 8.

227. Seyfried, *Beiträge zu den Expeditionen*, 157-8, no. 7.

228. J. Bourriau, in *Middle Kingdom Studies*, ed. S. Quirke (New Malden, 1991), 3-20.

229. S.J. Allen, in *Proceedings of the Seventh International Congress of Egyptologists, Cambridge, 3-9 September 1995* (ed. C.J. Eyre), Orientalia Lovaniensia Analecta 82 (1998), 39-48.

230. B.G. Trigger, B.J. Kemp, D. O'Connor, A.B. Lloyd, *Ancient Egypt, A Social History* (Cambridge, 1983), 112.

231. N. Farag, Z. Iskander, *The Discovery of Neferwptah* (Cairo, 1971).

232. Collier, Quirke, *The UCL Lahun Papyri: Letters*, 129.

233. J. Couyat, P. Montet, *Les inscriptions hieroglyphiques et hieratiques du Ouadi Hammamat*, 51-2 no. 48.

234. Gardiner, Peet, Černy, *The Inscriptions of Sinai II*, 37.

235. Habachi, *Elephantine IV*, 111, no. 100, pl. 190.

236. Franke, Heqaib, 61; von Pilgrim, *Elephantine XVIII*, 316, fig. 135.

237. Grallert, *Bauen – Stiften – Weihen*, 205.

238. S. Farid, *ASAE* 58 (1964), 90-5, pl. X.

239. J.E. Gautier, G. Jequier, *Memoire sur les fouilles de Licht*, MIFAO 6 (Cairo, 1902), 105, figs 131, 132.

240. W.M. Flinders Petrie, G.A. Wainwright, A.H. Gardiner, *Tarkhan I and Memphis V*, 23, 32, pl. LXXVII (top).

241. W.M. Flinders Petrie, *Ehnasya*, EEF 26, London 1905, 5-6, pl. XIV; PM IV, 119.

242. M. Pillet, *ASAE* 24 (1924), 65-8.

243. I. Matzker, *Die letzten Könige der 12. Dynastie* (Frankfurt am Main/ Bern/ New York, 1996), 170, 177, n. 24 (contains further literature).

244. Sadek, *Wadi el-Hudi I*, 41-3, nos 19-20; 96-7, nos 149.

245. Abd el-Raziq et al., *Les inscriptions d'Ayn Soukhna*, 44-7, no. 6.

246. F. Hintze, W.F. Reineke, *Felsinschriften aus dem sudanesischen Nubien* (Berlin, 1989), 146, nos 499.

247. Boston MFA 13.3967/20.1222; R.J. Leprohon, *Stelae* I, CAA Boston 2, (Mainz am Rhein, 1985), 90-2.

248. De Morgan, *Dahchour I*, pl. XX, 2.

249. BM 101, *Hieroglyphic Texts* II, pl. 2.

250. Roth, *Königsmütter*, 240-1, 581, fig. 111 (Roth restores the title 'king's wife').

251. Rio de Janeiro 645 (2435), Louvre C7, BM 258, Simpson, *Terrace*, 29; Franke, *Orientalia* 57 (1988), 119-20.

252. Gardiner, Peet, Černy, *The Inscriptions of Sinai II*, 125-7, no. 122.

253. Sadek, *Wadi el-Hudi I*, 44-5, no. 21.

254. Hintze, Reineke, *Felsinschriften* I, nos 502-4.

255. Simpson, *Terrace*, 29; Rio de Janeiro 645 (2435), K.K. Kitchen, *Catalogue of the Egyptian Collection in the National Museum, Rio de Janeiro* (Warminster, 1990), pls 3-4.

256. LD Textband II, 15; London UC 14337 – Stewart, *Egyptian Stelae, Reliefs and Paintings from the Petrie Collection II*, 16, no. 67.

257. Berlin Inv. No. 38/66; W. Kaiser, *Ägyptisches Museum Berlin* (Berlin, 1967), 42, no. 428.

258. For the blocks, see G. Daressy, *ASAE* XVII (1917), 34; L. Habachi, *ASAE* 52 (1952), 462.

259. L. Habachi, *ASAE* LII (1952), 463; W.M. Flinders Petrie, *Hawara, Biahmu and Arsinoe* (London, 1889), pl. XXVII, 12.

260. L. Habachi, *ASAE* LII (1952), 464.

261. L. Habachi, *ASAE* LII (1952), 458-61.

262. L. Habachi, *ASAE* LII (1952), 454.

263. E. 27135, E. Delange, *Statues du Moyen Empire* (Paris, 1987), 30-1.

264. Hintze, Reineke, *Felsinschriften*, 102, no. 382.

265. W. Grajetzki, *Harageh, An Egyptian Burial Ground for the Rich around 1800 BC* (London, 2004), 54-6.

266. W. Grajetzki, *Two Treasurers of the Late Middle Kingdom*, BAR International Series 1007 (Oxford, 2001), 24.

267. This might even be the end of the Thirteenth Dynasty. The following kings are perhaps the so-called Sixteenth Dynasty.

268. J. von Beckerath, *Untersuchungen zur politischen Geschichte der zweiten Zwischenzeit in Ägypten* (Glückstadt, 1964), 86-93.

269. Hintze, Reineke, *Felsinschriften*, 102, no. 382a.

270. Hintze, Reineke, *Felsinschriften*, 152, no. 508.

271. Hintze, Reineke, *Felsinschriften*, 152, no. 509.

272. J. Vercoutter, *Kush* 14 (1966), 139; S.T. Smith, *JARCE* 28 (1991), 118.

273. Hintze, Reineke, *Felsinschriften*, 151, no. 506.

274. Cf. discussion in Franke, *Orientalia* 57 (1988), 252-3.

275. Franke, *Orientalia* 57 (1988), 249, n. 5.

276. D. Franke, in H. Altenmüller, R. Germer (eds), *Miscellanea Aegyptologica,* Wolfgang Helck zum 75. Geburtstag (Hamburg, 1989), 67-87.

277. Franke, *Orientalia* 57 (1988), 251.

278. A. Dodson, N. Swelim, *MDAIK* 54 (1998), 319-34.

279. P. Vernus, *Le surnom au Moyen Empire* (Rome, 1986).

280. Von Beckerath, *Zweite Zwischenzeit*, 39-40, 231-2, XIII 9; Ryholt, *Second Intermediate Period*, 338, File 13/6 (collection of sources).

281. Von Beckerath, *Zweite Zwischenzeit*, 40-1, 230-1, XIII 7; Ryholt, *Second Intermediate Period*, 338, File 13/8 (collection of sources).

282. G. Castel, G. Soukiassian, *BIFAO* 85 (1985), 290, pl. 62 (Semenkare).

283. Ryholt, *Second Intermediate Period*, 337, File 13/3 (collection of sources).

284. Von Beckerath, *Zweite Zwischenzeit*, 42-3, 233-4, XIII 12; Ryholt, *Second Intermediate Period*, 339, File 13/13 (collection of sources).

285. K. Ryholt, *GM* 156 (1997), 95-100.

286. Von Beckerath, *Zweite Zwischenzeit*, 44-5, 234-5, XIII 14; Ryholt, *Second Intermediate Period*, 339-40, File 13/15 (collection of sources).

287. Von Beckerath, *Zweite Zwischenzeit*, 46-7, 235-6, XIII 15; Ryholt, *Second Intermediate Period*, 340-1, File 13/20 (collection of sources).

288. S. Quirke, 'Ways to measure Thirteenth Dynasty royal power from inscribed objects', forthcoming.

289. Von Beckerath, *Zweite Zwischenzeit*, 46-9, 235-6, XIII 15; Ryholt, *Second Intermediate Period*, 336, File 13/1 (list of sources; Ryholt placed the king here as the first of the Thirteenth Dynasty).

290. Von Beckerath, *Zweite Zwischenzeit*, 47-8; Ryholt, *Second Intermediate Period*, 319.

291. O.D. Berlev, *Palestinskij Sbornik* 25/88 (1974), 26-31.

292. W.C. Hayes, *A Papyrus of The Late Middle Kingdom in the Brooklyn Museum* (Brooklyn, 1955), 146-7; von Beckerath, *Zweite Zwischenzeit*, 99-100.

293. Quirke, in *Middle Kingdom Studies*, 132-5.

294. Von Beckerath, *Zweite Zwischenzeit*, 49-51, 238-9, XIII 17; Ryholt, *Second Intermediate Period*, 342, File 13/22 (list of sources). The king appears only on Louvre C 12 (ANOC 58.2).

295. Quirke, in *Middle Kingdom Studies*, 134.

296. Ryholt, *Second Intermediate Period*, 220.

297. G. Jequier, *Deux pyramides du Moyen Empire*, Fouilles à Saqqarah (Cairo, 1933), 28, fig. 21.

298. Grajetzki, *Two Treasurers*, 28-9, pl. 2.

299. Franke, *Orientalia* 57 (1988), 268, n. 60.

300. Cairo JE 37466, 37467; Ryholt, *Second Intermediate Period*, 342, File 13/23, 1.

301. W.V. Davies, *A Royal Statue Reattributed*, British Museum occasional papers (London, 1981), 24, no. 16.

302. Ryholt, *Second Intermediate Period*, 285, n. 1031.

303. Von Beckerath, *Zweite Zwischenzeit*, 54-5, 240-3, XIII 21; Ryholt, *Second Intermediate Period*, 222-5, 343 File 13/26 (list of monuments).

304. Grajetzki, *Two Treasurers*, 18-20.

305. Von Beckerath, *Zweite Zwischenzeit*, 55-7, 243-5, XIII 21; Ryholt, *Second Intermediate Period*, 225-8, 345-8, File 13/27 (list of monuments of Khasekhemre Neferhotep).

306. W. Helck, *Historisch-biographische Texte der 2. Zwischenzeit und neue Texte der 18. Dynastie* (Wiesbaden, 1975), no. 32.

307. London BM 428, belonging to the treasurer Senebi, is datable to the period; Grajetzki, *Two Treasurers*, 27-8, no. 1.4.

308. Dublin UC 1360, S. Quirke, *RdÉ* 51 (2000), 223-51.

309. Randall-MacIver, Wooley, *Buhen* I, 200-1 (tomb K8), pl. 74.

310. W.V. Davies, in H. Guksch, D. Polz (eds), *Stationen, Beiträge zur Kulturgeschichte Ägyptens, Rainer Stadelmann gewidmet* (Mainz, 1998), 177-9.

311. W.K. Simpson, *MDAIK* 25 (1969), 154-8; Ryholt, *Second Intermediate Period*, 349, File 13/29, no. 18 (year 7 is certain, 8 is also possible).

312. Sadek, *Wadi el-Hudi I*, 46-52, nos. 22-5; Sadek, *Wadi el-Hudi II*, 5-7, no. 155.

313. Von Beckerath, *Zweite Zwischenzeit*, 57-8, 246-50, XIII 24; Ryholt, *Second Intermediate Period*, 348-52, File 13/29 (list of monuments of Khaneferre Sobek-hotep).

314. Cairo CG 20086, Franke, *Heqaib*, 75.

315. M. Bietak, *SAK* 11 (1984), 59-75.

316. B. Fay, *MDAIK* 44 (1988), 67-77.

317. B. Jaroš-Deckert, *Statuen des Mittleren Reiches und der 18. Dynastie*, CAA Wien, Lieferung 1 (Mainz am Rhein, 1987), 39-48.

318. E. Delange, *Catalogue des statues égyptiennes du Moyen Empire* (Paris, 1987), 66-8.

319. Cairo CG 42034.

320. C. Aldred, *Middle Kingdom Art in Egypt* (London, 1950), 25.

321. C. Randall-MacIver, L. Wooley, *Buhen* I (Philadelphia, 1911), 200-1 (tomb K8).

322. Von Beckerath, *Zweite Zwischenzeit*, 58-9, 250, XIII 25; Ryholt, *Second Intermediate Period*, 353, File 13/31 (list of monuments).

323. Von Beckerath, *Zweite Zwischenzeit*, 59, 250-1, XIII 26; Ryholt, *Second Intermediate Period*, 353-54, File 13/32 (list of monuments).

324. Von Beckerath, *Zweite Zwischenzeit*, 59, 251-2, XIII 27; Ryholt, *Second Intermediate Period*, 354-56, File 13/33 (list of monuments).

2. Archaeology and Geography

1. This survey of Egypt in the Middle Kingdom is based on Gomaà, *Besiedlung* I; F. Gomaà, *Besiedlung* II, where further literature can be found. Further bibliography is supplied in these notes only for more recent research.

2. M. Baud, F. Colin, P. Tallet, *BIFAO* 99 (1999), 1-19.

3. H. Jaritz, *MDAIK* 43 (1987), 67-74 (the Middle Kingdom date is disputed).

4. H. Junker, *Bericht über die Grabungen der Akademie der Wissenschaften in Wien auf den Friedhöfen von El-Kubanieh-Süd, Winter 1910-1911* (Wien, 1919); H. Junker, *Bericht über die Grabungen der Akademie der Wissenschaften in Wien auf den Friedhöfen von El-Kubanieh-Nord, Winter 1910-1911* (Wien, 1920).

5. C. Eder, *GM* 178 (2000), 5-29.

6. Von Pilgrim, *Elephantine XVIII*, 134-41.

7. Von Pilgrim, *Elephantine XVIII*, 282-4.

8. Von Pilgrim, *Elephantine XVIII*, 251-2. Franke, *Heqaib* (for the local history of Elephantine in general).

9. The tombs are discussed in S.J. Seidlmayer, *Gräberfelder aus dem Übergang vom Alten zum Mittleren Reich*, SAGA 1 (Heidelberg, 1990), 63-8.

10. Cairo CG 404.

11. Naville, *XIth Dynasty Temple I*, 10-11; Arnold, *Der Tempel des Königs Mentuhotep von Deir el-Bahari I* (frontis).

12. D. Polz, A. Seiler, *Die Pyramidenanlage des Königs Nub-Cheper-Re Intef in Dra' Abu el-Naga: ein Vorbericht* (Mainz, 2003), 27-31, 73-88.

13. Franke, *Heqaib*, 40.

14. Cf. Grajetzki, *GM* 156 (1997), 55-62, esp. 60. In the article I refuted the identification of Wahka (II) with the person of the same name on the stela in

Stockholm based on the writing of a female grammatical ending 't' in the filiation, believing that Nakht was a woman's name. The 't' might be a simple mistake of the ancient writer. The Stockholm stela seems really to belong to Wahka (II) who therefore is datable to the time of Amenemhat III, whose name appears on the stela.

15. P. Montet, *Kêmi* V (1935-7), 131-63.

16. Perhaps also known from a stela found at Abydos (Cairo CG 20161).

17. J. Kahl, *Siut-Theben* (Leiden/ Boston/ Köln, 1999).

18. A. Roccati, *Oriens Antiquus* 13 (1974), 41-50; Franke, *Heqaib*, 22 (the text appears on a painted wall plaster fragment now in Turin; Torino Cat. Supp. 18351).

19. D. Magee, 'Asyût to the end of the Middle Kingdom: a historical and cultural study' (Oxford, 1989) (unpublished PhD thesis), 229-30.

20. Willems, *Chests of Life*, 84.

21. W.M. Flinders Petrie, *A Season in Egypt 1887* (London, 1888), pl. VIII, 211 (however, the inscription might belong to Senebi (II)).

22. A.M. Blackman, *The Rock Tombs of Meir II*, ASE 23 (London, 1915), pls III, VI.

23. A.M. Blackman, *The Rock Tombs of Meir III*, ASE 24 (London, 1915), pl. XIX.

24. Blackman, *The Rock Tombs of Meir III*, 20-1, pls X-XX.

25. A.M. Blackman, *The Rock Tombs of Meir VI*, ASE 29 (London, 1953), 2, pl. V.

26. A.B. Kamal, *ASAE* 11 (1911), 36.

27. Blackman, *The Rock Tombs of Meir VI*, 8-37, pls IX-XXXII.

28. A.B. Kamal, *ASAE* 14 (1914), 75-7.

29. Willems, *Chests of Life*, 86.

30. H. Willems, *Jaarbericht ex Oriente Lux* 28 (1983-4), 80-102.

31. Martin, *Seals*, no. 1773.

32. Martin, *Seals*, no. 406.

33. J.W. Wegner, in M. Bietak, E. Czerny (eds), *Scarabs of the Second Millennium BC from Egypt, Nubia, Crete and the Levant: chronological and historical implications* (Vienna, 2004), 233.

34. Gomaà, *Besiedlung* I, 309.

35. A.G. Shedid, *Die Felsgräber von Beni Hasan in Mittelägypten* (Mainz am Rhein, 1994), 13-15.

36. Simpson, *JARCE* XXXVIII (2001), 7-8.

37. Franke, in *Middle Kingdom Studies*, 51-67.

38. E.P. Uphill, *Pharaoh's Gateway to Eternity: The Hawara Labyrinth of King Amenemhat III* (London, 2000); I. Blom-Böer, *JEA* (2001) 87, 195-7; I. Blom-Böer, I. Uytterhoeven, *JEA* 88 (2002), 111-20.

39. G. Caton-Thompson, E.W. Gardner, *The Desert Fayum* (London, 1934), 138-40.

40. E. Bresciani, *Egitto e vicino oriente* 20-1 (1997-8), 7-48.

41. J. Bourriau, in S. Quirke (ed.), *Discovering Egypt from the Neva: the Egyptological legacy of Oleg D. Berlev* (Berlin, 2003), 51-9.

42. D. Arnold, *Antike Welt* 22/3 (1991), 154-60.

43. Arnold, *The Pyramid Complex of Senwosret III at Dahshur*.

44. D. Arnold, *Der Pyramidenbezirk des Königs Amenemhet III. in Dahschur/1: Die Pyramide*, AV 53 (Mainz am Rhein, 1987).

45. T. Bagh, *MDAIK* 58 (2002), 29-61.

46. Farid, *ASAE* 58 (1964), 85-98, fig. 4.

47. D. Eigner, in E.C.M. van den Brink (ed.), *The Nile Delta in Transition, 4th-3rd Millennium BC* (Jerusalem, 1992), 69-77.

48. E. Czerny, *Ägypten und Levante* XI (2001), 13-26.

49. S.T. Smith, *Askut in Nubia* (London, 1995), 66-9.

50. S.J. Seidlmayer, *SAK* 28 (2000), 233-42.

51. T. Schneider, *Ausländer in Ägypten während des Mittleren Reiches und der Hyksoszeit, II, Die ausländische Bevölkerung*, ÄAT 42 (Wiesbaden, 2003)

52. This changed in the Second Intermediate Period, from which there are several treasurers certainly coming from foreign (Asian) background.

53. B. Kemp, R. Merrillees, *Minoan Pottery in Second Millennium Egypt* (Mainz, 1980); P. Warren, in W.V. Davies, L. Schofield (eds), *Egypt, the Aegean and the Levant: interconnections in the second millennium BC* (London, 1995), 1-18.

3. Society

1. 'A class (a particular class) is a group of person in a community identified by their position in the whole system of social production, defined above all according to their relationship (primarily in terms of the degree of ownership or control) to the conditions of production (that to say, the means and labour of production) and to other classes .... The individuals constituting a given class may or may not be wholly or partly conscious of their own identity and common interests as a class, and they may or may not feel antagonism towards members of other classes as such' (definition after G.E.M. de Ste Croix, *The Class Struggle in the Ancient Greek World* (London, 1981), 43-4). The defining of classes in Middle Kingdom Egypt is very complicated, as we do not know very much about the ownership of land. Therefore the term 'class' is used in this chapter only very loosely, and is avoided for the 'lower classes'.

2. P. Sorokin, *Social and Cultural Mobility* (New York, 1959); R. Hermann, *Intelligenztheorie* (Hamburg, 1979); P. Bourdieu, *La noblesse d'état* (Paris, 1989), 82-4; M. Hartmann, *Der Mythos von den Leistungseliten* (Frankfurt, 2002).

3. Grajetzki, *Two Treasurers*, 77.

4. Cf. the Heqanakht papyri of the early Twelfth Dynasty: Letter I is written by Heqanakht to his household. It does not start with any special greeting formula. Letter III is written to a high official ('Overseer of Lower Egypt Herunefer') and starts with a long greeting formula; see J.P. Allen, *The Heqanakht Papyri* (New York, 2002), 15-18.

5. Papyrus Prisse column 6, line 11 to column 7, line 3 (E. Dévaud, *Les maximes de Ptahhotep: d'après le Papyrus Prisse, les Papyrus 10371/10435 et 10509 du British museum, et la Tablette Carnarvon* (Fribourg, Suisse, 1916).

6. Kemp, *Ancient Egypt*, 149-80.

7. Kemp, *Ancient Egypt*, 160-3, figs 57-8.

8. J.A. Wilson, *The Burden of Egypt* (Chicago, 1951), 123-4.

9. J.E. Richards, in J. Lustig (ed.), *Anthropology and Egyptology* (Sheffield, 1997), 33-42. Richards examined several Middle Kingdom tombs at Abydos, revealing that certain precious goods were accessible to a large number of people. She observed that some of the richest tombs were simple surface burials, while other poor (intact) burials were placed in more elaborate shafts. She is in opposition to the views of B. Kemp (Kemp, *Ancient Egypt*, 149-80) who saw in the Middle Kingdom a society which was regulated by the state; assuming that there were in a regulated state only rich and poor and no 'middle classes'. However, a look at the European communist states in middle and eastern Europe in the last century reveals that even in highly prescriptive states there was a wide spread of property and wealth. Therefore the observations on Abydos are important, but do not necessarily disprove the Kemp view.

10. Allen, *The Heqanakht Papyri*, 149.

11. S.J. Seidlmayer in *Grab und Totenkult im Alten Ägypten*, ed. H. Guksch (München, 2003), 68.

12. G. Brunton, *Matmar* (London, 1948), 2, 30; Seidlmayer, *Gräberfelder*, 128.

13. T. Säve-Söderbergh, *New Kingdom Pharaonic Sites, the Finds and the Sites*, Scandinavian Joint Expedition to Sudanese Nubia Publications 5 (Copenhagen, 1991).

14. H. Junker, *Bericht über die Grabungen der Akademie der Wissenschaften in Wien auf den Friedhöfen von El-Kubanieh-Süd, Winter 1910-1911* (Wien, 1919); H. Junker, *Bericht über die Grabungen der Akademie der Wissenschaften in Wien auf den Friedhöfen von El-Kubanieh-Nord, Winter 1910-1911* (Wien, 1920).

15. E. Czerny, *Tell el-Dab'a IX, Eine Plansiedlung des frühen Mittleren Reiches* (Wien, 1999).

16. Blackman, *Meir II*, pls VI, XI.

17. 'Slaves' are people who do not own their own labour power and the means of production they employ; 'serfs' are people who own some of their labour power and also some of the means of production they employ. G.A. Cohen, *Karl Marx's Theory of History* (Oxford, 1978).

18. H. Altenmüller, *SAK* 18 (1991), 12.

19. M. Collier, S. Quirke, *The UCL Lahun Papyri: religious, literary, legal, mathematical and medical* (London, 2004).

20. Franke, *Heqaib*, 177, 186.

21. J. Garstang, *El Arábah* (London, 1901), pl. V; J. Baines, in G. Dreyer, J. Osing (eds), *Form und Mass, Festschrift für Gerhard Fecht*, ÄAT 12 (Wiesbaden, 1987), 43-61.

22. Hayes, *A Papyrus of The Late Middle Kingdom*, 87-109; S. Quirke, *The Administration of Egypt in the Late Middle Kingdom* (New Malden, 1990), 147-9.

23. Berlev, *Trudovoe*, 7-27.

24. Berlev, *Trudovoe*, 96-146; but see for possible 'outsiders': O. Berlev, *Obshchestvennye otnosheniia v Egipte epokhi Srednego tsarstva* (Moscow, 1978), 63-73.

25. Translation follows S. Quirke, *Egyptian Literature 1800 BC, questions and readings* (London, 2004), 126.

26. Quirke, *RdÉ* 39 (1988), 83-106.

27. Cf. the discussion: R.B. Parkinson, in A. Loprieno (ed.), *Ancient Egyptian Literature, History and Forms*, Probleme der Ägyptologie 10 (Leiden, 1996), 137-55; and most important, D. Franke, *GM* 167 (1998), 33-48.

28. There is, for example, the term 'man of a town' which has been interpreted as an expression for a man without an administrative title, but with some standing; see S. Quirke, *Zeitschrift für ägyptische Sprache und Altertumskunde* 118 (1991), 141-9. For a different view, see P. Andrassy, *Proceedings of the Seventh International Congress of Egyptologists, Cambridge, 3-9 September 1995*, ed. J.C. Eyre, Orientalia Lovaniensia Analecta 82 (Leuven, 1998), 49-58.

29. For a summary of the problem, see Franke, *GM* 167 (1998), 33-48.

30. Richards, in J. Lustig (ed.), *Anthropology and Egyptology*, 33-42.

31. R. Engelbach, *Harageh* (London, 1923), pl. LIX (tomb register).

32. Collier, Quirke, *Letters*, 115.

33. Leiden 43; Florence 23 (time Amenemhat III, one son of the stela owner is also 'governor'); Cairo CG 20750 (two sons of the stela owner are 'governors', one son is 'overseer of troops'); London BM 577, *Hieroglyphic Texts of the British Museum* 4, pl. 35 (the son is 'overseer of priests' and 'governor').

34. M.A. Murray, *The Tomb of Two Brothers* (Manchester, 1910).

35. The whole matter needs to be researched. Perhaps the sons of the governors are for unknown reason never mentioned with their titles or perhaps this is just an accident of the surviving sources.

36. Cairo CG 20022.

37. Collier, Quirke, *Letters*, 200-1. There is also the possibility that some of these officials belonged to the central government, which was also present in Lahun.

38. W.A. Ward, *Index of Egyptian Administrative and Religious Titles of the Middle Kingdom* (Beirut, 1982), 153, no. 1317.

39. This needs to be researched, but cf. Grajetzki, *Die höchsten Beamten*, 176-7 (where families with mainly scribal titles are listed).

40. Grajetzki, *Two Treasurers*, 46 (the career of the high steward Titi started as 'cupbearer').

41. Quirke, *Administration*, 192.

42. Schneider, *Ausländer in Ägypten während des Mittleren Reiches und der Hyksoszeit, II.*

43. K. Hopkins, *Past and Present* 32 (1965), 20-1.

44. P.R.C. Weaver, *Familia Caesaris, A Social Study of the Emperor's Freedmen and Slaves* (Cambridge 1972), 1: 'They enjoyed a high rate of social advancement, which was often much greater than that of the free born proletariate.'

45. Franke, Doss. 587; H.G. Fischer, *Egyptian Titles of the Middle Kingdom*, 2nd ed, revised and augmented (New York, 1997), frontis.

46. Cairo CG 20145.

47. Franke, Doss. 533.

48. H. Carter, Earl of Carnarvon, *Five Years Explorations at Thebes* (London/New York, 1912), 54-5.

49. Wegner, in M. Bietak, E. Czerny (eds), *Scarabs of the Second Millennium BC from Egypt, Nubia, Crete and the Levant: chronological and historical implications* (Vienna, 2004), 222-7 (Bebi, Hathoraa and Nebetneheh, daughter of Rehuankh; a fourth woman named Ipi has the administrative title 'chamberlain').

50. Allen, *The Heqanakht Papyri*, 107-17.

51. Grajetzki, *Die höchsten Beamten*, 224.

52. 'Ser' might mean all bureaucrats, including the ministers, while 'semer' seems to refer exclusively to the people closest to the king; the officials with ranking titles.

53. Grajetzki, *Die höchsten Beamten*, 232-3.

54. C. Raedler, in R. Gundlach, A. Klug (eds), *Das ägyptische Königtum im Spannungsfeld zwischen Innen- und Außenpolitik im 2. Jahrtausend v. Chr.* (Wiesbaden, 2004), 308.

55. Franke, *Heqaib*, 17-18.

56. Stela Berlin 1204, Lichtheim, *Ancient Egyptian Autobiographies*, 98.

57. Franke, in *Middle Kingdom Studies*, 51-67.

58. G. Posener, *L'Enseignement Loyaliste, sagesse egyptienne du Moyen Empire* (Geneva, 1976), section 2.

59. Trigger, *Ancient Egypt*, 78.

60. The exceptions are some fragments from the tomb of the 'king's son' Amenemhat-ankh, son of Senusret I or Amenemhat II found at Dahshur. No woman is mentioned on these fragments; see Fay, *Louvre Sphinx*, 50-2.

61. Roth, *Königsmütter*, 366, table 2.
62. Ryholt, *Second Intermediate Period*, 38-9.
63. Ryholt, *Second Intermediate Period*, 239-41.
64. Berlin 7288, Grajetzki, *Two Treasurers*, pl. 6.
65. Berlev, *Palestinskij Sbornik* 25/88 (1974), 26-31.
66. Vatican MG 170 (ANOC 65.2).
67. R.J. Leprohon, *JARCE* 33 (1996), 165-71.

Appendix

1. The number of years in a coregency with the successor are in brackets.
2. Ryholt, *Second Intermediate Period*, 71.
3. Ryholt, *Second Intermediate Period*, 285, n. 1031.
4. Ryholt, *Second Intermediate Period*, 337, File 13/3.
5. Ryholt, *Second Intermediate Period*, 340, File 13/17.
6. Ryholt, *Second Intermediate Period*, 340, File 13/16; this Sekhemre-Khutawy is possibly identical with Sekhemre-Khutawy Amenemhat Sobekhotep II, who might have changed parts of his royal titulary.
7. Cylinder seal, Petrie Museum UCL 11532; Ryholt, *Second Intermediate Period*, 403, P/3.
8. List after Grajetzki, *Die höchsten Beamten*, 7-31; for additional discussions for the viziers of the early Middle Kingdom see: J.P. Allen, in N. Strudwick, J.H. Taylor (eds), *The Theban Necropolis* (London, 2003), 21-6.
9. After Grajetzki, *Two Treasurers*.
10. P. Tallet, *RdÉ* 54 (2003), 288-94.
11. P. Tallet, *GM* 193 (2003), 59-64.
12. There is a treasurer Ameny attested on a sarcophaghus found at Tanis, but originally perhaps from Hawara. The sarcophagus might belong to one of the treasurers with this name. A possible third treasurer with the name Ameny is known from a stela found at Abydos. However, the title is only partly preserved. The identification as treasurer at the royal court remains uncertain.
13. B. Gratien, *CRIPEL* 22 (2001), 50, fig. 1.

Further Reading

Bourriau, J., *Pharaohs and Mortals* (Cambridge, 1988).

Beckerath, J. von, *Untersuchungen zur politischen Geschichte der zweiten Zwischenzeit in Ägypten* (Glückstadt, 1964).

Franke, D., *Das Heiligtum des Heqaib auf Elephantine* (Heidelberg, 1994).

Garstang, J., *The Burial Customs of Ancient Egypt as Illustrated by Tombs of the Middle Kingdom* (London, 1907).

Gestermann, L., *Kontinuität und Wandel in Politik und Verwaltung des frühen Mittleren Reiches in Ägypten* (Göttingen, 1987).

Habachi, L., *Elephantine IV, The Sanctuary of Heqaib* (Mainz am Rhein, 1985).

Hayes, W.C., *The Scepter of Egypt I* (New York, 1953).

Matzker, I., *Die letzten Könige der 12. Dynastie* (Frankfurt am Main/ Bern/ New York, 1986).

Obsomer, C., *Sésostris Ier, Etude chronologique et historique du règne* (Brussels, 1995).

Quirke, S. (ed.), *Middle Kingdom Studies* (New Malden, 1991).

Richards, J.E., *Society and Death in Ancient Egypt: mortuary landscapes of the Middle Kingdom* (Cambridge, 2005).

Ryholt, K.S.B., *The Political Situation in Egypt during the Second Intermediate Period c. 1800-1550 BC*, Carsten Niebuhr Institute Publications 20 (Copenhagen, 1997).

Tallet, P., *Sésostris III et la fin de la XIIe dynastie* (Paris, 2005).

Wildung, D., *Sesostris und Amenemhet* (Munich, 1984).

Bibliography

ADAIK = Abhandlungen des Deutschen Archäologischen Instituts, Abteilung Kairo (DAIK), Glückstadt/Mainz

ÄA= Ägyptologische Abhandlungen, Wiesbaden

ÄAT =Ägypten und Altes Testament, Wiesbaden

ANOC = Abydos North Offering Chapel

ASAE = Annales du Service des Antiquités de l'Égypte, Le Caire

ASE = Archaeological Survey of Egypt, London

AV = Archäologische Veröffentlichungen, Mainz

BIFAO = Bulletin de l'Institut Français d'Archéologie Orientale, Le Caire

BiOr = Bibliotheca Orientalis, Leiden

BMMA = Bulletin of the Metropolitan Museum of Art, New York

CAA = Corpus Antiquitatum Aegyptiacarum, Mainz

Cairo CG = Catalogue Générale (of the Egyptian Museum in Cairo)

CRIPEL = Cahier de Recherches de l'Institut de Papyrologie et d'Égyptologie de Lille, Paris

EEF = Egypt Exploration Fund, London

FIFAO = Fouilles de l'Institute Français d'Archéologie Orientale (IFAO) du Caire

GM = Göttinger Miszellen, Göttingen

HÄB = Hildesheimer Ägyptologische Beiträge, Hildesheim

JARCE = Journal of the American Research Center in Egypt, New York

*JEA = Journal of Egyptian Archae*ology, London

JNES = Journal of Near Eastern Studies, Chicago

LD = R. Lepsius, *Denkmaeler aus Aegypten und Aethiopen* (Berlin, 1849-56).

MDAIK = Mitteilungen des Deutschen Archäologischen Instituts Kairo, Mainz

MIFAO = Mémoires publiés par les membres de l'Institut Français d'Archéologie Orientale (IFAO) du Caire, Berlin/Cairo

MMJ = Metropolitan Museum Journal, New York

OBO = Orbis Biblicus et Orientalis, Freiburg/Göttingen

PM = B. Porter, R. Moss, *Topographical Bibliography of Ancient Egyptian Hieroglyphic Texts, Reliefs and Paintings*, 7 vols, 1927-51 (2nd edn: 1960-), Oxford

PSBA = Proceedings of the Society of Biblical Archaeology, London

RdÉ = Revue d'Égyptologie, Paris

SAGA = Studien zur Archäologie und Geschichte Altägyptens, Heidelberg

SAK = Studien zur altägyptischen Kultur, Hamburg

ZÄS = Zeitschrift für ägyptische Sprache und Altertumskunde, Berlin

Abd el-Raziq, M., G. Castel, P. Tallet, V. Ghica, *Les inscriptions d'Ayn Soukhna*, MIFAO 122 (Cairo, 2002).

Allen, J.P., *The Heqanakht Papyri* (New York, 2002).

Arnold, D., *Gräber des Alten und Mittleren Reiches in El-Tarif*, AV 17 (Mainz am Rhein, 1976).

Bibliography

Arnold, D., *The Pyramid Complex of Senwosret III at Dahshur, Architectural Studies* (New York, 2002).

Badawy, A., *A History of Egyptian Architecture, The First Intermediate Period, the Middle Kingdom and the Second Intermediate Period* (Berkeley/ Los Angeles, 1966).

Beckerath, J. von, *Untersuchungen zur politischen Geschichte der zweiten Zwischenzeit in Ägypten* (Glückstadt, 1964).

Berlev, O., *Trudovoe naselenie egipta v epokhu srednego tsarstva* (Moscow, 1972).

Blackman, A.M., *The Rock Tombs of Meir II*, ASE 23 (London, 1915).

Blackman, A.M., *The Rock Tombs of Meir III*, ASE 24 (London, 1915).

Blackman, A.M., *The Rock Tombs of Meir VI*, ASE 29 (London, 1953).

Breasted, J.H., *Ancient Records of Egypt: historical documents from the earliest times to the Persian conquest* I (Chicago, 1906).

Clère, J.J and J. Vandier, *Textes de la première période intermédiaire et de la Xième dynastie*, Bibliotheca Aegyptiaca (Brussels, 1948).

Collier, M. and S. Quirke, *The UCL Lahun Papyri: Letters*, BAR International Series 1083 (Oxford, 2002).

Couyat, J., and P. Montet, *Les inscriptions hieroglyphiques et hieratiques du Ouadi Hammamat* (Cairo, 1912).

Davies, W.V., *A Royal Statue Reattributed*, British Museum occasional papers (London, 1981).

Delange, E., *Catalogue des statues égyptiennes du Moyen Empire* (Paris, 1987).

der Manuelian, P. (ed.), *Studies in Honor of William Kelly Simpson* (Boston, 1996).

Fay, B., *The Louvre Sphinx and Royal Sculpture from the Reign of Amenemhat II* (Mainz am Rhein, 1996).

Franke, Doss. = Franke, Dossier = Franke, *Personendaten aus dem Mittleren Reich*.

Franke, D., *Personendaten aus dem Mittleren Reich (20.-16. Jahrhundert v. Chr.)*, Ägyptologische Abhandlungen 41 (Wiesbaden, 1984).

Franke, D., *Das Heiligtum des Heqaib auf Elephantine*, SAGA 9 (Heidelberg, 1994).

Gardiner, A.H., T.E. Peet and J. Černy, *The Inscriptions of Sinai* II (London, 1955).

Gomaà, F., *Die Besiedlung Ägyptens während des Mittleren Reiches, I. Oberägypten und das Fayyûm* (Wiesbaden, 1986).

Gomaà, F., *Die Besiedlung Ägyptens wahrend des Mittleren Reiches, II. Unterägypten und die angrenzenden Gebiete* (Wiesbaden, 1987).

Grajetzki, W., *Die höchsten Beamten der ägyptischen Zentralverwaltung zur Zeit des Mittleren Reiches*, Achet A 2 (Berlin, 2000).

Grajetzki, W., *Two Treasurers of the Late Middle Kingdom*, BAR International Series 1007 (Oxford, 2001).

Grallert, S., *Bauen – Stiften – Weihen* (Berlin, 2001).

Habachi, L., *Elephantine IV, The Sanctuary of Heqaib* (Mainz am Rhein, 1985).

Hayes, W.C., *The Scepter of Egypt I* (New York, 1953).

Hayes, W.C., *A Papyrus of The Late Middle Kingdom in the Brooklyn Museum* (Brooklyn, 1955).

Helck, W., *Die Prophezeiung des Nfr.tj* (Wiesbaden, 1970).

Hieroglyphic Texts from Egyptian Stelae, etc. in the British Museum, Department of Egyptian and Assyrian Antiquities (London, 1911-).

Hintze, F. and W.F. Reineke, *Felsinschriften aus dem sudanesischen Nubien* (Berlin, 1989).

Jaroš-Deckert, B., *Das Grab des Jnj-jtj-f*, AV 12 (Mainz am Rhein, 1984).

Bibliography

Jequier, G., *Deux pyramides du Moyen Empire*, Fouilles à Saqqarah (Cairo, 1933).

Kemp, B.J., *Ancient Egypt, Anatomy of a Civilization* (London/ New York, 1989).

Kitchen, K.K., *Catalogue of the Egyptian Collection in the National Museum, Rio de Janeiro* (Warminster, 1990).

Lichtheim, M., *Ancient Egyptian Literature, A Book of Readings, I: the Old and the Middle Kingdoms* (Berkeley, Los Angeles/London, 1975).

Lichtheim, M., *Ancient Egyptian Autobiographies, Chiefly of the Middle Kingdom*, OBO 84 (Göttingen, 1988).

Martin, G.T., *Egyptian Administration and Private-Name Seals* (Oxford, 1971).

Middle Kingdom Studies, see Quirke, S. (ed.).

Morgan, J. de, *Catalogue des monuments et inscriptions de l'Égypte antique I* (Vienna, 1894).

Morgan, J. de, *Fouilles à Dahchour, Mars-Juin 1894* (Vienne, 1895).

Naville, E., *The XIth Dynasty Temple at Deir el-Bahari I*, EEF Memoir 13 (London, 1907).

Obsomer, C., *Sésostris Ier, Etude chronologique et historique du règne* (Brussels, 1995).

Petrie, W.M.F., *Abydos II* (London, 1903).

Petrie, W.M.F., G. Brunton and M.A. Murray, *Lahun II* (London, 1922).

Pilgrim, C. von, *Elephantine XVIII, Untersuchungen in der Stadt des Mittleren Reiches und der Zweiten Zwischenzeit*, AV 91 (Mainz am Rhein, 1996).

Polz, D. and A. Seiler, *Die Pyramidenanlage des Königs Nub-Cheper-Re Intef in Dra' Abu el-Naga: ein Vorbericht* (Mainz, 2003).

Quirke, S., *The Administration of Egypt in the Late Middle Kingdom* (New Malden, 1990).

Quirke, S. (ed.) *Middle Kingdom Studies* (New Malden, 1991).

Randall-MacIver, C. and L. Wooley, *Buhen* (Philadelphia, 1911).

Roeder, G., *Debod bis Bab Kalabsche*, 2 vols: *Les temples immergés de la Nubie VI*, 1+2 (Cairo, 1911).

Roque, M.F.B. de la, *Tôd (1934 à 1936)*, FIFAO 17 (Cairo, 1937).

Roth, S., *Die Königsmütter des Alten Ägypten*, ÄAT 46 (Wiesbaden 2001).

Ryholt, K.S.B., *The Political Situation in Egypt during the Second Intermediate Period c. 1800-1550 BC*, Carsten Niebuhr Institute Publications 20 (Copenhagen, 1997).

Sadek, A.I., *The Amethyst Mining Inscriptions of Wadi el-Hudi I, Text* (Warminster, 1980).

Sadek, A.I., *The Amethyst Mining Inscriptions of Wadi el-Hudi II, Additional text, plates* (Warminster, 1980).

Schenkel, W., *Memphis, Herakleopolis, Theben, Die epigraphischen Zeugnisse der 7.-11. Dynastie*, ÄA 12 (Wiesbaden, 1965).

Schneider, T., *Ausländer in Ägypten während des Mittleren Reiches und der Hyksoszeit, II, Die ausländische Bevölkerung*, ÄAT 42 (Wiesbaden, 2003).

Seidlmayer, S.J., *Gräberfelder aus dem Übergang vom Alten zum Mittleren Reich*, SAGA 1 (Heidelberg, 1990).

Seyfried, K.-J., *Beiträge zu den Expeditionen des Mittleren Reiches in die Ost-Wüste*, HÄB 15 (Hildesheim, 1981).

Simpson, W.K., *The Terrace of the Great God at Abydos: the Offering Chapels of Dynasties 12 and 13* (New Haven/ Philadelphia, 1974).

Smith, W.S., *The Art and Architecture of Ancient Egypt*, revised with additions by William Kelly Simpson (Harmondsworth/ New York/ Ringwood/ Markham/ Auckland, 1981).

Bibliography

Stewart, H.M., *Egyptian Stelae, Reliefs and Paintings from the Petrie Collection* II (Warminster, 1979).

Studies in Honor of William Kelly Simpson, see der Manuelian, P. (ed.).

Trigger, B.G., B.J. Kemp, D. O'Connor and A.B. Lloyd, *Ancient Egypt, A Social History* (Cambridge, 1983).

Wildung, D., *Sesostris und Amenemhet* (Munich, 1984).

Willems, H., *Chests of Life* (Leiden, 1988).

Žaba, Z., *The Rock Inscriptions of Lower Nubia* (Prague, 1974).

Illustration Sources

Plates

I. Cairo Egyptian Museum CG 415; from H. Evers, *Staat aus dem Stein, Denkmäler, Geschichte und Bedeutung der ägyptischen Plastik während des Mittleren Reichs*, München 1929, pl. 29.
II. Cairo Egyptian Museum; photo: Grajetzki. Compare W.M. Flinders Petrie, G.A. Wainwright, E. Mackay, *The Labyrinth, Gerzeh and Mazghuneh*, London 1912, p. 30.
III. Cairo Egyptian Museum CG 394; after J.H. Breasted, *Geschichte Aegyptens*, Stuttgart 1936, pl. 98.
IV. Petrie Museum UC 13202; photo © Petrie Museum, University College London.
V. Cairo Egyptian Museum CG 42034; photo: Grajetzki.
VI. Cairo Egyptian Museum JE 46307; photo: Grajetzki.
VII. Petrie Museum UC 8253; photo © Petrie Museum, University College London.
VIII. Cairo Egyptian Museum CG 409; photo: Grajetzki.
IX. Photo © Römisch-Germanisches Museum, Mainz O 2585, photo: Sabine Hölper.
X. Cairo Egyptian Museum CG 28033; photo: Grajetzki.
XI. Photo © Petrie Museum, University College London. Compare W.M. Flinders Petrie, *Gizeh and Rifeh*, London 1907, pp. 12-13.
XII. Photo © Petrie Museum, University College London.
XIII. Photo © Petrie Museum, University College London.
XIV. Photo © Petrie Museum, University College London.
XV. Photo: Grajetzki.
XVI. Photo: Grajetzki.
XVII. Photo © Petrie Museum, University College London.
XVIII. Photo © Petrie Museum, University College London.
XIX. Copenhagen Ny Carlsberg Glyptotek ÆIN 1539; photo © Petrie Museum, University College London).
XX. Photo © Petrie Museum, University College London.
XXI. Photo © Petrie Museum, University College London.
XXII. Photo © Petrie Museum, University College London.
XXIII. Metropolitan Museum of Art, New York 16.1.3; photo © Petrie Museum, University College London.

Figures

1, 5, 6, 14, 17, 21, 24, 25, 35, 38, 39, 41 are by the author.

2. G. Roeder, *Debod bis Bab Kalabsche*, 2 vols: *Les temples immergés de la Nubie VI*, 1+2, Cairo 1911, pl. 120a.
3. After Werner Kaiser, Martin Bommas, Horst Jaritz, Achim Krekeler, Cornelius v. Pilgrim, Michael Schultz, Tyede Schmitz-Schultz, Martin Ziermann, 'Stadt

und Tempel von Elephantine. 19./20. Grabungsbericht', *MDAIK* 49 (1993), 133-87.

4. W.M. Flinders Petrie, *Koptos*, London 1896, pl. X.

7. After S. Seidlmayer, in K.A. Bard (ed.), *Encyclopedia of the Archaeology of Ancient Egypt*, London/ New York 1999, 154, fig. 14.

8. After von Pilgrim, *Elephantine XVIII*, fig. 48.

9. PM V, 238-9.

10. De Morgan, *Cat. des Mon. I*, fig. on 155.

11. After K. Michalowski, Ch. Desroches, J. de Linage, J. Manteuffel, M. Ejmoejmis, *Tell Edfou 1939*, Cairo 1950, 91, fig. 52.

12. After Allen, *The Heqanakht Papyri*, pl. 1.

13. After L. Gabolde, 'Le "grand château d'Amon" de Sésostris Ier à Karnak: la décoration du temple d'Amon-Rê au Moyen Empire', *Mémoires de l'Académie des Inscriptions et Belles-Lettres, N.S.* 17, Paris 1998.

15. After J. Wegner, *Ägypten und Levante* X, 2000, 87, fig. 2.

16. After Wegner, in *Scarabs of the Second Millennium BC from Egypt, Nubia, Crete and the Levant:* M. Bietak, E. Czerny (eds), Vienna 2004, 224, fig. 2.

18. H. Steckeweh, *Die Fürstengräber von Qaw*, Leipzig 1936, frontispiece.

19. G. Brunton, *Qau and Badari III*, London 1930, pl. IV.

20. After Badawy, *A History of Egyptian Architecture II*, fig. 56.

22. P. Montet, *Kêmi* I (1928), 53-68, pl. II.

23. After Willems, *Chests of Life*, 87.

26. After D. Arnold, *Lexikon der ägyptischen Baukunst*, Düsseldorf 2000, fig. on 154.

27. Burial found at Qasr as-Saga (no. 31), late Middle Kingdom (reconstructed from the description in the publication).

28. After Badawy, *A History of Egyptian Architecture II*, fig. 76.

29. After D. Arnold, *The Pyramid Complex of Senusret I, South Cemeteries of Lisht III*, New York 1992, 54-57, pls 66-9.

30. After F. Arnold, in M. Bietak (ed.), *Haus und Palast im Alten Ägypten*, Wien 1996, plan 1.

31. Information from R. Stadelmann, N. Alexanian, *MDAIK* 54, 1998, 293-317.

32. After de Morgan, *Dahchour I*, 17, fig. 19.

33. After M. Bietak, *Tell el-Dab'a II, Der Fundort im Rahmen einer archäologisch-geographischen Untersuchung über das Ägyptische Ostdelta*, Vienna 1975, 161, fig. 33.

34. After M. Bietak, J. Dorner, *Ägypten und Levante* VIII (1998), 15, fig. 4.

36. W.M.F. Petrie, *Illahun, Kahun and Gurob*, London 1891, pl. XIV

37. After E. Czerny, *Tell el-Dab'a IX, Eine Plansiedlung des frühen Mittleren Reiches*, Wien 1999, 21.

40. After J. Wegner, *MDAIK* 57, 2001, 281-308, fig. 5.

Index

Aashyt (queen) 90, 176
Abdju, *see* Abydos
Abgig 41, 119
Abisko 20
Abu (Elephantine) 80
Abu Ghalib 129
Abu Handal 31, 33
Abu Simbel 27
Abukir 61
Abusir 125
Abydos 10, 13, 14, 20, 21, 24, 32, 36,
    38, 40, 43, 44, 47, 48, 55-7, 69, 71,
    72, 94-6, 131, 156, 157, 173, 187
Adj-zehui (treasurer) 174
Aegean 47, 92
Africa 84
Africanus (Christian writer) 2, 3
Ahanakht I (governor) 110, 172
Ahanakht II (governor) 110
Ahmose (king) 18
Akhiatef 147
Akhmim 97, 98
Amenemhat (father of official) 146
Amenemhat (governor) 42, 113
Amenemhat (royal sealer and
    governor) 43, 172
Amenemhat (vizier) 26, 172
Amenemhat I (king) 24-36, 38, 40, 42,
    44, 48, 77, 91, 92, 105, 110, 113,
    121, 123-5, 133, 169, 172, 173, 178
Amenemhat II (king) 28, 36, 43, 45-8,
    85, 99, 101, 108, 109, 114, 115, 121,
    125, 126, 127, 136, 146, 162, 169,
    172, 174, 179, 189
Amenemhat III (king) 51, 52, 55, 57-9,
    62, 65, 66, 70, 74, 85, 101, 102, 107,
    109, 111, 116, 118, 119, 126, 127,
    129, 169, 172, 174, 180, 186, 188,
    Pls. II, III
Amenemhat Intef Ameny 67
Amenemhat IV (king) 58, 59, 61, 62,
    119, 156, 160

Amenemhat Renseneb (king) 68, 170
Amenemhat Sobekhotep, *see*
    Sobekhotep II
Amenemhat V 67, 73, 171; *see also*
    Sekhemkare
Amenemhat-ankh ('king's son') 36,
    162, 189
Amenhotep (treasurer) 46, 174
Amenhotep I ('king's son') 72
Amenhotep III (king) 22
Amenu-sekhem 47
Ameny ('great one of the tens of
    Upper Egypt') 52
Ameny ('herald') 43
Ameny ('king's son') 36, 45, 114, 162
Ameny ('overseer of
    marshland-dwellers') 46
Ameny (official) 146
Ameny (treasurer) 60, 174, 190
Ameny (vizier) 60, 172, 173
Ameny Qemau (king) 64, 67, 128, 171
Ameny-seneb (governor) 86, 87, 133
Ameny-seneb (treasurer) 174
amethyst 26, 43, 74
Amun 15, 36, 38, 89, 91
Andjeti (nome) 130
Aniba 135
Ankh-Amenemhat 59
Ankhet (woman) 123
Ankhkhnumre (king), *see* Zegerzenti
Ankhtyfy (governor) 7
Ankhu ('overseer of fields') 55, 66, 67,
    163
Ankhu (governor) 85, 86
Ankhu (vizier) 68, 69, 73, 147, 158,
    162, 173
annal stone 45, 47, 172
Anu (governor) 105
Anubis 13, 105
Arabian Gulf 54
Armant 20, 24, 41, 46, 56, 79, 92, 102,
Arnold, Dieter 89

199

Artapanus (Jewish author) 72, 73
Asia (Asiatics) 19, 20, 22, 25, 31, 32,
    46, 54, 60, 64, 69, 73, 133, 136, 146,
    147
Aswan 31, 48, 80, 108, 134, 172
Asyut 8, 9, 34, 42, 97, 103, 105, 150
el-Atawla (Atfet, per-Nemty) 41, 103
Atfet 103
Atfih 117, 121
Athribis (Kem-wer) 130
Atum 71, 130
Auibre Hor (king) 64, 68, 73, 128, 171
Auitibre 170
Avaris, *see* Tell el-Dab'a
Ayn Soukhna 25, 26, 29, 33, 60

Bab el-Kalabsha 27
Badari 23, 28, 98, 144, 149
bak (servant) 147, 148
Baket I (governor) 112
Baket II (governor) 112
Baket III (governor) 112, 113
Balansura 104
Baset, *see* Bubastis
Bastet 32, 131
Bat 94
Batiu (Bayt) 94
Bebi (vizier) 22, 172
Bebi (woman) 189
Behedet (Delta) 130
Behedet, *see* Edfu
Beirut 61
Ben 20
Beni Hasan 21, 34, 35, 36, 42, 97-9,
    101, 102, 104, 107, 110, 111-16,
    150, 160, 162
Benu 131
Berlin 162
Berlin leather roll 36
Biahmu 59, 117, 119
Bilifya 41
'Book of the Two Ways' 110, 111
boundary stela 42
Brooklyn Museum 149, 173, 174
Brunton, Guy 144
Buau Mentuhotep (steward) 22
Bubastis 32, 41, 59, 131
Buhen 20, 42, 43, 71, 72, 74, 134, 135
Busiris (Djedu) 130
But, *see* Qattah
Buto 78, 130

Byblos 54, 57, 61, 71, 134, 136

Cairo 11, 40, 117, 130, 155
Cairo Egyptian Museum CG 394: Pl.
    III; CG 415: Pl. I; CG 20022: 189;
    CG 20145: 189; CG 20516: 33; CG
    20394: 163; CG 20750: 188; CG
    28033: Pl. X; JE 46307: Pl. VI
Canaanite 69
Chenephres, *see* Sobekhotep IV
Christ's thorn tree 97
Copenhagen Ny Carlsberg Glyptotek
    ÆIN 1539: Pl. XIX
copper 20, 46
Crete 134, 136

Dabod 47
Dagi (vizier) 22, 24, 90
Dahshur 46, 48, 51, 52, 54, 55, 57, 58,
    60, 63, 64, 67, 95, 117, 118, 121,
    125, 126, 161, 174
Dakla oasis 77
Dal 53
Dara 7
Dedetamen 163
Dedetanuqet ('king's daughter') 70
Dedumont Senebtyfy (vizier) 173
Dedusobek (official) 162
Deir el-Bahri 20-3, 56, 58, 89, 92, 172
Deir el-Ballas 20, 93
Deir el-Bersheh 34, 97, 104, 107,
    109-11, 115, 150, 172
Delta 9, 64, 72, 73, 75, 78, 129, 135,
    143
Denderah 11, 12, 16, 19, 20, 21, 93
Dep (Buto) 78, 130
Diospolis Parva, *see* Hiu
Dja, *see* Medinet Maadi
Djari (official) 13
Djeba, *see* Edfu
Djedet, *see* Mendes
Djedkheperu (king) 170, 173
Djed-ptah/Dedtuseneb (vizier) 173
Djed-sut (sa-ra-Teti) 125
Djedu, *see* Busiris
Djefa-Amenemhat 46
Djefa-Hapi I (governor) 42
Djefa-Hapi II (governor) 42
Djehuty-nakht (governor) 111
Djehuty-nakht VI (governor) 110
Djer (king) 94

Djerti, *see* Tod
djet-people (serfs) 147
Djoser (king) 46, 57
Dublin 71; UC 1360: 184

Edfu 35, 41, 79, 86-8, 130
Elephantine 11, 14-16, 20, 24, 37,
    42-4, 52, 59, 67, 73, 79-81, 83-7,
    145, 147
Elkab 20, 59, 70, 79, 88
'Eloquent Peasant' (work of literature)
    9, 84, 141, 142
Engelbach, Reginald 150
Esna 41, 79, 89
Ethiopia 77
Eusebius (Christian writer) 2
Ezbet Rushdi 132

famine 13, 42
Fadrus 144
Farras 135
Fayum 30, 41, 49, 57, 58, 60, 119
Florence 2540 A+B 42
fortress 42, 52, 53, 72

Gebelein 12, 19, 20, 34, 79, 89
Gebel Zeit 67, 68
Gebtu, *see* Koptos
Geregtawy (king), *see* Intef
Gizeh 117, 125
gold 20, 56, 61, 93, 156
'great enclosure' 148, 149
Gurob 144

Haankhef ('god's father') 71
Haankhef ('king's son') 71
Haankhef Iykhernefret ('king's son') 72
Hapidjefa I (governor) 105-7, 142
Hapidjefa II (governor) 106, 107
Hapidjefa III (governor) 107
Hapidjefa IV (governor) 107
Hapy 109
Harageh 116-18, 150
Harakhte (god) 40, 94
Hathor 18, 59, 89, 94, 107, 109, 129,
    136
Hathoraa (woman) 189
Hat-mehit (nome) 133
Hatnub 18, 43, 49, 104, 109, 172
Hatshepsut ('king's daughter') 163
Hatshepsut (ruling queen) 58, 62

Hawara 51, 55, 58, 60, 62, 63, 116-18,
    121, 190
Hekenmaat, *see* Amenemhat II
Heliopolis 14, 36, 40, 41, 47, 61, 130,
    131
Helwan 117, 131
hem nisut ('servant of the king') 147,
    148
hemet (female servant) 147, 148
Henenu (steward) 19, 22, 24, 90
Henhenet (queen) 176
Heny (deputy governor) 153
Heqa-andju (nome) 130
Heqaib (governor) 84
Heqaib I (governor) 84
Heqaib II (governor) 85, 86
Heqaib III (governor) 86
Heqaib sanctuary 11, 16, 82, 84, 85,
    102
Heqaib-ankh (governor) 86
Heqanakht papyri 142, 157
Heracleopolis 8, 9, 13, 22, 47, 56, 59,
    62, 84, 87, 98, 116
Herfu (treasurer) 174
Hermoupolis (Khemenu) 47, 104, 109,
    172
Herodotus 54
Herunefer (official) 187
Heryshef 116
Hesebu (nome) 130
Hetep (official) 125
Hetepibre (king) 67
Hetepibre Qemau-Sa-Horndjitef
    (king) 67, 171
Hetepkare (king) 170
Hetep-Senusret, *see* Lahun
Hetepti ('king's mother') 58, 61
Hetepti (official) 13
Hieraconpolis 14, 41, 56, 79
high steward 21, 26, 34, 35, 48, 54, 56,
    57, 74
Hiu 93, 94
Hor (high steward) 44
Horemkhauef (governor) 89
Horhotep (governor) 89
Hori (vizier) 173
Horus 15, 42, 62, 88, 89, 91, 130
Hotep-ka-Sobekotep 72
Hut-Ihyt 129
Hut-Sekhem, *see* Hiu
Hut-Waret (Avaris), *see* Tell el-Dab'a

Huy-imenti (nome) 130
Hyksos 64, 132

Iabti (nome) 131
Iah ('king's mother') 18
Iantin (governor of Byblos) 71
Iasy 46
Ibi (king) 7
Ibiau ('deputy treasurer') 72
Ibiau (vizier) 173
Ibt (treasurer) 174
Ibu (governor) 99, 101
Ihy (official) 125
Ihyseneb 146, 147
Ikkur 135
Imau, *see* Kom el-Hisn
Imentet (nome) 129
Imet, *see* Nebesheh
Imi ('king's mother') 25
In (king), *see* Qakare
Indian Ocean 54
Ineb-hedj (nome and town) 121, 124
Input (nome) 114, 116
Inpy ('overseer of the gateway') 51,
    117, 118
Inrety, *see* Gebelein
'Instruction of King Amenemhat I for
    his Son Senusret I' 28, 31, 33, 165
Intef ('god's father') 22
Intef (high steward) 44
Intef (king, 13th Dynasty) 69, 170, 171
Intef (local governors) 10, 12, 97
Intef (Nubian king) 27, 169
Intef (official) 19
Intef ('overseer of troops') 19, 22, 90
Intef (treasurer) 34, 173
Intef I (king) 11-13, 15
Intef II (king) 10, 11, 12, 13, 14, 15,
    19, 21
Intef III (king) 10, 11, 15, 16, 19, 59,
    162
Intefiqer (official) 31
Intefiqer (vizier) 27, 31, 34, 43, 91,
    159, 172, 178
Ipi (treasurer) 34, 173
Ipi (vizier) 34, 90
Ipi (woman) 189
Ipu, *see* Akhmim
Iqen, *see* Mirgissa
Iqer 93
Irer 151

Isis 94
Ita ('king's daughter') 45
Itakayt ('king's daughter') 36
Ita-weret ('king's daughter') 45
Iti (woman) 174
Iti-ib (local governor) 9
Itj-tawy 29, 30, 31, 44, 64, 68, 89, 121,
    124, 125, 134
Iuai 46
Iufni (king) 67
Iuhetibu ('king's daughter') 70
Iuhetibu ('king's mother') 70
Iu-nefer ('overseer of storerooms') 55
Iunu, *see* Heliopolis
Iunyt, *see* Esna
Iwy (vizier) 173
Iy ('king's wife') 68, 162
Iy (official) 174
Iy-ib-khenti-re (king), *see* Intef
Iykhernefret (treasurer) 55, 60, 159,
    174
Iymeru ('controller of the broad hall')
    74
Iymeru (official) 162
Iymeru (vizier) 173
Iymeru Neferkare (vizier) 72-4, 173
Izi (local god) 88
Izi (treasurer) 174

ka-house (chapel) 14, 24, 93
Karnak 10, 15, 36, 38, 42, 43, 56, 67,
    72, 74, 173
Kawit (queen) 90, 176
Kemeni 147
Kemeteni 147
Kemi ('king's daughter') 71
Kemi ('king's mother') 71
Kemi-nub (queen) 45, 46
Kemni (official) 61
Kemsit (queen) 90, 176
Kem-wer (nome) 130
Kem-wer, *see* Athribis
Kerma 60, 135
Khaankhre, *see* Sobekhotep I
Khabau (king) 173
Khahetepre, *see* Sobekhotep V
Kha-kau-Re ('king's son') 48, 49
Khakaure, *see* Senusret III
Khakaure-seneb (governor) 87
Khanferre, *see* Sobekhotep IV
Khasekhemre, *see* Neferhotep I

Kha-Senusret 41
Khasuu (nome) 130
Khatana 32
Khedjer ('king's son') 69
Khelua 117, 121
Khem 129
Khema (governor) 84
Khemenu, *see* Hermoupolis
Khendjer (king) 65, 69, 126, 170, 171
Khenmes (vizier) 173
Khenmet ('king's daughter') 45-7
Khenmet-nefer-hedjet-Weret I (queen)
    48, 51, 52, 127
Khenmet-nefer-hedjet-Weret II
    (queen) 127, 181
Khen-Nekhen 13, 78
Khenty-Iabti (nome) 131
Khenty-khety 130
Khenty-khety-em-sauef Seneb
    (treasurer) 174, Pl. XIX
Khenty-khety-wer ('overseer of the
    gateway') 47, 48
Kheperka (treasurer) 174
Kheperkare, *see* Senusret I
Khepesh (nome) 129
Khesu-wer (official) 129
khetem 83
Khety (governor) 107, 112
Khety (kings) 8, 13, 14
Khety ('overseer of sealers') 20
Khety ('overseer of the quarry') 22, 24,
    25
Khety (treasurer) 22, 23, 90, 173
Khety (vizier) 60, 146, 172
Khety I (governor) 9
Khety II (governor) 9
Khety-ankh (governor) 131
Khnem-sut-Kheperkare 41
Khnum 82, 102, 121
Khnum-aa (governor) 102
Khnumhotep (governor of
    Elephantine) 87
Khnumhotep (III) (vizier) 54, 56, 57,
    115, 128, 160, 161, 172
Khnumhotep I (governor) 32, 113, 114
Khnumhotep II (governor) 113-15, 152
Khnumhotep IV (governor) 113, 115
Khui (king) 7, 8
Khusobek (officer) 54, 135, 147
Khutawyre, *see* Wegaf
al-Kom al-Ahdar 130

al-Kom al-Ahmar, *see* Hieraconpolis
Kom el-Hisn 129
Kom Ombo 41, 80
Königsnovelle 40
Koptos 15, 24, 32, 35, 36, 38, 39, 92,
    93, 162
Kor 135
Korosko 31, 38
Krokodilopolis, *see* Shedyt
Kuban 135
al-Kubaniya 80, 81

Kumma 53, 60, 135
Kush (also Kash; Upper Nubia) 42,
    46, 52, 53, 114

Labyrinth 59, 62, 63, 118
Lahun 49, 51, 52, 58, 59, 92, 95,
    116-18, 121, 139-41, 146, 150, 151,
    153, 161, 165, 174
'Laments of Ipuwer' 144
Lebanon 136
Libya 31, 134
Libyan desert 77
Libyans 20, 31, 32, 94
Lisht 25, 26, 30, 34, 35, 36, 41, 44, 46,
    47, 57, 59, 117, 121, 122, 123, 172-4
Liverpool 69
London Petrie Museum: UC 8253: Pl.
    VII; UC 13202: Pl. IV; UC 32203:
    150; UC 42034: Pl. VI
London, British Museum 60, 85, 173;
    EA 428: 184; EA 577: 189; EA 614:
    175; EA 1203: 176
Louvre 62; Louvre C1: 33
'Loyalist Teaching' 45, 160

Maakherure, *see* Amenemhat IV
Madu, *see* Medamud
magical wands 115
Ma-Hedj (nome) 111
Manetho 2, 3, 54, 72, 164
Mari 137
mastaba 1, 22, 35, 50, 51, 56, 73, 118,
    172
Matariya 40
Matmar 98, 103, 144, 149
Mayanarti 135
Mayt (royal woman) 176
Mazghuneh 67, 125, 126, 128
Medamud 36, 68, 70, 92

Medinet el-Fayum 58, 62; *see also* Shedyt
Medinet Maadi 59, 61, 117, 119, 120
Medjay (Nubian tribe) 31, 84, 94
Meir 32, 35, 97, 101, 102, 104, 107, 146, 150, 152
Meketre (treasurer) 22, 26, 34, 35, 157, 173
'member of the elite' (title) 21, 26
Memphis 7, 17, 22, 23, 25, 30, 35, 47, 59, 64, 72, 74, 118, 124, 125, 128, 129
Menat-Khufu 57, 111-15
Mendes 133
Menes (king) 18
Menet ('king's daughter') 52
Men-merut, *see* Neferhotep I
Men-nefer 124
Mentiu (tribe) 54, 60
Mentuhotep ('god's father') 70
Mentuhotep ('king's son') 176
Mentuhotep (officer) 70
Mentuhotep ('overseer of the double granary') 42
Mentuhotep (treasurer) 36, 38, 40, 44, 45, 92, 122, 174
Mentuhotep II (king) 8-11, 17-25, 27, 29, 68, 88, 89, 92-5, 110, 169, 172, 173, 176
Mentuhotep III (king) 12, 17, 18, 22, 23, 25, 29, 30, 90-2, 95, 169
Mentuhotep IV (king) 25-9, 169, 172
Mentuhotep-aa (king) 11, 12, 169
Menu (nome) 97
Menu-hotep (vizier) 173
Merenre (king) 14, 52
Mereret ('king's daughter') 52, 127
Meresger (queen) 52
Merestekhi ('king's sister') 66
Mermesha (king) 69, 170, 171
Merneferre Iy (king) 64, 74, 170, 171
Meru ('overseer of sealers') 90
Mery ('sealer under charge') 43
Merykare (king) 8, 9
Merykau (treasurer) 47, 174
meryt-people (serfs) 147, 148
Mesehti (governor) 105
Meshy 147
Meydum 117
Min 32, 38, 92
Mirgissa (Iqen) 52, 71, 134, 135, 174

Moalla 7, 89
Mont 24, 41, 46, 68, 89, 92
Moses 72
Mostagedda 98, 103, 144, 149
mummy mask 80

Naga ed-Deir 97, 144
Nakht (governor) 113, 114, 186
Nakht (high steward) 44
Nakht (treasurer) 105
Nakht-ankhu (governor) 102, 103
Nakhti (governor) 101
Nakhtnebtepnefer, *see* Intef III
Naqada, *see* Nubt
Naret-khentet (nome) 116
Naret-resyt (nome) 130
Near East 1
Nebankh ('high steward') 74, 162
Nebesheh 131
Nebetiunet ('king's daughter') 72
Nebetmeheh (woman) 189
Nebhepetre, *see* Mentuhotep II
Nebit (vizier) 56, 128, 172
Nebkaure (king) 8
Nebnun, *see* Semenkare
Nebpu-Senusret (official) 60
Nebsenet 163
Nebsumenu (treasurer) 174
Nebsumenu (vizier) 173
Nebtawre, *see* Mentuhotep IV
Nebuau 41
Nebui (official) 155
Nebyt (Kom Ombo) 79, 80, 87
Nedjemibre (king) 67, 170
Nedjesankh/Iew (official) 163
Nedjfit (nome) 107
Nedjfit-Khentet (nome) 103
Neferhotep I (king) 64, 70-4, 87, 136, 155, 161, 162, 170, 171, 174, 184
Neferitatenen ('king's mother') 36
Nefer-khnum (governor) 102
Neferty (priest) 29
Neferu (name of several kings' mothers) 12, 13, 15, 162
Neferu (wife of Mentuhotep II) 18
Neferu (wife of Senusret I) 36, 45
Neferukau (queen) 15
Neferukayt (queen) 15
Neferu-Ptah ('king's daughter') 58, 70, 118
Nefret (mother of Amenemhat I) 29

Nefret (queen) 163
Nefret-henut (queen) 52
Nefrusi 111
Neheri (governor) 110, 113, 171
Neheri II (governor) 110
Nehesy (king) 73
Nehy ('soldier of the town') 71
Neith 130
Nekhbet (goddess) 13, 18, 88
Nekheb, *see* Elkab
Nekhen (nome and town) 13, 79, 88, 154
nemes headdress 62, 63, 97
Nemty 41, 103
Neni 70
Nen-nisut, *see* Heracleopolis
Nerikare 68, 170
Nesmont ('high steward') 56-7
Nesmont ('overseer of troops') 32
Netjernakht (governor) 114
Netjerui (nome) 92
New York, Metropolitan Museum 16.1.3: Pl. XXIII
Nimaa(t)re, *see* Khendjer
Nimaatre, *see* Amenemhat III
Nitokris 61
Nubhetepti (queen) 162
Nubhetepti-khered ('king's daughter') 73-4, 128
Nubia 1, 20, 27, 31, 33, 42, 43, 47, 52, 53, 60, 62, 65, 71, 72, 84, 85, 114, 133, 145
Nubians 20, 80, 27, 28, 47, 52, 53, 80, 84, 134, 135
Nubkaure, *see* Amenemhat II
Nubkaure-nakht, *see* Sarenput II
Nubt 93

oasis 71, 77, 84
obelisk 36, 41
obsidian 61
Ombos 93
Osiris 38, 40, 50, 60, 71, 72, 94, 95, 97, 130
Osiris-Khenty-amentiu 15, 24, 38, 43, 55, 56, 122

Paenhapy (governor) 111
palace façade 44, 98, 118
Palestine 19, 45, 65, 73, 115, 132, 133, 136

papyrus Boulaq 18: 68, 69, 92, 153, 159, 162, 173
Pe (Buto) 78, 130
Pepy II (king) 7, 74
Per-Nemty, *see* el-Atawla
Petrie, W.M. Flinders 50, 99
pottery style 44, 57
'Prophecy of Neferty' 2, 28, 29, 31, 45
Ptah 72, 122
Ptahwenenef (official) 146
Ptolemies (kings) 2
Punt 24, 93
pyramid 7, 8, 30, 36, 41, 43-50, 55, 58, 63, 64, 67, 116, 121, 123

Qakare (king) 27
Qantir 24
Qasr as-Sagha 117, 119, 120
Qattah 129
Qaw 23, 28, 98, 100, 144, 149, 153
Qaw el-Kebir 42, 97, 99, 100-3, 111
Qemau-Sa-Horndjitef, *see* Hetepibre Qemau-Sa-Horndjitef
Qemeny (vizier) 172
Qift, *see* Koptos
Qis 107
Qubbet el-Hawa 42, 84-6
al-Qusiya, *see* Qis

Ra-Henu, *see* Wadi Hammamat
Ramses II (king) 22, 45
Ramushenty (governor) 112, 113
Re 7, 15, 130
Red Sea 93
Redienptah (treasurer) 174
Redi-ui-Khnum (steward) 16
Rehuerdjersen 47, 174
Reisner Papyri 97, 172
Renenutet 61, 119
Renesres 155
Renseneb 96, 156
Renseneb, *see* Amenemhat Renseneb
Resseneb (vizier) 173
Retjenu (South Palestine) 54
Rifeh 98, 102, 103, 107, 152
Riqqeh 117, 121
Rome 155

Sadeh 176
Saff el-Baqar 16
Saff el-Dawaba 12

Saff el-Kisasija 15
saff-tomb 12, 15, 16, 17, 89, 90
Sahathor ('king's son') 72, 170, 171
Sahathor 46
as-Salamiya 92
Samont (official) 60
Samont ('scribe of the royal document') 48
Samont (vizier) 172, 173
Sankhkare, *see* Mentuhotep III
Saqqara 8, 30, 46, 62, 67, 69, 117, 118, 125
Sarenput I (local governor), 42, 84-6, 147
Sarenput II (local governor) 84
Sasatet (official) 53
Satet 14, 15, 16, 37, 80
Sathathor ('king's daughter') 52, 127
Sathathoriunet ('king's daughter') 50
Sathathormeryt 46
'Satire of Trades' (work of literature) 148
Satre (mother of Khety) 20
Sau (Sais) 130
Saut, *see* Asyut
scarab 70, 71, 101, 136, 173, 174
Schiaparelli, Ernesto 99
Scythians 54
seal impression 71, 86, 96, 173, 174
seal, *see* scarab
Seankhibre (king) 67, 170, 171
Seankhibtawy, *see* Mentuhotep II
Sebat ('king's daughter') 36
sed festival 22, 26, 34, 38, 43, 55, 59, 131
Sedjefakare Kay-Amenemhat (king) 68, 170, 171
Sedment 23, 28
Sehel 52, 56, 70, 71, 81
Seherutawy, *see* Intef I
Sehetepibre (king) 67, 170
Sehetepibre (official) 146
Sehetepibre, *see* Amenemhat I
Sehetepibtawy, *see* Amenemhat I
Sehetepkare (king, 13th Dynasty), *see* Intef
Sekhamaat 51
Sekhemkare (king) 66, 67, 170, 173
Sekhemre-Khutawy (king, cf. Sobekhotep II) 65, 66, 170, 171, Pl. IV

Sekhemre-Sewadjtawy, *see* Sobekhotep III
Sekhem-Sobeknofru 63
Sekhet-ad 133
Sekhet-hemat (Wadi an-Natrun) 77
Sekmen 54
Sema, *see* Amenemhat I
Semenkare 67, 163, 170
Semitic 69, 73
Semna 52, 53, 60, 61, 72, 134, 135
Sen-ankh (treasurer) 52, 174
Seneb (treasurer) 174
Seneb… (queen) 69
Senebef (treasurer) 174
Senebhenas (queen) 70
Senebi (treasurer) 71, 74, 174, 184
Senebi I (governor) 32, 108
Senebi II (governor) 108
Senebni (official) 155
Senebsen (queen) 71
Senebsimai ('king's sister') 162
Senebsumai (treasurer) 69, 71, 117, 159, 174
Senebtyfy 71
Senebtysy 71, 122, 147
Senefertawyf, *see* Qakare
Senen 147
Senet 91, 172
Senet-senebtysy ('king's daughter') 52, 125
Senitef ('overseer of the chamber') 48
Senusret (treasurer) 174
Senusret (vizier) 43, 172
Senusret I (king) 25, 28, 30, 31, 33, 34, 36-44, 46, 48, 53, 69, 78, 88, 91, 92, 95, 99, 105, 106, 111, 119, 121, 131, 134, 135, 147, 152, 169, 172, 174, 189, Pl. I
Senusret II (king) 48-51, 58, 59, 102, 110, 116, 117, 156, 164, 169, 172, 179, Pls. XV, XVI
Senusret III (king) 32, 51-7, 66, 68, 85, 92, 95-7, 101, 109-11, 115, 118, 123, 126, 127, 132, 134-6, 165, 169, 172, 174
Senusret-ankh (official) 122
Senusret-ankh (vizier) 172
Senusret-seneb-wer ('king's son') 48
Serabit el-Khadim 59, 136
serf 148, 149, 188
Serra East 135

servant 148
Seshemtawy, *see* Senusret II
Sesostris, *see* Senusret
Seth (king) 70, 93, 170
Setiu (Asiatics) 60
Sety I (king) 10
Sewadjkare 67, 170
Sha 102
Shalfak 135
Shas-hotep 102
Shat er-Rigal 22
ash-Shatb 102
Shedyt 59, 62, 117, 119
Sherit (queen) 52, 181
Siese (treasurer) 47, 125, 174
silver 47, 56, 92, 118
Sinai 25, 32, 33, 47, 56, 59, 61, 135, 136
Sinuhe (official) 31, 45, 136
slave 146, 147
Snofru (king) 29, 126, 128
Snofru ('overseer of the chamber') 48
Sobek 58, 119
Sobekaa Bebi (vizier) 173
Sobekemhat (vizier) 56, 128, 172, 174
Sobekemsaf ('herald of Thebes') 73
Sobekherhab (official) 71, 155
Sobekhotep (governor) 101
Sobekhotep (officer) 70, 163
Sobekhotep (official) 50, 87
Sobekhotep (treasurer) 44, 173
Sobekhotep Djadja ('king's son') 72
Sobekhotep I (king) 68
Sobekhotep II (king) 68, 69, 92, 162, 163, 173, 174
Sobekhotep III (king) 70, 163
Sobekhotep IV (king) 64, 71-5, 133, 155, 161, 162, 170, 173, 185
Sobekhotep Miu ('king's son') 72
Sobekhotep V (king) 74, 170, 171
Sobekkare, *see* Sobeknofru
Sobeknofru 51, 61, 62, 169
Sokarhotep (official) 131
Sopdu 146
Sopdumeri 147
sphinx 47, 61, 62
Steckeweh, Hans 99
Steindorff, Georg 99
steward 16, 21
Stockholm 101
Su 130

Suez 60
Syncellus, George (Christian writer) 2, 3
Syria 92, 136

'Tale of Sinuhe' 28, 31, 45, 136
Tall al Muqdam 130
Tall ar Ruba, *see* Mendes
Tanis 47, 61, 69, 72
el-Tarif 16, 17, 89
Tarkhan 117, 121
Ta-seti (nome) 13, 29, 78, 80
Ta-shi, *see* Fayum
Ta-wer (nome) 13, 94
'Teaching of Merykare' (work of literature) 9
'Teaching of Ptahhotep' (work of literature) 141
Tell ar-Rataba 31
Tell el-Dab'a 32, 62, 73, 131, 132, 133, 136, 145, 161
Tell Farun, *see* Nebesheh
Tell Ibrahim Awad 131
Tem (queen) 18, 23, 90, 176
Tep-ihu, *see* Atfih
Tep-resi 78
Ter-remu 130
Teti (king) 125
Thebes 1, 3, 8-11, 13, 14, 20-4, 26, 29, 32, 38, 43, 44, 50, 57, 59, 61, 68, 78, 71, 78, 79, 80, 89, 91, 92, 134, 141, 147, 149, 153, 156, 157, 172, 173
Thinis (This) 9, 13, 14, 19, 55, 94, 98
Thot 109
Thracians 54
Thutmose III 4, 10
Tihna el-Gebel 104, 111
Tjan (queen) 72
Tjeb-netjeret (nome) 130
Tjebu, *see* Qaw
Tjehemu (official) 20
Tjehenu (tribe) 31
Tjemeh (tribe) 31
Tjeni, *see* Thinis
Tjetji (treasurer) 14, 15
(el-)Tod 11, 15, 20, 24, 32, 41, 42, 46, 47, 70, 79, 92
tomb-robbery papyri 15
Turin 99, 174; Torino Cat. Supp. 18351: 186
Turin Canon 4, 5, 12, 13, 15, 23, 25,

43, 51, 54, 61-3, 65-9, 71, 72, 74, 180
turquoise 26, 33, 60

Ugarit 134, 136, 172
Ukh-hotep (official) 108, 152
Ukh-hotep II (governor) 108
Ukh-hotep III (governor) 107, 108
Ukh-hotep IV (governor) 101, 108, 109
Uronarti 53, 135, 173
Userhet ('warrior') 115
Userkare, *see* Khendjer
Uto 18, 130, 131

vizier 21, 22, 24-8, 34, 43, 48, 54, 56, 60, 68, 69, 72, 73, 90, 91, 110, 116, 128, 146, 147, 152, 158-62

Wadi Allaqi 135
Wadi an-Natrun 77, 143
Wadi el-Hudi 25, 26, 43, 44, 47, 56, 60, 61, 72
Wadi Gasus 47, 50
Wadi Hammamat 24-6, 43, 56, 59, 60, 72, 93, 152, 172
Wadi Tumailat 31

Wadj (governor) 121
Wadjit (nome) 16, 97, 99
Wadjit, *see* Uto
Wadjkare (king), *see* Zegerzenti
Wah (official) 157
Wahankh, *see* Intef II
Wahibre Ibia (king) 8, 74, 117, 170, 171, 173
Wahka I (governor) 101
Wahka II (governor) 99, 101, 185, 186
Wahka III (governor) 102
Wahsut 95, 156, 157
Walls-of-the-Ruler 31
Wawat 20
Wegaf (king) 65-7, 70, 163, 171
Wehem-mesut 29
Wenet (nome) 109-11
Wepemhab (treasurer) 174
Wepwawet 56, 103
Wepwawet-hetep 111
Wetjes-Hor (nome) 13, 87
Würzburg 68, 162

Zahi (official) 155
Zegerzenti (king) 27, 169

Made in the USA
Middletown, DE
20 February 2020

85080428R10130